International Joint Ventures

Theory and Practice

Aimin Yan and Yadong Luo

M.E. Sharpe
Armonk, New York
London, England

Library of Congress Cataloging-in-Publication Data

Yan, Aimin, 1956–
    International joint ventures : theory and practice / Aimin Yan and Yadong Luo.
      p. cm.
    Includes bibliographical references and index.
    ISBN 0-7656-0473-6 (alk. paper)
      1. Joint ventures. 2. International business enterprises. I. Luo, Yadong. II. Title.

HD62.47.Y355 2001
338.8′8—dc21   00-032979

Printed in the United States of America

The paper used in this publication meets the minimum requirements of
American National Standard for Information Sciences
Permanence of Paper for Printed Library Materials,
ANSI Z 39.48-1984.

BM (c)   10   9   8   7   6   5   4   3   2   1

To our wives, Huimin Lu and Cuihua Huang,
who have made tremendous sacrifices of their
own professional careers in supporting ours.

Contents

List of Tables, Figures, and Appendix

Tables

Figures

Appendix

Foreword

The past twenty years have witnessed a rapid increase in the number of joint ventures between companies from different countries. These international joint ventures (IJVs) are part and parcel of the movement toward global expansion. They offer an important alternative to international mergers and acquisitions by allowing for cooperation between firms without a loss of corporate identity. IJVs, however, share one important attribute with mergers and acquisitions: It has proved very difficult to realize the added value anticipated at the time of their formation.

Joint ventures are particularly problematic to manage, because by preserving the separate identity of their parent companies, they incorporate inherent sources of conflict. When joint ventures cross borders, differences in culture and management philosophy come into play and the challenge can become daunting. Quite a few managers therefore maintain that companies should only enter into IJVs failing any other alternative. Their instability and supposedly high rate of failure are often cited, and this leads many observers to wonder why so many new IJVs continued to be established every week.

One of the singular contributions of this important new book is to point out that we should be extremely careful before making simple judgments about the success of IJVs. Thus if we fail to recognize that many joint ventures are set up to achieve specific partner objectives, after which their dissolution may be envisaged, we could commit a fundamental error of judgment about their performance. The definition of what constitutes good joint venture performance, and the means to attain it, are contentious but core issues, which this books treats in a more sophisticated manner than other writings on the subject.

The two authors, Aimin Yan and Yadong Luo, enjoy considerable respect for their work on IJVs during the past decade. Their own joint venture of authorship exhibits the integration of complementary assets—expertise in the fields of organization and strategy, respectively—that makes collaboration so fruitful. In addition, they are well versed in the international aspects of business. As well as being noted scholars, Yan and Luo have kept in close touch with the practical experiences of IJVs through research and consulting. The authors' ability to draw upon their rich experience lends a further competitive edge to this book. They are able to relate their carefully reasoned argument to empirical case studies. Following the introduction, each chapter contains one or more case studies as well as frequent illustrations within the text. This approach assists the reader to appreciate the full relevance and utility of the argument. Yan and Luo do not need to rely on the platitudes or disjointed sound bites that characterize too many business books. They know their subject deeply and they are aware of how it manifests itself in business practice.

Although I am a co-author of a recent book on strategic alliances, which will enjoy friendly competition with *International Joint Ventures*, I am happy to admit that I have learned much from having the privilege of reading an advance copy of this book. I cannot wait to bring it to the attention of my class members, and I am sure you will have the same reaction once you have had this opportunity to read it.

John Child
Diageo Professor of Management
University of Cambridge

May 2000

Preface

International joint ventures are a rapidly growing organizational form. The number of joint ventures has dramatically increased worldwide in the past two decades. Interfirm partnerships announced in the 1980s exceeded the total number formed in all prior years combined (Anderson 1990). Growth of joint ventures both in number and in strategic importance in conducting international businesses has continued throughout the 1990s. In fact, it has been suggested that the business world is stepping into an "age of alliance capitalism" (Dunning 1995).

Not surprisingly, scholarly writings on joint ventures have been proliferating as well. As a matter of fact, joint ventures have been a topic of study in many academic disciplines, including business and management, economics, law, sociology, psychology, anthropology, and international relations. A quick glance over the table of contents of every issue of the major business journals will find subjects on joint ventures or interorganizational cooperation or partnerships. In addition, increasingly more books on the subject have been published, among which several have been well received, such as Contractor and Lorange's edited volume, *Cooperative Strategies in International Business* (Lexington Books, 1988); Lorange and Roos's *Strategic Alliances: Formation, Implementation and Evolution* (Blackwell, 1992); Bleek and Ernest's *Collaborating to Compete: Using Strategic Alliances and Acquisitions in the Global Marketplace* (Wiley, 1993); Yoshino and Rangan's *Strategic Alliances: An Entrepreneurial Approach to Globalization* (Harvard Business School Press, 1995); Gomes-Casseres's *The Alliance Revolution: The New Shape of Business Rivalry* (Harvard University Press, 1996); the three-volume *Cooperative Strategies* (New Lexington, 1997), edited by Beamish and Killing, on "North American Perspectives," "European Perspectives," and "Asian Pacific Perspectives," respectively; and Child and Faulkner's *Strategies of Co-operation: Managing Alliances, Networks, and Joint Ventures* (Oxford University Press, 1998).

Each of these books has unique features. For example, the edited volumes reflect a diversity of research ideas about cooperative ventures but tend to be quite loose in structure. On the other hand, many books were written from narrowly defined perspectives, for example, by stressing the strategic aspect of international joint ventures yet paying little attention to the managerial aspect. Except the most recent Child and Faulkner book, these works tend to address joint ventures as a generic phenomenon without specifying the particular challenges in managing such ventures in developing or transitional economies.

So, why this book? What does it offer in terms of value-added contributions?

There are three driving forces that have provided the strongest motivation for us to write this book, each originating in a different component of our professional lives connected with joint ventures: research, teaching, and consulting. First, as scholars, over a dozen years of research on the subject, we have each produced a number of articles and papers for publication and presentation. Each of them focuses on a specific area or aspect of joint ventures; no special effort has been made to integrate what in reality are coherent and mutually interdependent phenomena. Nowadays, most academic journals appreciate focused and deeply grounded papers, thereby discouraging efforts that are integrative and synthetic in nature. Also, through a deeper reflection on our research programs as well as on the entire joint venture literature, we have come to a better and finer understanding of the work conducted by numerous other scholars. We must admit that under a more critical than appreciative mentality in reviewing and reacting to others' work (another ironic tradition in journal publications), we have been more able to detect "gaps" than to articulate connections and interrelations between others' work and that of our own. As Paul Beamish and Peter Killing, the editors of the 1996 *Journal of International Business Studies* Special Issue on Global Perspectives on Cooperative Strategies suggest, it is time to "consolidate the current and future thinking on international cooperation." From a scholarly point view, therefore, in writing this book we take the opportunity to consolidate previous work, reconcile differences and inconsistencies in the literature, and thus contribute to joint venture research.

Second, as professors, we have been involved in teaching the subject of international joint ventures. Over the years, we found that it is particularly difficult to find a volume for a graduate-level class, which reaches deep into theory, incorporates a variety of perspectives, reports rigorously designed empirical work, and covers the entire process of international joint venturing. The typical international business textbook treats joint ventures as only one of its many subjects, therefore presenting some major concepts but leaving much of the important depth unexplored. On the other hand, more in-depth, scholarly books tend to cover a limited scope, such as partner selection or negotiations. Third, as business consultants, we have been involved in helping multinational companies, government agents, and other organizations form and manage joint ventures. The lack of in-depth studies of real world joint ventures in one type of book and the lack of systematic conceptual analysis in other types have not provided the practitioner with a great deal of help. Since business environments in different countries may vary significantly, most practitioners today demand not only sufficient details about how to proceed with a particular joint venture's establishment, but also the reflected and thus more generalizable knowledge about managing international joint ventures. A frequently asked question, for example, is "How is setting up a joint venture in China different from in Germany, and why?" Therefore, for a thoughtful practitioner, while "know-how" is important, "know-why" generates more insightful learning. From this consideration, we wanted to provide executives and managers involved or interested in joint ventures with a book that combines rich examples and data with systematic analysis.

This book has the following features:

First, it crystallizes both authors' decade-long theoretical and empirical research on international joint ventures and their consulting experience. The readers will find that many examples and data used in this book are drawn from joint ventures in Asia, particularly in China, to take advantage of the deep expertise of the authors. International joint ventures in China have been the primary subject for empirical study as well as providing consulting services for both authors.

Second, the book integrates multiple perspectives. Theoretically, we draw heavily upon theories of organization, strategic management, and economics in examining the key issues in joint ventures. The book takes a balanced approach to understanding joint ventures by accounting for both the foreign and the local partner's interests and perspectives, as well as interactions between them. Scholarly work on international joint ventures to date has over-represented the perspectives and interests of the multinational companies as venture partners, while the perspectives and roles of the local players—partners or government agents—have been consistently ignored or downplayed. This approach is particularly true for ventures found in developing countries. Recent studies have indicated that such ignorance can be dangerous and costly because it fails to recognize joint ventures as multiparty partnerships. A trademark feature of joint ventures, as different from single, independent firms, is that all strategic decisions are subject to negotiations among different parties, including the venture management, rather than unilateral decisions made by any single party. Practically, an "imperialist" approach imposed by the multinationals can prompt antagonism by the local players and interpartner conflict, which can significantly reduce the chances of joint venture success.

Third, in this book, we adopt a holistic view by examining the entire process of international joint venture development, from partner and ownership structure selection to the design of managerial control systems and venture performance assessment. In addition, we consider both the static and dynamic features of joint ventures by exploring the issues of evolution and stability of joint ventures over time. Finally, the book balances between academic and practical interests by providing both systematic theoretical analyses and in-depth descriptions of many real-world, cross-country partnerships as case studies and examples.

This book itself results from a joint venture. The partners involved in the project include two of us (similar to the overwhelming majority of joint ventures in which two partners are involved). The partnership possesses several characteristics that probably are critical to all joint ventures: (1) We are in a similar stage of professional development and thus share the same academic aspirations and development objectives. (2) We possess a common ground of experience so that we are able to understand and appreciate each other's perspectives and contributions. Both of us studied international joint ventures for our Ph.D. dissertations and since have published extensively, taught the subject at the undergraduate, graduate, and executive levels, and have been continuously involved in consulting on the subject. (3) Our home academic disciplines and scholarship have been sufficiently different (one in international business, the other in organization theory). Therefore, we each contributed to the collective pool of complementary intellectual resources. (4) We developed a consensus right from the beginning of the project on its goals, objectives, and key procedures of working together. Although one author is located in Boston, Massachusetts, and the other in Honolulu, Hawaii, the numerous electronic mail exchanges, telephone calls, and faxes, as well as physical meetings, helped us manage the project smoothly and without breakdowns of interpartner communication. Last but not least, we had had experience of successful collaboration before taking this venture, and over time personal friendship emerged. Once again, our experience shows that a long-term relationship and trust are quite effective in curbing opportunism in partnerships!

The book project would not be successful if we didn't have cooperators and supporters. First, we feel extremely grateful for Sean M. Culhane, M.E. Sharpe's editor responsible for this project, who initially served as a strong champion and since has been a wonderful facilitator for the project. Second, we would like to extend our deepest appreciation to Dr. John Child, the Diageo Professor of Management Studies of the University of Cambridge, who wrote the foreword for the book. John is an internationally well respected scholar in organization theory, strategic management, and international joint ventures, and his work on organizational strategic choices and organizational theory development in transforming economies has exerted significant influence on both of us. Third, since the book crystallizes the authors' multiyear research efforts, we are in debt to our co-researchers and co-authors on various research projects. The first author would particularly acknowledge his long-term cooperation with his gifted former dissertation advisor, Dr. Barbara Gray at Penn State. Their cooperative research on joint ventures over the past decade provided much of the ground on which this book was based. Several chapters of the book were based on joint research projects with Professor Gray. Therefore, we feel greatly indebted to her. The book also benefited from joint research with Xiansheng Duan, Oded Shankar, and Ming Zeng. All these scholars and friends have made valuable contributions. Fourth, we thank several doctoral students, Manuela N. Hoehn and Tatiana Manalova at Boston University and Wei He at Boston College, who carefully read the manuscript and provided a mix of respect and challenges for our ideas. Fifth, we want to acknowledge the institutional support each of us received from our schools during the writing of this book. The Human Resources Policy Institute of Boston University and its director, Dr. Fred Foulkes, especially provided much needed financial support to relieve part of the teaching duties of the first author.

Finally, we owe our families for their love and continuing selfless support. Over the years, our wives, Huimin Lu and Cuihua Huang, have made tremendous sacrifices of their own professional careers in supporting ours. Therefore, it is to them that we dedicate this book. We also appreciate our little ones, Linda, Esther, Edward, and Rosalie, for their understanding, love, and friendship.

Part I

Defining International Joint Ventures

——— 1 ———

Conceptualization and Formation Motives

In this chapter, we first define international joint ventures and explain why managing such ventures can be particularly challenging. Second, we identify several key areas of research that have emerged in the literature: motives for joint venture formation, partner/structural selection, governance and control, and venture stability and performance. Then we continue to discuss the first area of research by presenting the major practical and theoretical reasons for forming international joint ventures. Finally, we describe the structure of this book in terms of the fundamental questions to be addressed in each chapter.

International Joint Ventures Defined

In this book, we focus on equity joint ventures, as differentiated from nonequity, cooperative alliances in which the partners do not share ownership of capital resources. Equity joint ventures are legally and economically separate organizational entities created by two or more parent organizations that collectively invest financial as well as other resources to pursue certain objectives (Anderson 1990; Pfeffer and Nowak 1976). Among the different forms of interorganizational relations, joint ventures are unique and arguably the most complex type of arrangement. Interfirm contractual relationships such as licensing or franchising do not involve shared equity or joint capital investment by the participating firms, whereas corporate mergers and acquisitions result in a complete combination between two firms without creating a new organization existing in parallel to the merging firms. In comparison to the contractual forms of interfirm cooperation, joint ventures represent a longer-term collaborative strategy.

International joint ventures are broadly defined as joint ventures that involve firms from different countries cooperating across national and cultural boundaries. On some occasions, joint ventures formed by partners from the same country but located in a country other than their parents' are also considered as international joint ventures (Geringer and Hebert 1989). Although an overwhelming majority of international joint ventures involve only two parent firms, one from a foreign country and the other from the local country, some ventures may consist of multiple participants. For example, many early joint ventures in China were three-way partnerships including a local partner, a multinational partner, and a partner from Hong Kong. In other cases, a joint venture may include partners with more complex nationality or cultural backgrounds. For example, Xerox Shenzhen is a joint venture formed between Xerox China Ltd., Xerox's wholly owned holding company in China, and Fuji Xerox, which itself is a U.S.-Japanese joint venture in Japan. This Chinese joint venture without a Chinese partner was created to take advantage of the preferential government policies toward enterprises with an international joint venture status.

Complexities in International Joint Ventures

As legally and economically independent organizations, joint ventures operate like stand-alone firms and have to engage in all the different types of "regular" business activity and external relationships that any independent firm has to undertake. However, more complex than the single organization, joint ventures involve multiple "internal" interorganizational relationships: the relationship between the partner firms, the venture management's relationship with the foreign parent and with the local parent, and the relationship between the venture's managers nominated by different partners. Each of these relationships can be extremely difficult to manage. First, the most important and arguably the most problematic relationship is that between the joint venture partners. Above all, international joint ventures represent an intercultural and interorganizational linkage between two separate parent companies that join forces with different strategic interests and objectives. Importantly, "These parents, unlike the shareholders of a widely held public corporation, are visible and powerful and can and will disagree on just about anything" (Killing 1983, 8). Cross-cultural differences, diverging strategic expectations, and incongruent organizational strategies, structures, and operational processes between the partner firms have been frequently cited as sources of interpartner conflict, which in turn lead to the venture's instability and performance problems. As Davidson (1982, 46) argues, "Even more important than formal arbitration procedures, perhaps, is the nature of the relationship with the partner. A positive relationship that extends beyond legal contractual commitments is the principal goal of any joint venture agreement."

Similarly, it is quite a challenging task for the joint venture management to effectively create and maintain a healthy relationship with each of the parent firms. For example, when an unbalanced linkage with one parent (e.g., internal transfer pricing) is poorly managed, it can create serious dissatisfaction in the venture's other parents. In one of the U.S.-Chinese joint ventures that we studied, the American firm bought back some of the venture's products and, after minor modification, sold them in South Africa. From this deal, while the U.S. parent made a sizable profit, the joint venture lost money because the internal transfer price was set too low to cover the costs. This created a serious problem for the Chinese partner, who complained that the U.S. firm was making "dirty money" at the partnership's expense.

Finally, empirical evidence suggests that the working relationship between the two groups of managers at the joint venture, each nominated by and thus representing a different parent, is also very critical to the venture's operation, creating significant implications for interpartner trust as well as the venture's performance, as illustrated by Killing (1983, 9):

> The board of directors of one company in my study, consisting of American and British managers, continually disagreed vehemently about the amount of data required before a decision could be made. The British could not understand why the Americans wanted "all those numbers." The Americans, on the other hand, believed the British were totally "flying blind." This problem was serious, as it meant that either the Americans had to agree to proceed with what they considered to be insufficient information, or the British had to incur a delay and spend extra money collecting information which they did not feel was necessary. From this beginning the problem became even worse. . . .

In addition to the complex inter- and intra-organizational relationships that a joint venture has to manage, the external institutional environments in which the venture operates are also quite complex and hard to deal with. On the one hand, like a single, stand-alone organization, an international joint venture has to interact with the different components of the institutional environment in a local country. On the other hand, as a "child" organization, the venture is heavily influenced by the institutional environments of both of its parents. For example, from a legal point of view, the forms of incorporation, the structure of ownership arrangement, taxation regimes, and the governance mechanisms of joint ventures can be significantly different between the countries where the parent firms are found. Most international joint ventures, particularly ventures between partners from developed and developing countries, have to be furnished with two different accounting systems, one for the international firm and the other for the local tax authorities, because of the significant differences between the two accounting systems. In addition, the cultural environments are different. A joint venture has to hire local employees, including both managers and workers. In many cases, taking advantage of the cheap local labor is a major objective of companies from developed economies in forming joint ventures in developing countries. As a result, cultural and intercultural issues become a challenging task for joint ventures. Employer-employee relationships, as well as their mutual expectations, differ considerably in different cultural contexts. For example, Motorola in China found that it had to be engaged in building apartment buildings for employee families, a business that the company had never done before elsewhere in the world. At times, the social norms and expectations in different countries are so strong that ignorance can create serious management problems. For example, it is a widely shared, and many times taken for granted, practice in Taiwan, Hong Kong, and China that the employees receive a sizable bonus, frequently referred to as "the thirteenth month's salary," right before the traditional Chinese New Year. In one of our research fields (an Australian-Chinese joint venture hotel), the management's refusal to grant such a bonus prompted employee strikes during the holiday season.

The Key Areas of Research

As discussed above, the quite unique features of international joint ventures have made this organizational form both interesting and challenging. Since joint venturing is a process that involves multiple facets and dynamics, previous research has identified several key areas of study. In an effort to synthesize the vast and growing literature, Parkhe (1993) identified four major areas of research on international joint ventures: the motives for venture formation, partner selection, governance and control, and joint venture performance and stability. He further argued that although some of these areas have received enormous research attention, others continue to be understudied or virtually ignored. Relatively speaking, according to Parkhe, the various motives for creating international joint ventures have been extensively, if not systematically, explored. In contrast, research in other areas deserves more significant attention. In particular, the "choice of organizational structure, alliance structure design, and dynamic evolution of the cooperative relationship" represent the "three major areas await(ing) deeper theoretical insights" (p. 233).

Following Parkhe's suggestion, this book focuses on these understudied subjects. However, in order to provide the reader with a more complete picture, in the rest of this chapter, we summarize the previous work on the motives for forming international joint ventures from both the practitioner and scholarly literatures.

Practical Reasons for Joint Venture Formation

Why do firms choose joint ventures to conduct international business? The practitioner literature suggests the following reasons. First, joint ventures result from government insistence. Although the push for multinational firms to make direct foreign investment may come from forces associated with products (e.g., product offerings and value chains) and markets, many international joint ventures result from the pull by the local government. Governments, particularly in developing countries, exercise pressure on multinational companies to use the form of equity joint ventures rather than wholly owned subsidiaries. To the foreign firm, an alliance with a local organization, business or governmental, may be required in order to enter these countries. For example, the overwhelming majority of foreign investment projects in China during the first decade of the Open Door policy were framed as equity joint ventures, while the increase of wholly owned foreign subsidiaries is a quite recent phenomenon. It is important to note that oftentimes, institutional pressures for joint ventures, or for a particular type of joint venture, are imposed not in the form of formal laws or government regulations but in the form of strong social, cultural, or industrial norms. For example, the rise of the significant number of 50–50 shared equity joint ventures in China made the Western researchers and practitioners alike speculate that it was the Chinese law that required the equal split of equity ownership. In fact, the Chinese joint venture law in both the original 1979 version and the amended 1990 version states that the foreign partner's equity holdings should be "at least 25 percent" while no ceilings were stipulated. Therefore, joint ventures with majority foreign ownership have been legally allowed since the very outset of the policy. This type of venture, however, had been quite scarce until very recently. In fact, it was the prevailing political and cultural norm for interpartner "equality" promoted by the Chinese government and society that created the isomorphic, equally shared ownership structure in the overwhelming majority of Chinese joint ventures.

Second, gaining access to overseas markets has been a classic reason for firms to form joint ventures. This is true for both the multinational and the local partner firm. On the one hand, one advantage of a joint venture is that a foreign firm can piggyback on a local partner to gain access to the local market. On the other hand, in many cases, it is also the aim of the local partner to gain access to the international market. Without fully understanding the consumer behavior, distribution network, and marketing strategies and practices that are effective in a specific country, a foreign wholly owned subsidiary has many ways to fail. Japan is an obvious example. Its distinctive marketing and distribution practices encourage foreign companies to set up partnerships with Japanese companies as the most practical means of selling into the market.

Risk sharing is a third frequently observed motive for forming international joint ventures. First, if an investment project is financially too large or too risky for single firms to handle alone, they may join forces to share the financial risk. This is the case with oil exploration and commercial aircraft manufacturing where large, risky projects call for interfirm collaboration. Second, if the business environment in a host country is highly uncertain or unfriendly to foreign firms, a joint venture with a local firm may allow a multinational company to share political risks and to defuse xenophobic local reactions, a strategic action to amend the "liability of foreignness."

Fourth, formation of international joint ventures allows a firm to tap outside resources to build competitive strength at significantly reduced costs—with capital investment much lower than if the firm either developed it alone or achieved it through acquisition. For example, access to new products developed by a joint venture partner allows a firm to concentrate on its most competitive products while adding multiple related product applications. Access to a partner's technology enables a firm to enjoy the fruits of research and development while avoiding the rapidly escalating R&D costs. In addition to cost considerations, joint venturing is an effective, if not the most effective, avenue for companies in developing countries to learn about new business processes and to catch up with the substantial technological advantages possessed by their counterparts in developed economies.

Finally, joint ventures may be formed between partner firms in pooling resources to pursue a common interest or a symbiotic cooperative advantage. By sharing financial resources that otherwise are not available to each individual partner, two smaller companies in an industry can form a joint venture to achieve economies of scale similar to those that are enjoyed by their larger competitors. Alternatively, joint venture partners can cooperate to take advantage of pooled nonfinancial resources. It has been a classic rationale that a joint use of complementary resources, competencies, and skills possessed by different organizations can create synergistic effects, which none of the companies is able to achieve if acting alone.

Theoretical Explanations of Formation Motives

Previous scholarly work has offered a variety of theoretical perspectives on the formation incentives of international joint ventures, ranging from economic theories to organization theories and game theory. Below we focus on several most prominent perspectives, namely, transaction costs, organizational interdependence, and strategic behavior.

Transaction Costs

Williamson (1991) argues that there are three types of contract laws in business transactions, each accompanying a different mode of governance: (1) the classical contract law for markets, (2) the forbearance contract law for hierarchies, and (3) the neoclassical contract law for hybrid governance. The principal criterion for choosing among these alternative governance structures, according to Williamson, is minimization of transaction costs. Transaction costs are negotiating, writing, monitoring, and enforcement costs that have to be borne to allow an exchange between two parties to take place. The sources of these costs are the transaction difficulties that may be present in the exchange process (Williamson 1975). Jones and Hill (1988, 160) summarize six main factors producing transaction difficulties in interfirm transactions: (1) Bounded rationality: The rationality of human behavior is limited by the actor's ability to process information. (2) Opportunism: Human beings are prone to behave opportunistically, or to seek self-interest with guile. (3) Uncertainty and complexity: The real world is characterized by considerable uncertainty and complexity. (4) Small numbers: In the real world small numbers of trading relationships are frequently found (i.e., as in an oligopoly). (5) Information impactedness: Information pertaining to a transaction or set of transactions is frequently asymmetrically distributed between the parties to an exchange. Thus one party might have more knowledge than the other. Finally, (6) asset specificity: This refers to investment in assets that are specific to the requirements of a particular exchange relationship.

Previous research in the transaction costs tradition has explained why hybrid governance structures, including equity and nonequity joint ventures, are chosen among alternative structures for interfirm transactions. Comparing the three generic governance structures, Williamson argues that hybrid organizational forms, such as joint ventures, are more elastic than market transactions yet more legalistic than self-contained organizational hierarchies. Applying the principles of transaction costs theory to international entry decisions, Anderson and Gatignon (1986) argued that equity joint ventures represent an entry mode that renders substantial control to multinational companies. Empirically, they observed that joint ventures were more efficient than other entry modes. Other scholars (Hennart 1988, 1991; Kogut 1988) identified several theoretical scenarios in which an equity joint venture is necessary. First, strong motives for forming a joint venture are present when a focal firm is engaged in frequent transactions with a particular supplier and switching costs to other suppliers are high. The bilateral relationship between an aluminum firm and a particular bauxite mine is such an example, in which the refinery is usually designed around the characteristics of the particular ore (i.e., relationship specific asset investment). To conduct such transactions in the framework of spot markets would be hazardous, because after the investment has been made (and thus sunk costs have been incurred), the supplier could hold up the buyer by unilaterally raising the price of bauxite (e.g., opportunism). On the other hand, the option for the mining firm to establish a wholly owned refinery is not viable, because for an efficient size of operation, the refinery has to be so large that its output would go far beyond what the mining firm is able or willing to dispose.

Second, equity joint ventures are necessary when the interfirm transactions involve substantial transfer of tacit knowledge. In this case, the knowledge concerned is very difficult, if not impossible, to be specified in a nonequity technology transfer agreement.

> The problem with transferring tacit knowledge is that it is impossible for either party to know *ex ante* what the cost and the value of the transfer will be. The buyer does not know, by definition, what he is buying. He fears that the information he will be sold will be obsolete, or inappropriate. The seller does not know how much it will cost him to effect the transfer. (Hennart 1988, 366)

As a result, forming an equity joint venture may provide a mutual hostage situation (Kogut 1988) in which both partners are likely to have a fair deal: the transferor can make sure that the value of the knowledge is appreciated and appropriately compensated, while the transferee is ensured that its partner can be held responsible for making the knowledge work. The joint commitment of financial and other resources creates alignment of incentives between the partners and stabilizes the interpartner agreement on the division of profits or costs.

Third, future uncertainty associated with the transactional relationship calls for shared equity. In many cases, the outcomes of interfirm cooperation may not be available for distribution, or even for verification, when the contract is signed. Rather, they have to be jointly created after the agreement is reached. Therefore, the substantial uncertainty down the road can create fear for the parties. For example, new technical or human problems are likely to arise. Radical environmental events can take place during the execution of the agreement. These factors could not be foreseen when the contract is drafted, yet will have substantial impact on the successful execution of the agreement. In these circumstances, it would be difficult for the parties to distinguish *ex post* between poor luck and poor performance. As a result, they may exploit contract incompleteness and the difficulty in performance assessment to their own advantage (Hennart 1988).

A joint venture helps address the issue of uncertainty by creating a superior monitoring mechanism and alignment of incentives between the partners to reveal information, share technologies, make joint decisions, and achieve performance. Since joint ventures tie the partners together in the form of an equity relationship, unforeseeable uncertainties to both parties are dealt with collectively and both partners are motivated to make commitment to the venture's future development.

Interorganizational Interdependence

From an interorganizational relations perspective, modern business enterprises are embedded in interorganizational networks. The increasing interfirm interdependence presents a paradox: On the one hand, the firms strive for autonomy and independence of others (Burt 1982; Gouldner 1959; Guetzkow 1966). On the other hand, the increasingly turbulent business environments significantly constrain the firm's latitude for individualistic strategic actions (Astley and Fombrun 1983; Bresser and Harl 1986). As a result, collaborative efforts across organizational boundaries become necessary. Joint ventures emerge as a desirable form for coping with the paradoxical situation. They enable firms to pursue certain strategic goals at the collective level, while each still remains an autonomous entity at the corporate level. As Pfeffer and Salancik (1978, 154) note, "If the principal problem organizations face is competitive and symbiotic interdependence, then it can be presumed that joint ventures are undertaken to reduce uncertainty and promote stability in the environment."

The theoretical position taken by the interorganizational interdependence perspective is that joint ventures are established to manage the interdependence between the partner firms. This interdependence may take two different forms, mutual reliance for complementary resources and mutual needs for maintaining and managing an existing interfirm linkage, respectively. On the one hand, as resource dependence theory (Pfeffer and Salanci 1978) argues, no single organization is self-sufficient, each must be engaged in a variety of relationships with other organizations for critical resources in order to survive. Therefore, joint venture partners create the partnership to benefit from a synergistic effect to be derived from the joint use of their complementary resources (Chi 1994). This rationale is quite apparent in our explanation of the practical incentives for joint venture formation. On the other hand, Pfeffer and Nowak (1976) found that the need for managing the existing interdependent relationships between firms leads to the formation of joint ventures. They argue that "interdependence causes the creation of joint ventures to manage the interdependence, rather than the joint ventures themselves creating the interorganizational interdependence" (p. 400). More specifically, these authors argue that joint ventures are established to manage two types of organizational interdependence: competitive interdependence and symbiotic interdependence. "Competitive interdependence exists on a horizontal level among like organizations, while symbiotic interdependence exists between organizations vertically related in the production process." Further, they found empirical evidence that joint ventures are created either to reduce the level of competitive interdependence or to maintain and strengthen a symbiotic interdependence.

Strategic Behavior

This explanation for joint venture formation argues that joint ventures are formed for strategic reasons, that is, firms form joint ventures to enhance their competitive positioning in the market (Kogut 1988). From this perspective, the ultimate objective for a firm is to maximize profits through improving its competitive position vis-à-vis its rivals. Firms elect to form joint ventures whenever such a cooperative strategy enables them to gain a competitive advantage and thus increase their asset value. Harrigan (1988) argues that the increasing use of joint ventures "represents an exciting change in competitive behavior" that enable managers "to build strengths for their firms' business units." By forming joint ventures, firms "can change industry structures for the disadvantage of competitors." In the case of international competition, firms choose joint venturing as the most effective entry mode, a mode that maximizes profits rather than minimizes costs, as transaction costs theory posits.

There are numerous strategic reasons for forming joint ventures. Harrigan (1988) argues that "joint ventures can (1) exacerbate competition, (2) stabilize profit levels, or (3) precipitate structural changes in vertical integration, technological scale, or other industry traits." She further specifies how the different industry characteristics (e.g., demand growth, market attractiveness, market standardization, and uncertainty) and competitor traits affect the strategic use of joint ventures. In addition, many firms form joint ventures to deter entry or erode competitors' strategic positions. In his analysis of joint ventures as a way to deter entry through pre-emptive patenting, Vickers (1985) shows that, particularly for small innovations, joint ventures are an effective mechanism to guarantee the entry-deferring investment. More generally, Vernon

(1983) argues that joint ventures are a form of defensive investment by which multinationals hedge against strategic uncertainty, especially in industries of moderate concentration where collusion is difficult to achieve despite the benefits of coordinating the interdependence among firms.

Within the strategic behavior thesis of joint venture formation, a most recent and rapidly expanding argument is organizational learning. This explanation views joint ventures as a means by which firms learn from their partners to build strategic capabilities (Kogut 1988). In this view, joint venture partners are driven by a motive of acquiring knowledge, particularly tacit knowledge. Hamel (1991) in particular, argues that in joint ventures sponsors form horizontal alliances to extract and internalize the skills and competencies of their partners, and thus either strengthen their own competitive position or erode the competitive advantage of their partners. This learning-oriented motive for forming joint ventures, however, can create significant interpartner competition and conflict, which in turn can destabilize joint ventures.

Structure of the Book

In this chapter so far, we have provided a conceptualization of international joint ventures and conducted a review of previous work on the formation incentives of such ventures. The key questions we have answered are: "What is an international joint venture?" and "Why joint ventures?" Now we want to shift our focus to the other three major areas of joint venture research that Parkhe identified: partner/structural selection, governance and control, and venture stability and performance. To address these fundamental issues, we organize the book as follows.

The book is composed of four parts. In addition to the current chapter (as Part I), Part II (chapters 2–5) presents our analysis of the fundamental decisions in the venture's formation stage on partner selection, negotiations, structure of joint ownership, and structure of parent control. The questions addressed in these chapters are:

- What are the key issues involved in selecting an appropriate partner?
- How can the parties effectively handle the founding negotiations for the venture?
- What is the best arrangement of ownership sharing in joint ventures?

- What are the alternative structures in which the parent firms exercise managerial control over the venture's operations?

In Part III (chapters 6–9), we address the key challenges in managing the joint venture's operation and the multiparty relationship, and present empirical results with respect to the key variables. The questions addressed include:

- How do learning and knowledge transfers occur in joint ventures and what are their implications?
- How should an international joint venture's effectiveness and performance be measured?
- How can interpartner fit and synergy be created to enhance joint venture success?
- What is the empirical evidence for the relationships among bargaining power, control, interpartner relationship, and venture performance?

Finally, Part IV (chapters 10–12) focuses on joint venture evolution by exploring the dynamics, stability, and structural reconfiguration of joint ventures and the possible end-game strategies. The key questions concern:

- How do international joint ventures change over time?
- What are the driving and restraining forces for structural instability, and
- How can an international venture be appropriately disclosed or renewed?

Throughout the book, we will make a particular effort to incorporate the experiences of the real world joint ventures. We do this in three ways: (1) citing these experiences sporadically as examples for illustration, (2) reporting them as systematic case analyses, or (3) presenting them in the format of descriptive "mini cases" attached to the chapters. While most of these "mini-cases" were drawn on our own studies or derived from our syntheses of publicly available information, some were adopted from other sources. In the latter case, we have received permission for duplication and give full credit to the original authors.

Part II

Building International Joint Ventures

——— 2 ———

Partner Selection:
Criteria and Process

This chapter presents the criteria and process of partner selection in international joint venture formation. First, we delineate four broad areas in which interpartner compatibility is important: culture, strategy, organizational capabilities, and financial traits. The congruence between partners in these areas provides the key foundation for a successful international joint venture and will affect both the collective and the individual gains from the venture for the partners. Then, we develop a model of interpartner fit at a more specific and operational level by considering the parties' strategic objectives, resource contributions, commitment, and partner capabilities. We discuss each specific criterion, reiterate the possible influence of these criteria on joint venture operations, and, finally, describe the key aspects of partner selection process.

The Importance of Partner Selection

Few companies today believe that they, on their own, are able to develop, produce, and sell their products successfully over an extended period of time for the global business market. Increasingly, firms seek partnerships to stay ahead of the competition in today's global economy. As we presented in the previous chapter, multiple forces and incentives exist for companies to create international joint ventures and alliances.

The first major challenge for joint venturing is partner selection, which is critical to both the foreign and the local firm. Appropriate selection of a local partner can improve a multinational firm's disadvantage of "foreignness," and increase its competitiveness in the local market in general. For example, a desirable local partner can make it possible to invest in industries that are subject to local government restriction against foreign direct investment, and can help a multinational firm gain access to marketing and distribution channels that are available only to local businesses. In addition, a well-connected local partner can significantly reduce local political risks and gain political advantages in the host country. To the local firm, on the other hand, selection of an appropriate foreign partner is also critical. A desirable multinational partner can bring to the joint venture advanced technologies, know-how, management expertise, and channels to the international marketplace.

It is widely assumed that firms establish joint ventures only when the perceived additional benefits from joint venturing outweigh expected extra costs (Beamish and Banks 1987; Geringer 1991). These additional benefits will accrue, however, only through the selection and retention of a partner that can provide the complementary skills, competencies, and capabilities that assist the focal firm in accomplishing its strategic objectives (Buckley and Casson 1988; Hamel 1991; Harrigan 1985). From this perspective, partner selection determines the right mix of strategic resources of an international joint venture (Hamel, Doz, and Prahalad 1989; Harrigan 1985). In a dynamic market particularly, the importance of partner selection to the success of the partnership is magnified, because the right partner can spur the joint venture's adaptability, improve the strategy-environment configuration for both the venture and the parent firms, and reduce uncertainty in the venture's operation (Teagarden and Von Glinow 1990; Zeira and Shenkar 1990).

During the formation process, joint venture sponsors must appropriately identify the selection criteria, as well as the relative importance of each criterion (Geringer 1991). The criteria for partner selection are both extensive and divergent across firms, settings, and time (Beamish 1987). Previous researchers have identified two broad types of criteria: operation related and cooperation related (Geringer 1991). While operation-related criteria are associated with the strategic competencies and the skills of a partner, cooperation-related criteria often mirror the organizational or interorganizational traits. Examples of the former include absorptive capacity, product relatedness, market position, and industrial experience. Examples of the latter include previous interpartner collaborations, experience in overseas operations, organizational form, and firm size.

The Partners' Cultural, Strategic, Organizational, and Financial Traits

We argue that, at the outset, joint venture sponsors have to consider four broad yet fundamental factors in choosing an appropriate partner, which concern the cultural, strategic, organizational, and financial traits of the partners. The successful configuration of these factors requires not only an appropriate alignment of an international joint venture's organizational capabilities to the external industry or market and its strategic goals, but also a proper match between one partner's competitive advantages with the other's distinctive operational competencies. The operational competencies, mirrored in operation-related attributes such as market share, industrial experience, and relationship with the local government, constitute a necessary condition and a primary source for the venture's success in exploring market opportunities and exploiting product potentials in the host environment.

Fit between the partners with respect to their cultural, strategic, organizational, and financial traits warrants careful and systematic assessment in partner selection. Each category of traits is discussed in detail below.

Cultural Traits

Cooperation between partners from radically different cultures is a major challenge. For example, Americans tend to be individualistic and, generally, not group-oriented. This individualistic culture is in sharp contrast to that of the Japanese, whose cultural direction is highly collectivist and group-oriented. Even in joint ventures between the United States and Britain, in which, as the saying goes, "Two cultures are separated by the same language," the issue of cultural differences can be quite remarkable. As our example in the previous chapter illustrates, the American managers' heavy dependence on rational, rigorous data for decision making was interpreted by their British colleagues as "they trust the cold numbers much more than they trust their warm colleagues." However, cultural differences are not always a liability. For example, the mix of Toyota's team approach and General Motors' rigorous management systems contributed significantly to the high productivity at NUMMI, the first partnership between the two companies.

A danger to international joint ventures, however, is that one partner may unilaterally impose its own cultural values and norms on the other partner without considering the latter's cultural attributes. Or a partner may inadvertently relinquish its unique culture and strategic strengths to the other firm. For example, U.S. companies are generally not as skillful at learning from their venture partners as the Japanese are. Many foreign firms view joint ventures as an easy way of gaining access to

U.S. markets and learning U.S. technologies at the expense of U.S. firms. Not only do many foreign companies seek optimal benefit from their venture partners in the United States, but also the culture they originate from (especially the Japanese culture) is better equipped to accomplish this task.

In addition to the national culture, every company has its unique corporate culture. Potential joint venture partners need to assess and ascertain how well they can manage their differences in organizational culture, because the achievement of cultural synergy is a key factor in the building of mutual trust, which in turn contributes to venture success. Therefore, a company needs to take a close look at compatibility in organizational and management practices with a potential partner. Among the critical questions the top management should ask: "What are the differences between the two companies in organizational structure and business strategy? Are they centralized or decentralized in decision making? Are both managements flexible and committed to overcoming potential conflict? How compatible are their core values and philosophies?"

Hewlett-Packard's joint venture in China stands as a successful example in addressing the issue of cultural differences. Noticing the major differences in its Chinese partner's managerial and marketing practices, HP hired most of its middle managers from the local labor market. They were well versed in the Chinese business culture but not affected or imprinted by the partner's specific corporate culture. In fact, localization of middle management staffing is a common practice in all of HP's Asian operations. Expatriate managers from the United States were used on a limited scale, staffed only at the relatively senior positions and gradually replaced by locally hired managers.

A significant aspect of interpartner cultural fit is the chemistry between senior executives of the partner firms. As an experienced U.S. executive stated, "First and foremost, companies are people, not business or financial machines. The strength and success of a joint venture rest on the interactions of its people." The chemistry can be based on a variety of factors. For instance, in an Italian-U.S. joint venture, the venture's management attributed much of the venture's success to the compatibility and close friendship between the two chairmen of the parent companies. At the root of the close bond was that the U.S. firm's chairman was of Italian origin. When the American firm first sought a joint venture partner in Europe, the chairman zeroed in on the Italian company because of his personal desire to maintain strong ties with the country of his ancestors. As a result, the American chairman's personal role in the venture helped build an amiable and trusting relationship with the Italian partner, which contributed tremendously to the venture's success. Similarly, William Glavin, Xerox's president, stated, "Outside of the U.S., every Xerox entity commenced as a joint venture. Initially, I wondered how the success of a joint venture could weigh so heavily on simple trust. Yet, through the years, it proved accurate. Mutual trust at senior management levels has carried Xerox's ventures through some turbulent times."

Strategic Traits

Absorptive Capability

It has been noted in the joint venture literature that the complementary needs of the partners create interpartner "fit" that is expected to generate a synergistic effect on venture performance (Geringer 1991; Parkhe 1991). However, complementarity is not likely to materialize unless a certain threshold of skills is already in place. The success of a joint venture's operations and expansion will largely depend upon its partners' absorptive capability, or its ability to acquire, assimilate, integrate, and exploit knowledge and skills. Further, the firm's ability to process, integrate, and deploy new knowledge and skills depends significantly on how the newly acquired knowledge links, or fits with, the knowledge base already in place. Therefore, the knowledge bases possessed by the partner firms define the strategic and organizational fit between them (Beamish 1987), which in turn influences both the financial and operational synergies at the joint venture (Buckley and Casson 1988). As a result, a partner's absorptive capability is likely to be positively associated with the joint venture's profitability and sales growth.

Market Power

Because a major objective of foreign investors is to preempt market opportunities and business potentials in a host market, a local partner's market power is a key asset for joint venture development. A local partner's market power often represents its industrial and business background, market position, and established marketing and distribution networks. Market power also enables the firm to mitigate some industrywide restrictions on output, increase bargaining power, and offer the advantages of economies of scale. Moreover, a local partner's strong market power can strengthen an international joint venture's commitment to local market expansion. Furthermore, strong market power can lead to greater bargaining power with the government, which can help the joint venture reduce political risks and business uncertainties.

Product Relatedness

The product diversification relationship between the partners and the joint venture can influence the venture's economies of scale and scope and efficiency of transaction costs (Harrigan 1985). This relationship may also affect the joint venture's ability to develop its product mix as well as to expand in the local market. For example, product relatedness between the local partner and the joint venture determines how much the venture can utilize the existing distribution channels, product image, industrial experience, and production facilities already established by the local partner (Geringer, Beamish, and da Costa 1989). Unique values associated with related diversification (vertical or horizontal) are not expected to occur when the local parent's products are unrelated to the venture's. Economic rents arising from economies of scale and from a local partner's existing distribution channels, marketing skills, consumer loyalty, and production facilities are predicted to be greater in related product diversification than in unrelated diversification. In addition, a related product link between a partner and the joint venture can be very helpful in establishing the venture's long-term, desirable relationships with suppliers, distributors, customers, and government agencies.

Market Experience

A partner's market experience and accumulated industrial knowledge are of great value for achieving joint venture goals. A partner's established history and strong background in a market often result in a good reputation or high credibility in the industry, and signify the building of a solid marketing and distribution network. It therefore is not surprising that the joint venture's business activities can be immensely facilitated by its parent firms' connections and relationship networks.

Organizational Traits

Firm Size

A partner's ability to contribute to its joint venture's survival and growth is positively associated with its organizational size, a variable closely related to economies of scale, market power, process innovation, and organizational image (Geringer 1991). It also influences an international joint venture's ability to overcome entry barriers stemming from minimum efficiency scale, a factor critical to the venture's profitability and market growth (Killing 1983). Moreover, greater organizational size implies higher capabilities to reduce risks and mitigate uncertainty (Scherer and Ross 1990). However, from a managerial point of view, a joint venture may not receive the same level of strategic attention and commitment from a large conglomerate parent that operates multiple overseas ventures as it otherwise would receive if the parent were a smaller company.

International Business Experience

The partners' experience in conducting international business is critical to the success of cross-cultural and cross-border venturing activities. International experience affects interpartner fit both in the early stages of joint venturing (Zeira and Shenkar 1990) and in the changes of fit over time as the venture evolves (Geringer 1991). Because the business atmosphere and commercial practices differ among different countries, mistrust and opportunism often occur during joint venture operations. For example, a local partner's international experience, through import and export businesses or cooperative projects with other international players, proves to be a very desirable attribute. This experience represents wider perspectives, advanced knowledge and skills, and widely accepted standards of modern business and management practices. Similarly, a multinational firm's business experience in the specific host country is also highly valued by the local partner to which this experience may well mean the firm's familiarity with the local culture and business practices, adaptability, and willingness of cooperation.

Previous Cooperative Experience

Previous experience between the same partners increases the chances of joint venture success. First, as the length of the interaction between partners increases, the economic transactions become increasingly embedded within the social relations of the partners, which helps establish trust and deter opportunism (Barney and Hansen 1994; Grannovetter 1985). Second, successful previous cooperation between the partners leads to the development of skills and routines that are specific to the relationship. These relationship-specific assets include knowledge about the strategy, structure, and operation of the partner organization, familiarity with its executives and managers, and the unique strengths as well as weaknesses of the partner firm (Levinthal and Fichman 1988). As Hamel et al. (1989) note, the operation and management of joint ventures can be greatly facilitated if the partners have well understood and correctly assessed each other's strengths and weaknesses. Past or existing relationships between the partners can therefore prove to be a fine asset to the proposed joint venture. Such relationships can also foster the climate of openness among the venture's managers, which is essential for problem solving and decision making in the joint venture.

Organizational Skills

In an international joint venture, people with different cultural backgrounds, career goals, compensation systems, and other differences have to work together with little advance preparation. This "people factor" can halt the joint venture's progress, sometimes quite significantly. Because of the existence of cultural barriers, the use of a large workforce, and the reliance on both local and expatriate managers, a collective strength in human resource management is critical. These skills include not only the ability to effectively blend cultures and management styles, but also specific techniques and capabilities of job design, recruiting and staffing, training, performance appraisal, compensation and benefits, career development, and labor-management relations. Among these attributes, the abilities to overcome cultural barriers, recruit competent employees, and establish incentive structures are particularly important. For example, international joint ventures often encounter pressure from the local government to hire what they perceive as redundant or unqualified people, pressure from trade unions to set minimum or maximum wage rates, and pressure from labor departments to implement bureaucratic regulations concerning human resource management. Under these circumstances, a well connected, politically influential, and skillful local partner is crucial. Similarly, to a local partner that is interested in acquiring advanced technology and in exporting the venture's products to the international market, a foreign partner's strength in R&D, experience in operating international operations, and exposure to global marketing network is particularly valuable.

Financial Traits

Investment Assessment and Capital Budgeting

As a joint venture partner, a firm's ability to conduct effective investment assessment and capital budgeting is critical. Since these capabilities are highly country specific, it is crucial that the local partner be able to understand effective allocation of financial resources in the country. Financial managers need to be able to gauge the total risk of a capital project and to develop appropriate risk-adjusted discount rates to be used in assessing the project. When a local partner is versed in calculating the riskiness of these cash flows, the joint venture tends to be more stable and liquid. As the complexity of investment opportunities increases in a cross-country setting, a local partner's ability to evaluate, analyze, and budget host country investment opportunities directly contributes to the joint venture's growth and profitability.

Risk Management

A partner's risk management ability affects an international joint venture's vulnerability to external hazards and internal stability. Risk reduction in the form of hedging and risk sharing largely determines an international joint venture's stability and pattern of growth. For example, fluctuations in currency exchange rates can significantly accentuate the volatility of earnings and cash flows. Such volatility can in turn distort management information systems and incentives, hinder access to capital markets, jeopardize the continuity of supplier and customer relationships, and even put the company into bankruptcy. Exchange rate fluctuations also affect the value of returns to the venture's international partner. In addition, management of foreign exchange risks often calls for frequent adjustments of important operating variables such as pricing, output, and sourcing. It may also involve strategic changes such as altering asset ownership structures, relocating plants, and restructuring the entire organization to improve the corporate-wide ability to respond to exchange-rate shifts. To undertake such strategic responses, the partners will require each other's superior ability of risk management.

Exposure Hedging

Economic exposure has become increasingly complex when a host market is dynamic and volatile. This is because economic and operational exposures, largely derived from hostile institutional environment and volatile market demand, are more long-term than typical foreign exchange transactions. Since local firms are generally more knowledgeable in avoiding or attenuating economic exposure, finding a local partner with considerable hedging experience helps the foreign partner ensure cash flows from its expected return of investment and protect the joint venture in the unpredictable institutional environment. A local partner's knowledge in market segmentation, indigenous sourcing, and prediction of foreign exchange fluctuations also helps mitigate economic exposure for the joint venture.

Financing Ability

In many foreign markets, multinational firms are constrained in obtaining local financing resources. A local partner that maintains superior relationships with local financial institutions and knows optimal ways to secure local financing is of critical importance to both the venture and the foreign partner. This ability not only enables the optimal structure of debt and equity that will minimize costs and risks, but also affects the joint venture's profitability, liquidity, working capital structure, leverage, and cash positions, all of which influence a firm's financial position and structure. In general, a desirable local financing strategy meets the venture's need for funds at the lowest possible cost, with due regard for the currency and political risk, and with provisions for flexibility in meeting unanticipated financial needs without excessive delay or costs.

In practice, many foreign investors investigate their local partner's financial capabilities by checking each of the following areas: (1) profit making, including the ability to exercise cost control, increase revenue, reduce taxes and expenses, and maximize operational efficiency; (2) allocation and utilization of capital, including the ability to allocate and use working capital, attain local financing, use and control debts, and manage risks; and (3) assets management, including the ability to optimally deploy assets and resources, manage accounts receivables and cash flows, and manage fixed and intangible assets.

Summary

Interpartner fit in a joint venture depends on the complementarity and congruence of the strategic, organizational, and financial traits of the partners. Strategic fit refers to the degree to which an international joint venture's partners augment or complement one another's strategies and capabilities in light of industry, market, product, customer, capital, or technology-related issues. This, in turn, involves a configuration comprising the interpartner arrangements, external environment, and joint venture effectiveness. Organizational fit can be defined as the match between each partner's administrative practices, control mechanisms, cultural practices, and personnel characteristics, which may directly affect the efficiency and effectiveness of the partnership. A partner's strategic strengths influence the operational skills and resources needed for the joint venture's competitive success. A partner's organizational strengths affect the efficiency and effectiveness of interfirm cooperation. Conceptually, both strategic and organizational strengths are crucial for joint venture performance. A partner with superior strategic traits but lacking organizational strength can make the joint venture unstable, while the possession of desirable organizational attributes without corresponding strategic competence leaves the joint venture unprofitable. From a process perspective, the mid-range linkage between partner selection and joint venture success may lie in interpartner fit (Parkhe 1993a). While strategic attributes may affect strategic fit between partners (Ellis and Shenkar 1996), organizational traits are likely to influence organizational fit (Li and Shenkar 1996).

Finally, financial fit concerns the degree of match in cash-flow position and capital structure between partners. Reducing uncertainty in operational cash flow is usually one of the major reasons for joint venture formation. The reduction of default risk depends on the correlation of the pre-venture cash flows of the two partners. A larger firm, as a result of an alliance, will have better access to capital markets and lower financing costs. This cost advantage implies a reduction in the firm's risk from the lender's viewpoint, which can be achieved by corporate diversification or a conglomerate merger. Tax-savings on interest payments or transfer pricing are another source of benefits from financial fit. An additional gain can be derived from a lower systematic risk premium in world capital markets than in the domestic market, which is caused by the less-than-perfect correlation of national capital market returns.

Financial fit is far more critical to international than domestic joint ventures. Financial issues such as foreign exchange earnings, risk hedging, foreign currency financing, and currency swap are less than major concerns for managers of domestic ventures. These issues, however, are so fundamental to international joint ventures that mishandling them will give rise to venture instability, interpartner conflict, and even dissolution.

Interpartner Fit at the Operational Level

Our above discussion of interpartner compatibility in cultural, strategic, organizational, and financial traits depicts a broad contour of congruence between potential partners for a joint venture, which serves as a fundamental prerequisite of a successful partnership. The discussion, however, has focused heavily on the static features of the individual parent firms without considering how the partners work side by side in co-managing the specific venture in terms of its strategic mission, organizational features, and managerial practices. For example, while most scholars as well as practitioners tend to agree that partnerships between culturally distant countries are more challenging to manage than ventures between culturally similar countries, an undeniable fact is that among joint ventures formed between the same countries—whether it is between the United States and Britain, France and Italy, the United States and Japan, or Japan and China—there exist significant differences in venture performance. To explore interpartner fit more specifically, below we identify four operational-level criteria for partner selection: compatibility of partner goals, complementary resources, commitment of the partners, and partner capability.

Goal Compatibility

Joint ventures flourish in an atmosphere of interpartner cooperation and forbearance but are hindered by opportunism and conflict. The compatibility of goals set for an international joint venture between its parents

affects the extent to which they behave cooperatively or opportunistically (Parkhe 1993b). Having different goals about joint venture development and evolution plants the seeds for subsequent opportunism and
conflict (Geringer and Hebert 1989). When strategic goals between parties diverge, firms are more likely to use distributive rather than cooperative strategies during joint venture operations. In contrast, goal
congruence reduces a player's uncertainty about what another player
will do, which can in turn facilitate making the best response to the
partner's predicted strategies (i.e., Nash equilibrium). Goal congruity
thus propels organizational fit and strategic symmetry between foreign
and local parents (Park 1996; Parkhe 1993b). It may generate more financial or operational synergies because every party is highly motivated
to move in the same strategic direction. Additionally, goal congruity
stimulates the commitment of resources by each party.

Goal differences exist among the parents of joint ventures in both
developed and developing countries. For instance, many Japanese firms
seek Western partners' product innovation via joint ventures, whereas
their counterparts pursue market expansion or process innovation in Japan (Hamel 1991). Luo (1997), Osland and Cavusgil (1996), and Yan
and Gray (1994) suggest that while foreign parents want joint ventures
in China to focus on preempting market opportunities and benefit from
the release of pent-up demand long stifled by ideology-based governmental intervention, local parents see joint ventures as channels to acquire foreign technologies and organizational skills. Beamish (1993)
demonstrated that interfirm conflict resulting from goal difference makes
many joint ventures in China unsuccessful. Brouthers and Bamossy
(1997) suggest that joint ventures in Eastern Europe often fail because
goal incongruity deters the benefits of sharing resources.

According to Williamson (1979, 239), goal congruity harmonizes the
interests between parties that would otherwise give way to antagonistic
subgoal pursuits. This congruity is particularly critical in relational contracts of high complexity and with a long-haul orientation. Therefore,
no matter how elegant the strategic business concept is behind a cooperative deal or how capable the participants are, the partners have to
be able to work together. Otherwise, there is only a slim likelihood
that the venture will stand the test of time and cope with changing market and environmental conditions. Each company should evaluate the
objectives of the partner and identify whether or not they are compatible to its own.

The situation that holds the most promise for compatibility is one in which strategic goals converge while competitive goals diverge. For example, Du Pont and Philips have a strategic alliance in which both manufacture compact discs, yet respect each other's market boundaries. Unfortunately, not all joint venture goals are as compatible. Large companies sometimes send a string of employees to smaller partners for the sole purpose of gaining knowledge. To avoid the pitfall of ambiguous or different goals, participants should make sure they synchronize to begin with, then review what has been accomplished in terms of their original goals at least every three to six months. The success of a consortium between Boeing and three Japanese heavy industry companies to design and build the 767 and future Boeing aircraft is partially attributable to goal compatibility. Boeing sought foreign partners to ease its financial burden and operational risks while the Japanese tried to expand their role in the aerospace industry. The Japanese are now increasing their participation in the industry significantly, providing an ever-increasing portion of production parts and assembly. Boeing has reduced the risks of development by adding a large potential customer and by lowering the financial commitment required for production.

It is important to note that goal compatibility does not necessarily mean goal identity. Joint venture partners may, and many times do, have very different goals and expectations. However, as far as the partners understand and respect each other's goals and the two sets of goals are not in direct conflict (e.g., one partner is interested in local market while the other is interested in export), different goals still can be compatible. For instance, many multinational firms are interested in the Russian market while Russian firms are looking for advanced Western products and technology. If managed well (i.e., setting up a joint venture in Russia that produces technologically advanced products for the local market), both parties' strategic expectations can be met simultaneously.

Resource Complementarity

It is well recognized that the greater the resource complementarity between joint venture partners, the greater the operational and financial synergies to be achieved in the venture. Resource complementarity also reduces governance and coordination costs and stimulates information exchange during diversification. More importantly, interpartner complementarity improves the learning curve, thus providing additional benefits to the joint venture. In essence, an international joint venture is a mechanism for the partners to pool complementary assets and to seek skills that each individually lacks but considers vital for the fulfillment of its strategic objectives. For example, JVC depended on a number of joint ventures in its successful effort to make VHS the industry standard for the video industry. JVC stocked RCA with machines carrying the RCA label, set up licensing agreements with Japanese manufacturers, and formed alliances with Germany's Telefunken and Britain's Thorn-EMI Ferguson to help with manufacturing the video recorders. JVC's alliance with Thompson allowed it to learn how to succeed in the fragmented European market, while Thompson benefited from JVC's product technology and manufacturing prowess. As a result, Sony, once JVC's strong competitor, conceded defeat in 1988, discontinued its production of Betamax, and began manufacturing VHS machines.

Similarly, complementary strengths were a major driving force behind the formation of the 50–50 joint venture between Clark Equipment and Volvo. In the construction equipment business, neither partner individually had sufficient geographic presence and distribution capabilities to compete with the market leaders, Komatsu and Caterpillar. However, Volvo had roughly 70 percent of its sales in Europe and the Middle East, while Clark had 70 percent of its sales in North America. By pooling marketing resources, each partner resulted in a much broader geographic scope.

What exactly constitutes complementarity remains vague in the literature. Harrigan (1985) takes a broad view, applying complementarity to missions, resources, and managerial capabilities. These complementary skills can create a strategic fit in which the bargaining power of the venture's sponsors is evenly matched. Arrangements involving complementary assets include vertical quasi-integration, in which each partner contributes one or more distinct elements in the production and distribution chains, as well as horizontal linkages among partners with strengths in different geographical areas, product lines, and so forth.

The case for complementary skills seems to be particularly strong when the partners represent developing and developed economies, respectively. In such ventures, the developed country multinationals typically contribute manufacturing technology, product know-how, patents, business expertise, technical training, and management capabilities, while the local partner "commonly contributes some combination of capital, management, knowledge of the environment of the country and the market, contacts with the government, financial institutions, local suppliers and labor unions, and marketing capabilities" (United Nations 1989, 59). Specifically, Beamish (1988) categorizes partner needs in ventures involving developing and developed country partners into five groups: readily capitalized items, human resources, market access, government/political access, and knowledge needs. An appropriate mix or complementarity of these resources was found a critical factor in joint venture success.

Commitment

Finding a partner with an equal sense of commitment to the joint venture is the keystone to success. Even if partners appear generally capable and compatible, the chances of the venture's weathering changing market conditions are slim unless they are both willing to invest time, energy, and resources in the alliance. Without this commitment, a partner's resources, complementary or not, cannot help the venture realize its strategic objectives. Without commitment, compatible goals and commensurate risks remain uncultivated. A partner's commitment also affects ongoing trust building and maintenance. Commitment counters opportunism and fosters cooperation. For instance, at HP Medical Product Co. Ltd. in Qingdao, China, the partners were highly committed to joint product development for the local market. A recent eighteen-month R&D project on a new electrocardiogram was extremely successful, reducing product costs from $10,000 to only $3,000. The Chinese engineers contributed their knowledge of production that fits the demands of Chinese consumers in the most cost-effective way with the maximum local content. Similarly, Shanghai Foxboro, a joint venture manufacturing industrial control equipment, benefited significantly from its U.S. parent firm's continuing commitment to transferring updated technologies to the venture over time.

When joint ventures face unexpected environmental changes and market dynamics, partner commitment serves as a stabilizing device offsetting contextual uncertainties. For example, interpartner conflict is inevitable in joint ventures. If commitment from both partners is reasonably high, interpartner conflict may not seriously impair the stability of the joint venture. If partner commitment is low, however, serious and frequent conflicts will become a primary source of instability. For example, GM and Daewoo blamed each other for the lackluster performance of the Pontiac LeMans, a product of their joint venture in South Korea. Daewoo accused GM of failing to market the LeMans aggressively in the United States, while GM maintained that the Daewoo was not fully committed to improving the quality of the car and sourcing with more reliable suppliers. Lack of commitment from both parties ended this joint venture in 1992.

Interpartner learning and communication are important ingredients of dynamic commitment. Japanese-American Seating Inc. (JASI), a 65–35 joint venture established in 1987 between Kasai Kogyo Ltd. (seat manufacturer based in Tokyo) and Banting Seat Corporation (seat assembler headquartered in Detroit), is a good example for bilateral learning. Kasai spent much time teaching American managers and training American workers on the Just-In-Time (JIT) system. Kasai helped to design work cells for the new plant to allow quick, easy changes and short set-up times. It sent its best managers to monitor the joint venture. In a six-month period of time, Banting sent three groups of two to three salaried managers and technicians to Japan to learn about Kasai's production system, and to see the same seats they would be making being built at the Tokyo facility. Besides, the managers from Banting were committed to work with American suppliers to adopt JIT, so that JASI could get JIT supplies. Further, both companies established effective communication systems on the issues of product quality, customer service, engineering changes, and development and testing of prototypes, among others. They also communicated cultural issues with which the Japanese managers were unfamiliar, such as donations to a local charity or staging a company party for employees and their families. Most importantly, Kasai and Banting worked cooperatively to resolve conflicts between the two groups of employees.

Capability

As noted earlier, multifaceted capabilities of a potential partner are of prime importance. In general, what a company looks for in a partner is the ability to contribute complementary strengths and resources to the joint venture. It seeks a partner that can help overcome any weaknesses that have prevented the firm from achieving its business objectives. Without distinctive competencies, it is impossible to realize complementarity of resources, even though the two firms might have compatible and complementary goals. Resource complementarity affects collaborative synergies only within a specific period of time, and it alone is insufficient to support ongoing joint venture development. Organizational capability, by contrast, provides an essential supply base for the resources needed in the development of long-term partnerships. One of the examples showing the importance of partner capability is UPS Yamato Company, an equal-equity joint venture between United Parcel Service (UPS) and Yamato Transportation Company of Japan. The joint venture started out with international air transport of general cargo, letters, documents, small parcels, and other items. Both UPS and Yamato were the leaders in their own domestic markets. UPS employs 398,000 people, maintains a vehicle fleet of more than 157,000 trucks and an air fleet of more than 500 planes, and handles more than 3 billion packages and more than 5.5 percent of the country's gross domestic product. Combining the strength of two partners allows the venture to offer truly seamless transportation services. Unlike other delivery service companies, such as DHL and Federal Express, which are largely linked to transport of letters or business documents, the venture could handle anything from letters right up to automobiles or heavy machinery. This was a key advantage for the venture to compete with other transportation groups in the market of express delivery.

Joint venture partners need to determine which capability to seek from each other. The value-creating logic should guide the assessment of capability contribution. In general, it is critical for joint ventures to possess the ability to tilt the competitive balance in favor of the coalition and to allow members to gain competitive strength. For instance, in its battle against Sony for leadership in the VCR market, JVC brought a new standard, new products, and the Japanese manufacturing advantage to its coalition. In Europe, JVC co-opted several relatively weaker, yet not minuscule, competitors, such as Thomson, Thorn, and Nokia. Although these firms were individually weak, they were collectively powerful enough to gain large-scale access to the European markets and to lobby their respective governments and the European Community. Fujitsu followed a similar approach in its co-option of ICL, Nokia, Amdahl, and other mainframe computer makers against IBM.

In evaluating a partner's capability, managers must ask, "What can my potential partner bring that is unique?" According to Doz and Hamel (1998), uniqueness has three aspects: (1) unique capabilities that cannot be traded easily across companies, (2) unique capabilities that cannot be easily substituted, and (3) unique capabilities that cannot be independently developed or replicated within a reasonable time frame. The nontradable capabilities would lose their value if transferred or sold. *Guanxi* (interpersonal relationship) with the business community and governmental authorities is such a capability. It is individually embedded and organizationally extended, and cannot be sold to another company, particularly to a foreign one. Nonsubstitutable capabilities are resources and skills possessed or controlled by a partner that are hardly accessible by other firms. To continue the government-relationship example, a local partner with such good relationships is an absolute necessity for selling in government-controlled markets, for example, the automobile market. The third type of capability concerns capabilities that cannot be independently developed or replicated within a reasonable time frame. For instance, it is extremely difficult, if not impossible, for GE, as an American company, to independently develop a close relationship with the powerful European players. GE therefore had to turn to SNECMA, a company that had a strong French identity and was closely linked with Airbus and Airbus's French and German partners.

Partner Selection Process

It is always important to tackle the partner selection process head on. According to a survey conducted by the Conference Board in 1997, there is a positive relationship between the partner selection process and the success of joint ventures. The more rigorous and disciplined the partner selection process, the more successful the joint venture. Moreover, multinational companies that are faring well are twice as likely to do systematic partner assessments as less successful companies. These results suggest the importance of institutionalizing partner selection process for joint venture formation. This process can further promote subsequent institutionalization of partner capabilities that are needed for business development. According to Emerson Electric's chairman and CEO, Charles F. Knight, when certain rigorous pre- and post-venture guidelines are followed, "you can succeed where others have failed." During the past five years, Emerson has acquired nearly $2.4 million in sales through joint ventures—about 25 percent of the company's total sales. One of the key points in Knight's pre-venture guidelines is about the partner selection process. Specifically, Emerson followed four rules: (1) Do not get into business with a company in a turnaround situation; (2) do not do business with a company that does not have good management; (3) stick to core competencies; and (4) do a lot of due diligence work.

At a more general level, we provide below a checklist for firms pursuing international joint ventures. The seven activities are intended to help these firms form a concrete action plan in the partner selection process.

First, before seriously approaching any prospective ally, the capabilities of the targeted candidates should be subjected to a rigorous test. Many joint venture practitioners recommend establishing a team of experts to undertake a feasibility study on each candidate. The team's composition and the delineation of its investigation will, of course, depend on the nature and scope of the venture. In general, it should be a multifunctional team that includes operating managers plus functional experts in areas such as finance, business law, and taxation. For instance, over the years, Corning established more than fifty joint ventures, most of which have been successful. Samsung-Corning in Korea is one of these successful stories. Samsung, the Korean partner, sought to expand its television manufacturing, while Corning wanted to access to the high-growth markets of Asia. The joint venture's sales in 1996 exceeded $500 million, and Corning enjoyed a major market share in the dynamic Asian marketplace. James R. Houghton, Corning's chairman and CEO, attributed the venture's success to the following factors: (1) It started with a solid business opportunity; (2) both partners made comparable contributions; (3) the venture had a well-defined scope and had no major conflicts with the parents; (4) there was interpartner trust; (5) the management of each parent firm had vision and confidence to support the venture through rough spots; and (6) an autonomous team conducted a thorough assessment of the joint venture partner.

Second, partner assessment must be tough, critical, and thorough, and cannot be solely based on the partners' own descriptions. In fact, some multinational firms, such as Emerson Electric, sometimes form two teams to evaluate a proposed joint venture—one in favor and the other opposed—as a strategy for decision making and for avoiding the "deal fever." Naturally, all companies try to present themselves in the best possible light. A potential partner may characterize itself as possessing strengths in technology, management expertise, sales staff, and distribution networks. Investigations, however, may reveal significant differences between how the company describes itself and what the firm actually looks like. A former ICI executive noted that companies should not make the mistake of letting apparent compatibility interfere with a thorough analysis of capabilities and resources. Using the marriage metaphor, he warned against becoming "too starry-eyed or in love with your partner. A company has to take a hard look at its potential mate to ascertain whether it has the capabilities and resources to combat adverse market conditions." He recalled one of ICI's experiences with a Spanish joint venture in basic chemicals: "Although we had an excellent working relationship with our Spanish partner, the venture still collapsed. We had overestimated the market potential for the venture's products and the speed of reaching plant capacity, and we underestimated the joint venture's capital requirements. When both firms were required to contribute additional capital, our Spanish partner could not meet its financial obligations because it had run into serious financial problems. Despite our 'compatibility,' we had to withdraw from the venture."

Third, partner selection should be integrated with the focal company's strategic goals. For example, if a foreign company seeks long-term market growth, the importance of a local firm's marketing competence, market position, technological skills, industrial experience, organizational rank, and asset efficiency may outweigh other attributes. If a foreign company seeks cost minimization via export, such attributes as learning ability, foreign experience, and ownership type may be more critical than others. If a foreign company seeks short-term profitability, it should attach a higher value to a local partner's relationship-building skills, strategic orientation, profitability, and liquidity. Lastly, if a foreign company seeks reduction of financial risks and operational uncertainty, more weight may be placed on attributes such as corporate image, organizational leadership, human resource skills, and financial leverage. Sinopec-Honeywell joint venture in Tianjin, China, is a good example. In January 1993, Honeywell and the Chinese National Petroleum Company (Sinopec) entered a joint equity company, with Honeywell owning 55 percent of the equity. Honeywell's key goals for this joint venture are threefold: (1) geographic expansion, (2) market share, and (3) risk diversification. Honeywell needed a strong local partner that could ensure its smooth development of operations in China. Sinopec, a decade-old customer of Honeywell, was the leading, best-known state-owned company, with thirty-five refineries and petrochemical plants around the nation. It had dominated the Chinese hydrocarbon processing market for years and maintained leading industrial experience and technological skills among Chinese rivals. The company's strong relationship with the central government served as what Michael R. Bonsignore, Honeywell's chairman and CEO, called the "proprietary asset" to the venture.

Fourth, potential joint venture firms should obtain as much information as possible about their potential partner. For example, the business license of a local firm can provide information about its legal capacity, registered capital, business scope, and the name of the legal representative. It is also necessary to obtain a copy of the company's brochure and find out about the industry and the candidate firm's competitors (which may also serve as a good source for potential partners beyond the current candidate). The foreign partner may inquire whether the candidate had ever received any honors or awards from local authorities or professional organizations, because such awards may reflect the firm's professional reputation.

Fifth, the search for a joint venture partner should always start with the existing cooperative relationships. Forging an international joint venture with a company with which a previous relationship exists has a number of advantages: (1) The history of the relationship provides proof of how well the two companies can work together; (2) it is always easier to strengthen personal ties that are already in place than to start anew; (3) each company will have a fair idea of the capabilities, business ethics, and culture of the other company; and (4) the partner will be well versed in operating collaborative ventures. On a cautious note, some companies warn of the danger of relying too heavily on extending existing relationships. By restricting one's scope to existing partners, one may not find the optimum partner for a new business venture. Avoiding the grueling processing of seeking new partners may lead to a compromise in which you work with a familiar firm that has adequate but not superlative resources. Further, some firms fear that they could lose their autonomy or independence if they are too closely associated with a very limited number of partner firms. Such a tight bond can diminish a firm's chances of attracting other partners.

Sixth, a site visit is critical, as reliable information can often be obtained only by first-hand observation. During the site visit, attention should be given to employee attitudes, the morale of managers, operation efficiency, technologies and equipment, cash flows, overall financial health, and the effectiveness of the management systems. In addition, it is a frequently recommended practice that multiple candidate firms are visited on the same field trip. This helps the company increase bargaining power during joint venture negotiation, because, from the power-dependence perspective, the more alternatives a party can exercise, the more powerful it is in a bi-party bargaining. Another highly recommended practice is for the foreign partner to visit the local government officials as early as possible in the partner selection process. This is particularly important if the project is large in investment or has to be ratified by the host country government. Seventh, it is always important to understand, as early as possible, the key objectives and expectations of the potential partner. When a firm's expectations do not align with one's own, a rational assessment should be conducted in terms of whether the partners collectively are able to reconcile the differences. Caution should be exercised whenever a potential partner puts its own interests above those of the partnership, bets the venture's success too heavily on the political ties with the government, or intentionally hides its strategic agendas. These behaviors signal a strong tendency toward opportunism or lack of cooperation at best. Beijing Jeep is a good example of diverging expectations between the partners. Barely a year after the joint venture's formation, the Chinese partner felt that AMC had reneged on the terms of the contract, which called for joint design and production of a new Jeep, when the exhaust system, noise controls, and speed of the vehicle failed to meet international standards. The breakup between AT&T and Olivetti, one of the most publicized divorces in the joint venture arena, also demonstrates how differences in management objectives and styles between partners can impede the joint venture's success.

Lastly, the integration of partner selection with other investment strategies such as location selection, entry timing, and sharing arrangement needs to be investigated. Given the economic, cultural, and historical diversity of a host market, firms cannot use homogenous criteria in evaluating and selecting partners for joint ventures in different regions. The importance of each criterion may also differ because of the timing of investment, variations in the environment, and the strategic priority of the firm at the time.

Mini-Case Examples

Case 1: Burger King and Japan Tobacco

As McDonald's and Kentucky Fried Chicken have become firmly established in Japan, Burger King's penetration efforts appear to be at least ten years late. In 1993, Burger King partnered with Seibu Railways Corporation to take advantage of the local transportation company's access to high-traffic areas in Tokyo. By 1996, Burger King's penetration was limited to just five restaurants, compared with approximately 1,860 McDonald's and 1,200 Kentucky Fried Chicken restaurants in Japan. Burger King attributed this slow growth to Seibu's conservative views on expansion. In May 1996, Burger King announced the formation of a joint venture with Japan Tobacco Inc. (JTI), called Burger King-JTI. The new venture started with an acquisition of thirty-five outlets from Morinaga & Co.'s struggling Love Burger Chain. While no one could have predicted a partnership between the United States' no. 2 fast food restaurant and Japan's former tobacco monopoly, the pair appeared confident that they could break into Japan's fast food market. At formation, the venture faced these two largest competitors—McDonald's, which had half of Japan's burger market with 1,860 stores and sales topping $2.3 billion, and Mos Burger, a local chain that had 25 percent of the market share.

An evaluation of JTI reveals the following attributes:

Strategic Attributes

Like most Japanese companies, the tobacco firm showed a high degree of absorptive capability. It is widely reported that Western firms in general have difficulties in applying knowledge gained from international collaborations, while Japanese companies are particularly good at learning from their joint venture partners. Out of their international joint ventures, Japanese firms usually emerge stronger than their Western partners as a result of learning. This was not a concern to Burger King because Japan Tobacco had had no practical experience in the hamburger industry. Second, JTI's industrial experience may prove very important. Being a former government-run monopoly, JTI is familiar with and has maintained its informal ties with the Japanese government. Before its privatization in 1985, the firm was one of the largest public corporations in Japan, contributing 3.3 percent–4.8 percent of the national general account during 1965–1969. In fact, at the formation of the joint venture with Burger King, the government still owned two-thirds of JTI.

JTI's strategic orientation can be classified as a Prospector, in Miles and Snow's (1978) terminology. Since 1987 when import tariffs on foreign cigarette manufacturers were relieved, JTI has steadily lost its market share. Meanwhile, foreign brands have expanded from a scant 2 percent to more than 22 percent of the Japanese market. This increased competition, along with declining cigarette consumption worldwide, has prompted JTI to look for other markets to diversify its holdings. The new businesses the firm has explored include pharmaceuticals, foods, agribusiness, real estate, and engineering. Burger King assessed that JTI's Prospector orientation would be beneficial to the partnership because a high-growth strategy in the Japanese market needs a partner that is proactive and adaptable.

JTI possessed no experience or market presence in the fast food industry. However, the firm did have a small presence and some experience in the beverage industry through its "Half-Time" line of beverages, although this business has little in common with the service-oriented fast food industry. Thus, JTI scored negatively on market power and product relatedness, from Burger King's judgment. Another negative strategic attribute would be JTI's brand image. While JTI is a respectable company, its main line of business is cigarettes, which could potentially be in conflict with Burger King's core customer groups, including teenagers and their parents, who may not approve of an affiliation with JTI.

In sum, the assessment of JTI's strategic attributes revealed mixed results. The company is favorable in terms of absorptive capability, industrial experience, and strategic orientation. On the other hand, it scored negatively for market power, product relatedness, and corporate image. Therefore, JTI had a questionable strategic fit with Burger King.

Organizational Attributes

One of JTI's positive organizational attributes is its size. JTI employed 22,700 employees and its sales in 1997 were $29.8 billion, an increase of 35.2 percent over 1996. It also has international experience from pharmaceutical research with a U.S. firm, Agouron Pharmaceutical Inc.

Negative organizational attributes include a lack of past collaboration experience with Burger King and the likelihood of a low priority being given to the joint venture. Past collaboration would have been beneficial, but the lack of it would not be severely detrimental to the partnership. On the other hand, since JTI's core business is the tobacco industry, which has accounted for 98 percent of company revenues, the joint venture may find itself near the bottom of JTI's strategic agenda. This concern is not unreasonable because JTI has already encountered increasingly tough competition from battle-hardened foreign cigarette manufacturers in the Japanese market. Firms such as R.J. Reynolds and Phillip Morris had been reducing their investment in the United States due to high litigation and legal restrictions, then turning to Asia where restrictions were practically nonexistent. If JTI has to defend its core business in cigarette making, its commitment to the hamburger joint venture would be questionable. As a result, its attractiveness as a joint venture partner decreases from Burger King's perspective.

JTI has another questionable organizational attribute: organizational leadership. As a former government monopoly, the firm's leadership was highly political. Public corporations in Japan usually have a large number of civil servants occupying key management positions. Even after privatization, the companies still are under significant government influence. For example, three out of the thirteen presidents and chairmen of the Japan Railways group are former Ministry of Finance officials. This organizational attribute may have both positive and negative implications. On the one hand, ties with the government could provide preferential treatment to Burger King, such as easing of restrictions, granting of prime locations, and access to key government officials. On the other hand, the lack of autonomy as a result of these ties could prove detrimental. For example, dealing with bureaucratic government departments can slow down business decisions. In addition, there might be situations in which JTI have to acquiesce to the government at the expense of the joint venture's business interests.

Financial Attributes

Analysis of JTI's financial attributes over the last four years provides insight into the company's profitability, liquidity, leverage, and asset efficiency. The gross and net profit margins provide measures of the company's profitability. JTI had enjoyed a steady increase in gross profitability over the four years prior to the joint venture (Table 2.1). The firm's liquidity had experienced relatively small fluctuations over time and an increase in liquidity for 1997. The firm's asset efficiency had shown improvement during the four-year period. Overall, JTI demonstrated very favorable financial traits to Burger King.

In conclusion, JTI's financial health was very appealing to Burger King. The company's strategic and organizational strengths were less impressive. On the strategic side, the highly focused business in the

Table 2.1

JTI's Key Financial Attributes (1994–1997)

	1994	1995	1996	1997
Gross profit margin	0.15	0.16	0.16	0.17
Net profit margin	0.02	0.02	0.02	0.02
Current ratio	2.80	2.70	2.45	2.51
Quick ratio	1.50	1.55	1.50	1.67
Debt-assets ratio	0.06	0.06	0.05	0.05
Debt-equity ratio	0.09	0.09	0.08	0.08
Inventory turnover	5.50	5.90	6.10	6.95
Fixed-asset turnover	4.40	4.30	4.31	4.55

tobacco industry made the firm vulnerable, especially in the wake of the increasingly unfavorable public image of the industry overall. The Japanese general public has become aware of the health risks of cigarette smoking and the government has begun considering some regulative actions. On the organizational side, JTI, as a recently privatized government enterprise, will feel increased pressure from its foreign competitors that are larger in size and more efficient in technology and management.

Case 2: BNP and China's Industrial and Commercial Bank

The French-based Banque Nationale de Paris (BNP) holds a unique position in Asia by offering the scope of a truly transnational bank in combination with services tailored to meet the needs of regional markets. BNP has established offices in Beijing, Shanghai, and Guangzhou, and branches in Shenzhen and Tianjin. Most recently, BNP has embarked upon the first-ever Sino-foreign joint venture bank with the Shanghai branch of the Industrial and Commercial Bank of China (ICBC). This new bank would be known as the International Bank of Paris and Shanghai. BNP's international expertise and breadth (with operations in eighty countries) is a natural fit with ICBC's domestic experience and tacit knowledge.

This joint venture would allow BNP to continue to diversify its product and service line outside of its staple trade finance into merchant, corporate, and private banking. This would also allow the French bank to evolve with the changing environment in Asia, better meet the needs of its clientele, and enlarge its geographic scope. On the other hand, the partnership would enable the local partner to gain access to the rich experience and networks of the foreign partner in terms of managing global financial product portfolio. The Chinese bank admired its French partner's knowledge and technical expertise in managing a portfolio high in variety and complexity and truly global in scope. As China gradually moves toward a free market, the value of teaming up with a world-class player such as BNP and learning its tacit knowledge cannot be overstated.

The local partner, ICBC, brought several operations and task-related attributes to this corporate marriage. Strategically, it offered strong market power, highly complementary products and services, rich and extensive domestic industrial expertise, and a respectable corporate image. The local partner also contributed important organizational strength. ICBC's large size, leadership position in the local market, tight connection with the local government, and high reputation are especially invaluable. On the other hand, BNP brought to the partnership many attractive items. Strategically, BNP possessed a huge absorptive capacity—it is backed by the French government and possesses a massive asset base. BNP's market power is strong and its product portfolio truly global. BNP contributed to the venture its worldwide "five star–AAA" corporate reputation. Especially in Asia, corporate image, track record, and reputation are of the utmost importance. As a worldwide leader in profitability, asset efficiency, and liquidity, BNP also brought to the venture its extensive expertise in cash flow and financial management. Finally, BNP's familiarity with the local governmental and regulatory authorities was invaluable in operating in a highly regulated institutional environment.

Synergy seems to be the key feature of this joint venture. This partnership was expected to give BNP greater access to the local markets, faster entry and payback (a risk-reducing factor) due to increased efficiency, and a significant increase in its competitiveness in China. The increased operational scale of the bank could also improve its bargaining power in negotiating with its business partners, strengthen economies of scope and scale, and reduce risks through both product portfolio and geographical diversification. Further, the joint venture would also enable BNP to piggyback ICBC's wide access to the local labor market, fine brand recognition, and major clients.

An important feature in this case is that the foreign partner had had a long history of operation in Asia and fully understood the importance of sensitivity to the Chinese culture. BNP's valuable experience in Asia obviously helped a great deal in its partner selection in China. The French bank was locally well known for its high commitment to its joint ventures and for having never abandoned an Asian partner. In addition, over the years of operating in a quite dynamic area of the world, BNP has built a high level of adaptability.

In summary, it seems that in this joint venture, the parent firms possessed only desirable features. With these features, there is little doubt that the venture would face a promising start to success.

3

Founding Negotiations

This chapter tackles a prominent issue in the dynamic, evolutionary process of international joint venture development: contract negotiations during joint venture formation. Building on a socio-psychological perspective together with transaction cost theory, this chapter presents an integrated conceptual framework of joint venture negotiations in a general context where relevant antecedent, concurrent, and consequent factors are interlocked and mutually influential in sequence. It articulates three levels of antecedents of joint venture negotiations (environmental, organizational, and individual), three core concurrent factors (term specificity, issue diversity, and contractual obligatoriness), and three sequential consequences, including the immediate outcome (formation satisfaction), intermediate effect (process performance), and ultimate effect (overall performance).

Introduction

Negotiation is a decision-making or problem-solving process accomplished jointly by two or more parties. International interfirm negotiations involve a complex process of deliberate interactions between two or more firms originating in different nations and seeking to define their interdependence. Cultural differences, legal pluralism, monetary factors, ideological diversity, and greater uncertainty distinguish international business negotiations from domestic ones (Adler, Brahm, and Graham 1992; Brett and Okumura 1998; Moran and Stripp 1991). Different groups employ different negotiation behaviors and styles shaped by geography, history, religion, and politics. Discussions are often impeded when parties to a negotiation seem to pursue different paths of logic (Salacuse 1991; Tung 1988). The complexities involved in creating and managing an international joint venture—a hybrid, multi-ownership organizational form—are reflected in the negotiations leading to its establishment. Interpartner conflict often arises due to different perceptions, preferences, behavioral styles, and goals, with transaction hazards precipitated by opportunistic behavior in search of private interests (Parkhe 1993a; Ring and Van de Ven 1994).

Negotiations concerning joint venture formation are especially daunting. An international joint venture is typically established by two or more partners undertaking joint investment and risk and benefit sharing according to negotiated terms. From a bargaining perspective, the anticipated need for interpartner cooperation will influence the negotiation strategies used by each of the parties (Yan and Gray 1994). When the parties act in an adversarial manner, holding each other at arm's length, they generally use a distributive strategy in which limited information is exchanged while each party works independently to gain an information-based advantage in the negotiation (Pruitt and Lewis 1975). Distributive strategies are less likely in joint venture negotiations, however, because such ventures involve interpartner learning and future interdependence. Joint venture partners are more likely to use integrative strategies that allow the parties to freely exchange information and produce a mutually beneficial outcome. The integrative or problem-solving strategy does not preclude, however, the necessity to explicitly define relevant conditions for joint venture establishment and operations (Fayerweather and Kapoor 1976).

When operating in a highly complex, dynamic environment, an interfirm network becomes more vulnerable to environmental changes and interparty conflict (Hill 1990; Park 1996). This vulnerability requires strong bonds between the parties in order to sustain honest transactions. Joint venture management must develop mechanisms for facilitating interpartner learning and collaboration because the norms of reciprocity and trust alone are insufficient to control the venture or make the best use of its unique benefits (Hamel 1991; Yan and Gray 1994).

Negotiating joint venture formation is difficult and costly. The goals and expectations of one partner are often incongruent or incompatible with those of the other. Because an international joint venture entails mutual commitment of strategic assets in an uncertain, complex environment, transaction costs during formation and subsequent operations are high (Ring and Van de Ven 1994). Normative specifications and stipulations are necessary for all parties to ensure control of their respective strategic resources while benefiting from possible financial or operational synergies generated from the venture. Joint venture negotiation is also a social and political process affected by cultural distance and government pressure or hindrance.

To anticipate interpartner conflict, specifying terms during negotiations is imperative to joint venture formation and operations. During the formation stage, goal heterogeneity, low trust, and resource homogeneity are endogenous factors driving subsequent interfirm conflict. During the operations stage, significant uncertainties can emerge. For example, changes in the partners' strategic goals can result in conflicts. Furthermore, the growth of a network through a dynamic cyclical process contains the seeds of disintegration (Park 1996). The increase in resource transactions between partners over time implies that their domains will shift from being complementary to being similar, which further increases the likelihood of territorial disputes and competition. Well specified terms in the venture's founding negotiation can both prevent subsequent interpartner conflict and set up mechanisms to resolve such conflict if it does occur.

International joint venture negotiations differ from those of other international businesses because firm motivation, project longevity, and resource commitment are different for joint ventures. The resulting terms, clauses, and conditions are distinctive, venture-specific, and complex. Because it concerns the establishment and development of a new, independent entity involving long-term commitment, negotiating the contract for an international joint venture is a long range *ex ante* governance mechanism for attenuating opportunism and facilitating collaboration. By contrast, contract terms for other international businesses, such as import and export, are generally more standardized.

The process of international business negotiation has been extensively addressed. Graham's (1987) process model addresses the importance of successive interactions between negotiators and the impact of context on negotiations. Fayerweather and Kapoor's (1976) framework highlights the role of the "negotiation situation," arguing that environmental and organizational variables affect negotiation patterns. Kochan and Katz's (1988) bargaining model incorporates institutional factors such as government intervention and interfirm goal congruity as predictors of negotiation behavior. Tung (1988) treats the political and cultural factors in the negotiation context and business characteristics as critical antecedents of negotiation processes and outcomes. Similarly, Thomas (1976) views behavioral predispositions and incentive structures as determinants of negotiation procedures. Finally, Weiss (1993) regards conditions (e.g., circumstances, capabilities, culture, and environment) as exogenous factors affecting both negotiation behavior and interfirm relationships.

Although previous studies have shed light on international business negotiations in general, they have been deficient in modeling the specificity of contract negotiations for international joint ventures. In order to redress this deficiency, below we provide a conceptual model of the antecedent, concurrent, and consequent factors of joint venture contract negotiations. We first elaborate various antecedents of joint venture negotiations at the contextual, organizational, and individual levels. Then, we present our analysis of three concurrent factors, namely, issue diversity, term specificity, and contractual obligatoriness. Finally, we discuss the consequences of joint venture negotiations, including immediate, intermediate, and ultimate effects.

Antecedents of Negotiations

Social psychology theorists argue that situational constraints and the individual characteristics of the negotiator influence the process of negotiations, which in turn affects negotiation outcomes (Brett and Okumura 1998; Rubin and Brown 1975; Strauss 1978). Situational constraints include contingencies at both the environmental and organizational levels. The characteristics of the negotiator also have a direct bearing on the process and outcomes of negotiations.

Environmental Antecedents

Various contextual factors from the political, economic, sociocultural, and regulatory environments may affect the process of a negotiation. First, possible agreements between parties from different countries must be examined within the context of the political relations between the two countries. For example, formation of joint ventures between countries that do not maintain a normal diplomatic relationship can be considerably more difficult than such formation between two friendly nations. In many countries, particularly in developing countries, joint venture contracts cannot take effect unless they are ratified by the governmental authority.

There are three sets of economic variables that are critical to joint venture negotiation: (1) the host country's economic system (e.g., market, centrally planned, or mixed economies), which determines the nature and form of economic cooperation that can take place; (2) the level of economic development in the country, which indicates the availability of capital (especially foreign exchange), technological know-how, and skilled labor; and (3) the objectives or priorities of the host country as defined in its long-term plans and industrial policies.

The cultural environment also influences negotiations in several important ways. It affects how people process and interpret information and how they make decisions during the negotiation. Cultural differences are reflected in ways of problem solving, negotiation styles, and the choice of conflict resolution methods. Tung (1982) found major differences in these respects between Americans, Japanese, and Chinese. The ability to bridge cultural differences is often found important to the success of joint venture negotiations and the lack of such ability is a major contributor to failure.

Lastly, the regulatory environment influences joint venture negotiations in two major ways. First, it provides a legal framework with which the various terms and conditions specified in the contract must accord (Brouthers and Bamossy 1997). Normally, governmental regulations have an impact on a variety of areas such as market orientation (export ratio policy), material sourcing (localization policy), technology transfer, equipment import (import license policy), accounting, finance, taxation, and employee recruitment and compensation (labor, union, and employment policies). Both foreign and local partners must familiarize themselves with the host government's policies concerning foreign direct investment and be able to assess the impact of these policies on the focal project. It is also necessary to review corporate and joint venture laws enforced in the host country. Such legalities directly impact how the joint venture should be formed and what must be stipulated in its contract.

Contractual terms must be aligned with additional control exercised by the local government authorities. Following is a list of areas in which government control is often exercised.

Entry mode control. That is, foreign investors are allowed to only enter certain industries or through specific entry modes such as joint ventures, coproduction, or technology transfers.

Equity control. Foreign investors are restricted from holding a certain percentage of equity in the joint venture. For instance, foreign players in the Chinese auto assembly industries cannot maintain more than 49 percent of equity in a venture.

Location control. Foreign-invested projects may be required to be located in certain geographical regions. This is intended to help boost regional economies by launching heavy investment in certain areas, as planned by the central or local government.

Duration control. Each joint venture contract has to specify the term (number of years) of operation. Although this term can be renewed, such renewal is not automatic but is usually subject to a new round of approval by governmental authorities.

Partner control. Certain projects must include local firms assigned by the government. These firms may or may not have a previous cooperative history with the foreign investor.

Timing control. The host government may freeze or ration the approval of joint venture projects for certain periods of time. This often occurs when government agencies have overapproved the number of projects that are needed for economic development.

Project orientation control. Each project must be identified in its registration as belonging to one of the following categories: export, technologically advanced, infrastructure, import-substitution, or local market. There are different priorities and treatments attached to each category. In general, the first three enjoy preferential treatment, including lower income tax and tariff rates, refunds on value-added taxes, lower financing costs, better infrastructure access, government support, and cheaper land rent.

Size control. Projects of different investment sizes have to be ratified by different levels of the government. The greater the size, the higher the rank of the authority in charge. When a project plans to increase its investment size, it usually has to receive approval by the same authority that previously ratified the project.

Organizational Antecedents

The organizational context of joint venture negotiations refers to the structural properties and interorganizational bargaining power conditioning the course of the negotiation (Olekalns, Smith, and Walsh 1996). First, the relative balance of bargaining power between negotiating firms may have a significant influence on the interparty dynamics at the negotiation table. For example, negotiations between partners with equal bargaining power may be characterized by a strong mode of bargaining, compromising, and consensus building. In contrast, negotiations between unequal parties may be dictated by the more powerful or dominant partners' agendas. For example, with its exclusive technological know-how, Boeing possessed stronger bargaining power in its joint venture negotiation with Japan Civil Transport Development Corporation. The Japanese firm, as a result, had to make significant concessions, including adapting to the American partner's negotiation style and agenda.

Second, previous collaboration between the same partner firms is expected to affect joint venture negotiations. As the length of the interactions between partners increases, interpartner relationships and trust emerge. Previous collaboration fosters a climate of openness at the negotiation table, which helps the partners engage in joint problem solving. Since past cooperation often implies repeated negotiations, negotiating parties tend to be more accommodating, cooperative, and honest than parties engaged in one-shot transactions.

Options for avoiding or discontinuing negotiations will likewise influence each party's dedication to the negotiations. For example, a party that has such options is less motivated to work toward an agreement. However, when both parties perceive the cessation of negotiations as detrimental to their interests, they will be more willing to compromise and to commit themselves to a joint exploration of alternative solutions. Each partner's options for discontinuing negotiations rely on its dependence on the partner firm. In general, a party has a chance to dominate joint venture negotiations if it has alternative partner candidates, stronger technological or organizational skills, and other complementary competencies that the partner firm wants to acquire.

Third, the nature and complexity of the transaction affect the length and process of negotiations. Complex transactions usually require longer negotiations and call for more specificity in the contract. An international joint venture project increases in complexity as it requires a large amount of start-up cost and capital investment, potentially involves substantial operational uncertainties, or faces vigorous governmental interference.

Lastly, interpartner goal congruence may simplify joint venture founding negotiations. From a game theory perspective, when the interests in the venture are shared between the partners, the parties envision less uncertainty about each other's strategies and tactics at the negotiation table, which in turn may facilitate an atmosphere of joint problem solving. In contrast, when the partners diverge in terms of their strategic goals for forming the joint venture, negotiators are more likely to use distributive rather than cooperative strategies (O'Connor 1997). This often gives rise to a negotiation dilemma, which Kelley (1966) referred to as "the dilemma of honesty and openness."

Negotiator Antecedents

Joint venture negotiations, although an interfirm activity, are often subject to influences by the individual traits of the negotiators, because negotiations are, after all, conducted by and between individuals. The personality characteristics of a negotiator that can possibly affect his negotiation strategy and style may include the following: (1) introversion versus extroversion (e.g., extroversion can promote openness, while introversion helps analysis and reflection); (2) experience in international business (such that more experienced negotiators may meet with greater success); (3) internationalism versus isolationalism (e.g., internationalists tend to be more cooperative than isolationalists in negotiations); and (4) value systems (as a negotiator's values can dictate her choice of strategy, perception of efficacy, and range of possible options).

Interpersonal relationships are also important to negotiation success. Choice of strategies is influenced by the relationships that exist between negotiators representing different parties. Where the negotiators trust and respect their counterparts on the opposite team, the issues under discussion can be more easily defined and narrowed, thus facilitating a meeting of minds at the negotiation table (Tung 1988). Rubin and Brown (1975) define a high interpersonal orientation as one in which the parties are responsive and interested in variations in one another's behavior. Low interpersonal orientations are characterized as nonresponsive and uninvolved in aspects of the relationship. In countries with a strong relational culture (e.g., some Asian and Middle Eastern countries), this trait becomes even more critical. Companies in these countries tend to have a warm-up period of information exchange before contract negotiations begin. This period is actually an effort to construct an interpersonal relationship between the negotiators. Making such social investments is enormously worthwhile because it not only facilitates the focal negotiation but also nourishes a cooperative culture for the forthcoming joint venture. This is particularly important because, in many cases, the individuals participating in the venture's founding negotiations will later become the venture's senior managers.

The cultural background of the negotiators is expected to influence joint venture negotiations. Fewer cultural barriers make accurate interpretations of transaction terms and conditions more likely. A narrow cultural distance promotes information exchange, which is conducive to negotiation. By contrast, firms from countries separated by great cultural distance are likely to negotiate relatively ambiguous initial contracts, planning to make necessary adjustments to these terms over time as they become more familiar with each other. This flexibility is sometimes necessary. For instance, Shenkar and Ronen (1987) report that Confucian philosophy continues to provide the foundation for Chinese cultural values. The tenets of harmony, hierarchy, developing one's moral potential, and kinship affiliation have relevance for interpersonal behavior. These cultural values lead to (1) building flexibility into contractual arrangements in order to avoid lawsuits and save face in the future; (2) emotional restraint and politeness as basic styles of communication; (3) an emphasis on social obligations; and (4) an interrelationship of the life domains of work, family, and friendship.

Lastly, the loyalty and knowledge of a negotiator may affect the process and outcomes of joint venture negotiations. Negotiators who are loyal to their employers will have more zeal and take more initiative. This leads to more dedication to the process and consequences of negotiations. In fact, one of the strategies widely observed in joint venture negotiations is that one negotiator attempts to reduce his counterpart's loyalty to his or her firm. This may be done by strengthening personal relationships or offering personal favors. In order to enhance the loyalty of one's own negotiators, headquarters should delegate them enough power, respond quickly to requests for instruction, and reward them after they return. Additionally, knowledge about the transaction and familiarity with the partner organization and host market can stimulate a negotiator's bargaining power and win her more respect from the other party, thus placing her in an advantageous position during negotiations.

Concurrent Factors

Although the negotiation process is, in practice, hard to divide into clear-cut phases (Fisher 1980), contract negotiations can be considered as consisting of four stages (Graham 1987): nontask sounding out (e.g., establishing a rapport), task-related exchange of information, persuasion, and concessions and agreement. Below, we focus primarily on the last two, arguably the most substantive and critical stages of joint venture negotiation. We argue that concurrent factors of joint venture contract negotiations include term specificity, issue diversity, and contractual obligatoriness. Since these concurrent factors are all related to the content of joint venture contract negotiations, we first introduce the major terms of a typical joint venture contract. This will help clarify the concurrent factors discussed afterward.

Major Terms of an International Joint Venture Contract

Following is a brief introduction to the major terms stipulated in a greenfield, equity joint venture agreement that involves only two parties, one local and one foreign. Obviously, a full range of terms and their specifications would be determined by the situation, environment, and firm involved in a given negotiation.

Joint venture name, legal nature, and address. In most cases, the organizational form of a joint venture is a limited liability company in which each party is liable to the joint venture company within the limit of the capital subscribed by each party. The profits, risks, and losses of the venture company are shared by the parties in proportion to their contributions of registered capital.

Scope and scale of production. When the investment is in a highly regulated industry, the scope of its business is subject to restrictions. The joint venture contract should specify the intended scope of the business in accordance with these regulations and policies. The expected production scale for the beginning period as well as for the ultimate capacity must be stipulated.

Investment amount, unit of currency, and equity distribution. The total amount of investment contributed by all parties is often not the same as the registered capital. Some host countries may have rules concerning amounts of registered capital or the maximum difference between the amount of investment and registered capital. Investors sometimes strategically increase or decrease the amount of registered capital for tax reasons. As the unit of currency specified in the agreement may not be the same as the one a foreign investor actually remits, timing of cash contributions is also specified. Further, the contract often specifies the payment method (e.g., how many installments are allowed).

Forms of contribution. Joint venture parties may contribute various kinds of assets as their investment. These include, but are not limited to, cash, machinery and equipment, technology, land, factories, patents, trademarks, proprietary knowledge or skills, and other industrial or intellectual property rights. The contract should state explicitly what particular forms will be contributed and when. When contributing industrial or intellectual property rights, parties usually include a separate contract clarifying the nature of these investments as part of the main contract.

Responsibilities of each party. These responsibilities are project- and situation-specific. In a typical two-party joint venture, the local partner and the foreign partner's roles are clearly specified so that a shirking of responsibilities can be unequivocally detected and measured.

Technology or knowledge transfer. In many cases, a separate agreement that governs the interpartner exchange of skills and technology is signed between joint venture partners. Technology transfer agreements also are often signed between the joint venture and one of the parent firms.

Marketing issues. This clause usually specifies the targeted market (local or international), marketing channels and approaches (e.g., direct marketing, contracts with sales agents, or setting up sales branches or representative offices in major locations), and the joint venture trademark.

Composition of the board of directors. This generally stipulates (1) the total number of directors and the number of nominees from each party; (2) nomination of the chairman and vice chairman of the board; (3) the key functioning of the board and its decision rules (e.g., majority rule or consensus), and (4) the frequency of board meetings. Usually, the chairman of the board is the legal representative of the joint venture.

Nomination and responsibilities of venture management. The agreement should specify which party has the right to nominate the general manager (or president) and several deputy general managers (or vice presidents). The terms of such appointments are usually approved by the board. The responsibility of these top-level managers should be described. Departmental or divisional managers are usually appointed by the top management. This term also gives the board of directors the power to dismiss the general manager or deputy general managers in case of graft or serious dereliction of duty.

Project preparation and construction. In most cases, before the formal opening of the joint venture, an interim office needs to be set up to take pre-venture responsibilities on behalf of the partners. A major task for such an office is to manage the construction of the venture's physical facilities. The composition of managers in this office is normally decided by the board of directors.

Labor management. This item defines the key terms of the labor contract between the joint venture and the relevant authorities, such as a trade union or a government agency. Typically, it covers such details as recruitment, employment, dismissal and resignation, wages, labor insurance, welfare, rewards, and penalties for the joint venture employees. The procedures for appointing high-ranking managers and deciding their compensation are also specified.

Accounting, finance, and taxes. This term regulates the fiscal year period, dividend policies, allocation of retained earnings, currency and language used in bookkeeping and financial statements, auditing, financing policies, working capital management, and so on. Some joint venture agreements specify that venture management should submit to the board the operational plan and financial budget early each fiscal year, and submit a proposal concerning the disposal of profits.

Venture duration. This clause stipulates the joint venture's number of years of operation. The establishment of the joint venture usually starts from the date of issuance of its business license. Its duration can be extended, subject to the needs of both parties. In general, an extension is proposed by one party but requires approval by the board of directors.

Disposal of assets after expiration. Upon the expiration of the joint venture agreement, or termination before the date of expiration, liquidation will be carried out according to the relevant laws of the host country. Liquidated assets will be distributed in accordance with the proportions of investment contributed by respective parties. It a common practice that when a party of the joint venture sells all or part of its investment to a third party, consent has to be obtained from the other party of the venture. In this case, the other party usually has preemptive rights to buy the ownership.

Amendments, alterations, and discharge of the agreement. The conditions for amending and terminating the joint venture contract are usually stated in the contract. Amendments to the contract usually come into force only after a written agreement is signed by both parties and approved by the board. In case of an inability to fulfill the contract, the joint venture and its contract may be terminated prior to the time of expiration.

Liabilities for breach of contract. This article specifies the responsibilities of the party that breaches the contract as well as the measures the joint venture will undertake facing contract breaches. For example, if one party fails to pay its contracted contributions on schedule, the other party may have the right to terminate the contract and claim damages from the party in breach.

Force majeure. The contract usually includes articles that specify how the parties deal with delays or failure in executing the contract due to unexpected natural disasters such as an earthquake, typhoon, flood, fire, or war.

Applicable laws. The formation of the joint venture contract or agreement, its validity, interpretation, execution, and settlement of disputes shall be governed by the relevant laws of the host country.

Settlement of disputes. This term specifies the settlement method if any disputes arise. Methods may include consultation, arbitration, or legal procedures. These methods may be used in a sequential manner. That is, firms often strive to settle disputes through negotiation in the first place. In a case where no settlement can be reached, the dispute may be submitted for arbitration to an impartial arbitration institution, as agreed upon by both parties.

Effectiveness of the contract and miscellaneous concerns. The date on which the contract becomes effective should be clearly stated in the contract. Relevant appendices may also be included as integral parts of the joint venture contract.

Term Specificity

A key facet of negotiation content is term specificity, namely, the degree to which major terms, clauses, and conditions of transactions are specified during negotiations and incorporated in the subsequent contract. According to transaction cost theory, the specification of major terms during the negotiations and their eventual codification in a contract provide a safeguard against *ex post* performance problems because they mitigate each party's ability to act opportunistically over the course of significant, long-term investments, as in joint ventures (Hill 1990; Williamson 1979).

As one of the major *ex ante* mechanisms by which conflicts may be overcome and performance enhanced, term specificity serves to reduce managerial complexity by coordinating activities for collective goals (Hill 1990). Collaborative ventures can fail because of transaction hazards precipitated by opportunistic behavior on the part of each partner or because of high bureaucratic costs involved in coordinating interfirm exchanges (Williamson 1985). The importance of this specificity is elevated when investment uncertainty is high, duration is long, and commitment is heavy. Thus, term specificity concerning joint venture investment in a dynamic emerging market is of paramount value to the success of the partnership.

Where there is rivalry between parties, trust building is attenuated and opportunism instigated, thus generating further conflict (Buckley and Casson 1988). These threats increase the need for *ex ante* specifications governing each party's rights, duties, and benefits, which are reflected in the binding terms, clauses, and conditions negotiated and agreed upon by all parties. Negotiation ambiguity, by contrast, leaves contractual terms blurred or generalized, lacking clear bounds with respect to the benefits and responsibilities of all parties. This ambiguity creates a breeding ground for shirking responsibility and shifting blame, raising the likelihood of conflict between parties. It also hinders each party's ability to coordinate activities, utilize resources, and implement strategies (Ring and Van de Ven 1994).

To illustrate term specificity in joint venture contracting, in a hypothetical joint venture, the incorporating contract may describe each partner's responsibilities in a highly explicit and detailed manner such as the following: The local partner is responsible for (1) handling the joint venture's approval applications, registration, business licenses, land use, and other formalities concerning the establishment of the joint venture; (2) organizing the design and construction of the project; (3) assisting the foreign partner in processing customs declarations for the imported machinery and equipment; (4) assisting the joint venture in procuring equipment and materials and arranging for basic utilities, such as water, electricity, and transportation; (5) recruiting local employees for the joint venture and providing the expatriate employees with necessary assistance. On the other hand, the foreign partner is described as having responsibility for (1) procuring machinery, equipment, and industrial property for the venture; (2) handling matters relating to foreign markets; (3) providing necessary technical personnel for the installation, testing, and trial runs of equipment; and (4) assisting the local partner in recruiting and training managerial as well as technical personnel for the joint venture.

Another example of term specificity involves the venture's technology transfer agreement. Such an agreement may include the following specifics: The technology transferor guarantees that (1) the technology and the associated know-how will be up to date, reliable, and sufficient for the joint venture's operations and be able to meet the quality standards and production capacity stipulated in the contract; (2) the technology and know-how will be fully transferred to the joint venture; (3) it will compile a detailed list of the technology and technological services provided at various stages comprising an appendix to the contract; (4) drawings, technological conditions, and other detailed information are part of the transferred technology and shall be offered on time; (5) within the valid period of the technology transfer agreement, the transferor will provide any improvement or amendment to the technology without charging separate fees; and (6) the technical personnel in the joint venture will be trained to master the technology within a specified period of time. The agreement will also include articles that specify the technology transfer fees (as royalties or lump-sum payments) as well as penalties in case the transferor fails to carry out the agreement.

To summarize, term specificity serves as an institutionalized mechanism for mitigating opportunism and increasing forbearance (Buckley and Casson 1988). It helps each party ensure the most effective and efficient use of its distinctive resources and knowledge, thus optimizing the benefits of these resources in the joint venture. Moreover, term specificity helps protect the firm from premature disclosure of its strategies, technological core, or other proprietary knowledge. It is clear that the integration, exploitation, and protection of each investor's tacit knowledge or strategic resources are critical management issues in joint ventures.

Issue Diversity

Issue diversity is the degree to which relevant issues are included in contractual negotiations. One of the effective ways to shape negotiation processes and outcomes is to control the agenda of the discussions (Salacuse 1991). The party who manipulates the scope of negotiable issues will be in an advantageous position during later formation, operations, and management of the joint venture. Controlling the scope enables the party to avoid discussing issues that may be unfavorable to the firm, while promoting those topics and terms that are relatively advantageous (Weiss 1993). Thus, control of the issues to be negotiated as an *ex ante* mechanism can facilitate *ex post* operational and organizational controls after the formation of the joint venture. A party's relative bargaining power has a strong impact on controlling topic diversity. While the firm's strategic stake in the partnership prompts its intention to control, its bargaining power enables it to actually exercise control.

Ex post hazards of opportunism arise during long-term cooperation within an uncertain world. In order to mitigate opportunism, *ex ante* safeguards, such as complete coverage of relevant terms, are essential (Williamson 1979). There is widespread agreement in both the law and economics literatures (Williamson 1979) concerning the effectiveness of the discrete transaction paradigm, that is, "sharp in by clear agreement and sharp out by clear performance." A high degree of issue inclusiveness reduces the likelihood that the project will deviate from its desired course. Although a perfect contract is practically impossible, the degree of completeness of a joint venture contract positively contributes to joint venture success.

Contractual Obligatoriness

Contractual obligatoriness can be defined as the extent to which each party involved in joint venture negotiations is restrained by the binding force of the contract. Without such obligatoriness, the contract is incomplete no matter how specific and inclusive the terms are in contractual negotiations. Concluding an international joint venture agreement differs from signing an import or export contract in two primary ways. First, the terms stipulated in an international joint venture contract are more flexible than those in an export sales contract. Second, the parties to an international joint venture are less legally restrained than the parties in an export contract. In other words, joint venture partners have more leeway in stipulating relevant terms and clauses in order to align with their specific needs and interests. For instance, parties to an export contract must accept certain international definitions of standardized terms such as the types of payment (e.g., L/C, D/P, or D/A) and the kinds of pricing (e.g., FOB, CIF, or C&F). International joint venture agreements, however, are not constrained by such standards. International joint venture partners also have the right to ask for revisions after the agreement is concluded. This flexibility is often embedded in a special clause of the contract concerning the degree of obligatoriness in defining the terms, under what conditions a revision is called for, and how a revision process would proceed.

The governance structure, as the institutional matrix within which transactions are negotiated and executed, plays an important part in guiding joint venture establishment and development (Williamson 1979). Harmonizing interests that would otherwise give way to antagonistic subgoal pursuits appears to be an important governance function. Williamson (1979) suggests that simple governance structures should be used in conjunction with simple contractual relations, while complex governance structures should be adopted for complex relations. Contractual negotiations concerning joint venture establishment are a complex process, characterized as long-term or recurrent (rather than occasional) and idiosyncratic (project-specific). In this situation, contractual obligatoriness is one of the *ex ante* internal levers that can mitigate future opportunism and conflict. It legally constrains each party during subsequent stages of joint venture operations.

Under the classical contract law scheme, it is important to enhance discreetness and intensify "presentiation," meaning that both parties should make an effort to perceive or realize all terms at present (Williamson 1979). The economic counterpart to complete presentiation is contingent-claims contracting, which entails comprehensive contracting whereby all relevant future contingencies pertaining to the supply of a good or service are described and discounted with respect to both likelihood and futurity. The scheme's emphasis is placed on legal rules, formal documents, and self-liquidating transactions. It generally discourages third-party participation and narrowly prescribed remedies if the contract cannot continually proceed due to various reasons. The governance mechanism of the classical scheme is often too rigid for long-term businesses under uncertainty, as in the case of joint ventures, but does point up the importance of clarifying obligations in the contract.

The neoclassical contract law scheme emphasizes both contractual obligatoriness and governance flexibility. It should be noted that high governance flexibility does not mean low contractual obligatoriness. Instead, this flexibility is created in lieu of either leaving in contractual ambiguity or gaps or trying to plan too rigidly. Governance flexibility is devised to cope with changes in environmental contingencies by providing guidelines, which are legally binding to both parties, in the event of external changes. Normally, in long-term contracts executed under conditions of uncertainty, complete presentation is apt to be prohibitively costly if not impossible. Under such conditions, obligatory contractual terms containing governance flexibility assist in preventing breakdowns in the classical contract for long-term investment such as joint ventures. They also foster enforcement of the agreement and eventual payoff for both parties. In the neoclassical scheme, third-party (e.g., arbitrator) assistance in resolving disputes often has an advantage over litigation, and serves the functions of flexibility and filling contractual gaps. Recognition that the world is complex, agreements are incomplete, and some contracts will never be reached unless both parties have confidence in the settlement machinery thus characterizes neoclassical contract law. Neoclassical contract law has more power than the classic scheme to explain contractual obligatoriness in joint venture establishment.

Obligatoriness can be influenced by both the environmental and the firm-level antecedents. For example, unexpected changes in the institutional context can prompt interpartner conflict, which calls for the partners' obligatoriness to create boundaries and suggests solutions. Similarly, obligatoriness can also help the partners to adapt to changes in the partners' relative bargaining power, stakes, motivation, and strategies. Finally, with respect to negotiator antecedents, an individual's value system and cultural background can influence her attitude and approach to contracted obligations (Brett and Okumura 1998). People with a strong interpersonal relationship orientation (e.g., *guanxi* in China, *wa* in Japan, and *inhwa* in Korea) may not favor having high obligatoriness. Instead, they may pursue some way to provide for flexibility under terms in which both parties have confidence (Frances 1991).

Negotiation Consequences

Both transaction cost and social exchange theories maintain that negotiation outcomes are determined by negotiation process factors (Rubin and Brown 1975; Williamson 1985). As major concurrent constructs of contract negotiations, term specificity, issue diversity, and contractual obligatoriness protect a partner's strategic resources, mitigate against interfirm opportunism, and reduce operational and financial uncertainties (Williamson 1985). These benefits in turn reduce transaction costs, enhance economic rents, and improve financial and operational synergies from interpartner cooperation. As important *ax ante* contractual mechanisms and institutional systems, these concurrent factors benefit joint venture performance, which ideally benefits both parties.

Broadly, the consequences of joint venture negotiations fall into three sequentially interrelated categories: (1) immediate effect, (2) intermediate effect, and (3) ultimate effect. Because contingencies, both internal and external, will arise as an international joint venture evolves (Ring and Van de Ven 1994), we can assume that the impact of contract negotiations will abate over time, implying that it is stronger immediately rather than intermediately or ultimately.

Immediate Effect

The sociopsychological perspective suggests that negotiation outcomes are sequential (Pruitt and Lewis 1975; Rubin and Brown 1975; Strauss 1978). First, the immediate outcomes of a joint venture negotiation, in the event of a successful agreement, may be reflected in the extent to which negotiators are satisfied with the joint venture contract. Second, in the event of a deadlock, one may examine whether alternative strategies can be devised to help unblock the stalemate. Third, in the event of a complete breakdown between joint venture partners, both parties can withdraw and dissolve the negotiations. Therefore, the immediate effect is best manifested in satisfaction with joint venture formation, ranging from high in the first case to low in the third.

A successfully signed contract plays a pivotal role in the joint venture's founding because all major issues concerning the venture's formation, including construction, registration, and commencement, are stipulated in the contract. These terms provide explicit guidelines on how to set up an international joint venture. However, settling the contract does not necessarily guarantee a successful operation of the venture because operational outcomes are contingent on additional factors that cannot be fully articulated in contractual terms and clauses.

Intermediate Effect

The intermediate consequences of a negotiation rest on the process-based performance of an international joint venture. By "process-based performance," we mean the venture's effectiveness in establishing and executing the organizational procedures and operational routines through which the venture's business outcomes are generated. These may include technological development, product design, quality control, productivity, managerial and administrative efficiency, customer responsiveness, information flow, cost and budget control, and marketing effectiveness. Contract negotiations and specifications create explicit rules and measures for operational efficiency. In addition, contractual stipulations and codification derived from completed negotiations provide guidelines to an international joint venture's administration of major functional processes such as marketing, production, human resource management, accounting and finance, and management. This effect is intermediate, because it links a negotiation's immediate effect (i.e., the degree of satisfaction with the agreement) to the venture's ultimate business performance.

Ultimate Effect

The ultimate effects of the founding negotiation reside in the financial and overall performance of an international joint venture. Needless to say, success in the venture's founding negotiation is a necessary condition for joint venture eventual success. It provides a sound basis for interpartner cooperation, managerial rules, conflict resolution, and strategic direction, all of which are critical to the eventual success of the joint venture. This success may be gauged in such conventional measures as profits, sales, market share, growth, and overall competitiveness. Such ultimate effects are linked with intermediate effects in that the latter serve as enablers and predictors of the joint venture's eventual performance. Without success in production, operation, and management processes, a joint venture cannot attain high financial performance.

In conclusion, contract negotiation is an important determinant of joint venture success. Negotiating is a complex process that involves multilevel antecedent, concurrent, and consequent factors. These factors interact with each other, and jointly produce the consequences of joint venture negotiation. However, the framework we proposed in the chapter should be subject to further scholarly validation as well as practical verification.

A Mini-Case Example

Suzuki-Maruti Dispute: Negotiation Ambiguity

The joint venture between India's state-owned Maruti Udyog Limited and Japan's Suzuki Motor Corporation had been successful for sixteen years. Recently, however, the Indian government and Suzuki were involved in a bitter dispute over the appointment of the firm's next managing director. Factors contributing to the problem included an ambiguous contract, incongruent goals, scare tactics, dissatisfaction over the sharing arrangements, and other external factors. Although the disagreement did not lead to termination of the joint venture, it had resulted in an extremely difficult time in the venture's history. To a large extent, the problem the venture faced might have a significant effect on the future of the entire automobile industry of India.

On October 2, 1982, Maruti Udyog Limited (MUL) and Suzuki Motor Corporation (SMC) signed a joint venture contract to manufacture a modern and fuel-efficient "people's car," which included a license agreement, a commercial agreement, and a management agreement. These agreements set the background on which the joint venture began production. The joint venture duration was expected to be ten years. Initially, the partners agreed that Suzuki would serve as a minority owner with a 26 percent of capital investment, but its share could be increased upon mutual agreement. In 1988, when MUL restructured its capital base, Suzuki raised its ownership to 40 percent. Finally, in 1991, under India's new economic policy, Suzuki was allowed to increase its stake to 50 percent, making the joint venture an equal equity partnership. Despite this, Suzuki decided not to seek repatriating dividends because of the difference in the yen and rupee, which caused balance-payment problems for India.

In the joint venture contract, Suzuki agreed to transfer technology, engineering design, and development; help the venture manufacture and sell an 800cc, four-door, four-seat passenger car as well as a pickup van; allow access to improvements and modifications in Suzuki technology during the life of the agreement; and provide support to the venture in building up its engineering and design capacities. While it tried its best to meet the Indian government's requirements, Suzuki refused to enter into a buy-back arrangement with the government. The Indian government accepted Suzuki's terms to start production of the Maruti 800cc in December 1983.

Over the first several years, the joint venture performed well above its competitors. The advanced technology transferred from Suzuki allowed the venture to operate as a virtual monopoly in India's economy. The Maruti 800cc model was fuel-efficient and trouble free, with technology and reasonable pricing that were far superior to any other automobile in its class. When the liberalization plan was launched in 1991, the joint venture was far ahead of its newly entered rivals. As a result, the venture was able to capture 80 percent of the automobile market in India.

Since 1996, however, the partnership has experienced a bumpy ride. Externally, the automobile industry in India faced an influx of fourteen major automobile manufacturers. Therefore, competition has become increasingly intense. Internally, Suzuki and the Indian government have been unable to reach an agreement on how to fund a 15-billion-rupee ($415 million) expansion plan. Suzuki took a strong stance in wanting to raise its equity share. The government rejected its offer and proposed to fund expansion through increasing debt. The final decision to increase equity led the Indian government to believe that Suzuki was attempting to buy out MUL. Not surprisingly, interpartner trust was lost and in its stead there emerged distrust between the partners. As a result, the Indian government developed a strong desire to exercise more control over the joint venture.

On August 27, 1997 the Indian government appointed Mr. Bhaskarudu as the MUL venture's managing director, giving Suzuki only thirty minutes prior notice before a board meeting. Quite expectedly, Suzuki was strongly against the appointment, arguing that the nomination had violated a contractual agreement and occurred without prior consultation. Suzuki also argued that Bhaskarudu was incompetent and incapable of acting as managing director.

Back in 1992, Suzuki and the Indian government had agreed that the partners would alternately appoint the venture's chairman and managing director for a five-year tenure. That is, when one partner nominates the managing director, the other partner will nominate the chairman. However, it happened that, in 1992, when Suzuki nominated Mr. Bhargava as managing director, the Indian government did not select a chairman until 1996. Therefore, Bhargava virtually acted as both chairman and managing director. Because of this history, in 1997 Suzuki believed that it had the right to appoint a chairman as the Indian government was nominating a managing director. The Indian government, however, insisted that since its chairman had served only for one year, he had four more years to serve. This meant that both positions had to be filled with the local government's nominees.

The disagreement prompted both partners to consult with the original joint venture contract. However, the contract did not clarify selection procedures and used ambiguous terms open to differing interpretations. Suzuki saw the selection process as a periodic function. That is, the chairman and the managing director had to be nominated simultaneously for the same term, leaving no possibility that both positions would be filled by the same party's nominees. The Indian government, however, assumed that each appointment would take place every five years and that the nomination for the two positions does not have to be a related decision.

Throughout negotiations over the appointment of Bhaskarudu, Suzuki and the Indian government opposed each other with belligerence. Since the government remained inflexible, Suzuki attempted to demonstrate its leverage by freezing all work on technological upgrades that were intended to improve existing MUL models to meet India's emission goals for the year 2000. Suzuki also discontinued the production of diesel models and the development of a new car model. These scare tactics lengthened negotiations and further hampered relations between the partners.

As a 50–50 joint venture with a local government, decision making at MUL was based on consensus, and disagreements usually take long to resolve. This, in fact, is a rather generalized phenomenon—strain between foreign investors and local parent firms is usually multiplied by government involvement because the government often has nationalistic agendas and stringent rules. The dispute over the appointment of MUL's managing director delayed production despite the prospect of stiff competition. Suzuki was eventually forced to seek settlement through the Indian court, where it was ruled that the International Court of Arbitration would determine the MUL chairman selection problem.

—— 4 ——

Structure of Joint Ownership

Structure of joint venture ownership has a strong effect on risk sharing and resource commitment of the partners and the vulnerability and strategic flexibility of the joint venture. This chapter addresses the importance of ownership structure, identifies its various determinants, and analyzes its effect on management control over the venture. We elaborate in concrete terms how the ownership structure of an international joint venture should properly align with a variety of variables, such as environmental dynamics, governmental policies, and the partners' organizational experience, complementary needs, strategic intention, commitment, bargaining positions, knowledge protection, and global integration. Instead of arguing about which type of ownership structure outperforms others, we suggest that the configuration between ownership structure and the above variables may have significant impact on joint venture performance.

Importance of Ownership Structure

The ownership structure of an international joint venture is generally defined as the division of the equity investment in the joint venture among the sponsoring firms. Terms such as "equity ownership," "sharing arrangement," and "structure of equity holdings" are often used interchangeably. When only two partners are involved, a joint venture is majority-owned when one partner's equity stake is greater than the other partner's. If equity is equally split between the partners, the joint venture is a co-owned, equal partnership. Majority-minority or equal ownership can also occur when the joint venture involves multiple participants.

Ownership structure has critical and direct implications for the venture's operation. First, it is a common practice that a joint venture's ownership structure is linked to the venture's profit remittance scheme. In other words, ownership structure serves as a simple, yet many times exclusive, formula in which the joint venture's profit, or loss, is distributed among the partners. Second, ownership structure reflects a partner firm's investment strategy, because the majority or minority holdings in joint ventures are closely tied to the firm's capability to contribute strategic resources to the partnership and to the firm's established business practices. For example, many Western companies have corporate policies that prevent the firm from contributing proprietary resources to minority-owned joint ventures. Therefore, it has been a highly recommended strategy that firms increase their ownership holdings in joint ventures in order to protect their nonequity, proprietary resources committed to the joint venture (Blodgett 1991). Similarly, many companies strive for a majority, or at least a symbolic majority, holding (e.g., a 51 percent ownership) simply for the purpose of corporate consolidation. The ownership structure in a particular joint venture may also have impact on the firm's overall strategy with respect to its strategic control over international subsidiaries, bargaining power with local interests, and globally integrated synergy.

Third, ownership structure is expected to have a significant effect on the structure of control over the venture's operations. In the previous literature, researchers have correctly differentiated ownership control and managerial control at the conceptual level (Killing 1983; Lecraw 1984; Yan and Gray 1994). However, empirically, a joint venture's ownership structure has been found a critical factor in the structure of managerial control exercised by the partners. This is particularly true in the international context. For example, in Killing's (1983) study of joint ventures in developed countries, 70 percent of the "dominant control" ventures were majority owned by the managerially dominant partner. Using the same research framework, Beamish (1985) found that 76 percent of the "shared control" joint ventures were equally owned by their parent firms. Lecraw (1984) and Yan (1993) each found a significant positive correlation between the two variables, 0.57 and 0.60, respectively. In addition, in a field survey, Harrigan (1985) found that joint venture practitioners held a strong belief that ownership is closely linked to control. For example, most managers participating in the survey expected a minority (25 percent or less) owner of a joint venture to be passive, or inactively involved, in the venture's management. Despite the widely reported positive relationship, the linkage between ownership and control is more complex than it seems to be. We will further explore this relationship later in this chapter.

Fourth, in the process of international expansion, value-generating assets are increasingly dependent on created assets (e.g., human capital) rather than natural assets. Most of these created assets are intangible and ownership-specific, and often constitute the major contribution of a partner to a joint venture. Under these conditions, the equity distribution within a joint venture is critical, particularly when the partner firms are pooling core competencies in the venture.

Finally, a joint venture's relative strength within an interdependent, multinational network can reduce its vulnerability to host government intervention. The reverse is also true. That is, the higher the degree of dependence of the venture on local relationships, the more the venture is prone to political or other contextual risks. In general, if a joint venture's interaction with the local environment is high, the parent firms tend to decentralize decision making-power and disperse more resources to the venture. Conversely, since the foreign partner's control over local operations is positively related to its equity status, higher ownership will lead to a lower degree of dependence on local relationships. As a result, it is likely that the greater the portion of equity owned by foreign investors, the lower the risks and uncertainty assumed by their joint ventures.

Assessment of Different Ownership Structures

From the perspective of each individual joint venture partner, there are three generic types of ownership structure to choose: (1) majority ownership, (2) minority ownership, and (3) equal split of ownership (50–50 percent in the case of two partners). Not surprisingly, each structure has its strengths as well as its own problems.

It has been a prevailing assumption that whenever possible, multinational firms should go wholly owned in their international business operations. If such options are not possible, and thus a joint ownership is necessary, however, they should by every means strive for a majority ownership. This assumption is consistent with transaction cost theory, which posits that multinational firms should assume a majority equity position in order to gain dominance, and that a minority equity position is the worst possible arrangement for multinational firms entering a developing country, because without dominant control, foreign firms cannot effectively minimize transactional risks. The key argument is that a majority-owned joint venture can be operated as if it is a wholly owned subsidiary of the majority owner. Unlike equally owned partnerships in which continuing interpartner negotiations and bargaining characterize the decision-making process, majority-minority joint ventures do not suffer from the heavy transaction costs because, presumably, the joint venture will be operated as a one-party show by the majority owner. In a highly uncertain foreign environment, firms especially render the issue of control critically important, and therefore often adopt majority equity ownership as a traditional yet effective vehicle to gain management control.

This assumption, however, has been challenged by recent studies. For example, our own field work (Yan and Gray 1994) suggests that joint venture partners can voluntarily take equal-owner or minority-owner positions. Many foreign companies prefer, or at least are willing, to enter an equally owned partnership to take advantage of the local partner's expertise, know-how, and networks, as the following comments by an executive from an eminent U.S. firm suggest: "We could go wholly owned, but I am against it. I don't see we have a brilliant future with a wholly owned foreign enterprise. You go there as a foreign company, and you really have nothing to work with."

Moreover, majority ownership does not come free. In many cases, a foreign partner has to pay painful costs, such as making compromises on important issues, to gain a majority status. For example, 3M gained its full ownership in its early operations in China under the condition that the U.S. firm was not allowed to sell in the local Chinese market. Virtually 100 percent of the products manufactured in China had to be sold in international markets. Similarly, Xerox achieved a symbolic majority (51 percent) ownership in its first joint venture in Shanghai. However, the U.S. company had to agree that the venture's profit would be equally divided between the partners as if it were a 50–50 joint venture. Another implicit cost a majority owner has to pay is strategic inflexibility. Since a majority-equity holding means that the partner has more at stake in the venture than its partner, it takes more risk, and has to make more significant commitment than its minority partner. The partners' unbalanced stakes in the joint venture may, over time, change the equilibrium of dependence between the partners such that the majority owner becomes more dependent on the partnership relationship and thus loses its relative bargaining power (Emerson 1962; Yan and Gray 1994).

Furthermore, a majority-minority ownership structure may bring problems to the joint venture's routine management. Even in the case in which the majority owner well understands that majority control does not mean that it can ignore the importance of the goodwill and inputs from the local partner, many majority-holding international firms cannot refrain from forcing resolution of issues by taking them to a vote. As a result, the local minority partner may reduce its commitment to the venture, become passive, and ration its contribution to the joint venture. This potential loss may be significant because the venture risks losing the local partner's access to land; labor; financial resources; supply networks; marketing channels; and, very importantly, the local government bureaucracy.

Usually, however, the ownership structure often ends up equally split when both partners want to be a majority equity holder. It is not surprising that equal ownership was advocated by Killing for joint ventures in developed countries (Killing 1983). As Harrigan (1985) pointed out, a 50–50 ownership split ensures that neither partner's interests will be quashed. It best captures the spirit of partnership and is particularly desirable in high-technology joint ventures as insurance that both partners will remain involved with the venture's technological development. Equally distributed ownership is the only way that top management from each parent firm will stay interested enough to avert problems in the venture. In fact, the use of equal ownership accounts for 50 percent or more of joint ventures in developed countries (Beamish 1985).

Co-owned ownership structure can ensure equal commitment from each partner. Decision making must therefore be based on consensus. This often means a prolonged decision process that can lead to deadlocks. The success of 50–50 equity ventures relies strongly on the synergy between partners over issues ranging from strategic analyses to daily management of the venture. It is important that partners speak a common language, have similar background knowledge, and share a set of short-term and long-term objectives. By contrast, partners coming from diverse market environments, with different business backgrounds and conflicting goals, often have a harder time making a 50–50 venture a success. For example, when one partner is from a developed country and the other from a developing country, they are more likely to have divergent attitudes that can result in decision-making impasses (Killing 1983). Such joint ventures have a higher rate of failure than those formed between two firms both originated in developed countries (Beamish 1985). A 50–50 equity share is more likely to lead to problems in the internal management of the venture when it is necessary to carry out tasks on which the partners do not fully agree. Leadership and coordination systems in general become difficult. However, equal ownership accounts for a significant proportion of joint ventures in developing countries, varying from 30 percent in Latin American countries (Beamish 1985) to close to 80 percent in China (Yan 1993).

The issue of which structure of ownership best ensures joint venture success has been a puzzle to both academics and practitioners alike. We maintain that the relationship between equity ownership and joint venture performance is not a simple, linear linkage. Rather, it is a complex, nonlinear association in which many other factors may affect each of the variables or moderate the relationship between them. Recognizing this complexity, we suggest a few approaches to understanding the ownership-performance relationship. First, it should be understood that settling an appropriate ownership structure is a critical task in international joint venture negotiations. It is certain that ownership is a primary source of bargaining power and management control and a predominant means to protect the firm's proprietary knowledge and strategic resources. Second, ownership structure is not equally important to all joint venture sponsoring firms. In fact, different firms may attach varying levels of importance to equity ownership in joint ventures depending upon their strategic goals, integration requirements, resource dependence, and firm experience, as well as upon the venture's growth potential. For instance, a firm that has alternative ways to gain bargaining power and to exercise control over the venture's management may not consider equity ownership as too critical a variable. Since ownership structure is not the only contributor to bargaining power and managerial control, it is important for the firm to optimize its overall gains of control by considering multiple means of control and by reaching the most effective and efficient combination of these means. Similarly, firms with different national backgrounds may have different preferences in ownership positions in joint ventures (Erramilli 1996; Parkhe 1991, 1993b; Shane 1993). For example, Beamish and Delios (1997) found that Japanese multinational firms showed a higher propensity to secure dominant ownership positions in joint ventures than North American companies.

Determinants of Ownership Structure

A joint venture's ownership structure is influenced by numerous factors, including both environmental dynamics and organizational contingencies. The appropriate alignment of ownership structure with such external and internal contingencies is a key factor in venturing success. We argue that the configuration between ownership structure and contextual and organizational dynamics exerts a significant effect on joint venture performance. The various external and internal contingencies are discussed below.

Environmental Dynamics

Joint ownership structure is associated with the level of risk exposure as perceived by the firm. Joint venture equity arrangements may be structured to control exposure to uncertainty and mitigate risk taking. The transaction cost implications of the degree of integration, reflected in the extent of asset ownership, become increasingly complicated under conditions of uncertainty. When uncertainty is high, a greater ownership potentially entails greater switching costs, should undesirable events occur. The ownership of productive assets may deprive the owner of the flexibility of a low-cost exit from the market. Therefore, firms tend to shun ownership under such conditions. Unlike contractual risks resulting from the exposure of transaction-specific assets, which can be neutralized or mitigated through internalization of intermediate markets, uncertainty and risks embodied in the contextual environment are usually beyond the control of the firm. This will also cause the firm to shy away from majority ownership. When operating in a foreign location, investment in productive assets is nonredeployable. Facing a significant risk in a host environment, foreign investors are less likely to invest in such assets. This implies that the multinational partner in a joint venture would favor a lower level of equity ownership as risk increases. More generally, a firm's preference of equity ownership in joint ventures may be inversely related to the expected environmental uncertainty, complexity, and hostility.

Governmental Policies

Regulations and rules on ownership structure enacted by a host government have a direct impact on a firm's choice of ownership level. These regulations and rules are normally manifested in joint venture laws, foreign direct investment policies, or general industrial policies. Foreign direct investment often encounters more cumbersome treatment and constraints in developing countries than in developed nations. Today, countries such as China, Russia, and most Southeast Asian nations have allowed foreign firms to invest in a variety of their domestic industries, including those that were previously prohibited or restricted, such as airlines, mining, insurance, and health care. However, multinational firms entering these newly opened industries generally have to accept the joint venture mode, as opposed to whole ownership, and, more importantly, have to maintain a minority status. On the positive side, a minority equity holding may help multinationals mitigate its vulnerability to environmental uncertainty, thus reducing its economic exposure to external contingencies. On the negative side, minority equity impedes the multinationals' growth potential in these regulated industries.

Organizational Experience

When a multinational company enters uncharted waters, it will be less proactive in its commitment to local operations. This is further reflected in its equity structure. Specifically, firms will be more prudent and tactful in undertaking investment and resource dispersal to local ventures when they are unfamiliar with the dynamics of the local environment or have not yet accumulated enough culture-specific experience in the host country. Suffering from the liability of foreignness, firms tend to be circumspect and evolutionary in building an appropriate alignment with external contingencies. Since the level of equity ownership is positively associated with investment commitment, discreet behavior will result in a lowered level of equity investment. However, as the multinational partner in a joint venture accumulates experience in a host country over time, it will increase its equity commitment to the local venture.

Mutual Needs and Bargaining Position

When the foreign partner of a joint venture depends heavily on the local partner's strategic inputs or on the partnership in general, it may not possess sufficient bargaining power to install a favorable ownership structure. The factors contributing to a local firm's bargaining power include availability of alternative partners, strong market power and distribution channels, superior industrial linkages, superlative reputation and product image, and excellence in country-specific knowledge. In this case, the learning-oriented foreign firm faces a tradeoff between gaining access to its local partner's resources and achieving a desirable level of ownership control over the joint venture. When the importance of acquiring the local firm's tacit knowledge outweighs that of maintaining equity control over the venture, the multinational firm is likely to accept a minority-partner position. In fact, the foreign company may not need to maintain majority equity control if its intention is merely to secure these distinctive resources and proprietary knowledge.

Strategic Intention

Any international investment strategy must configure with the firm's strategic motivations. As ownership structure is associated with risk-taking propensity and resource commitment, it is quite logical that joint venture partners prefer that the venture's equity ownership be structured such that it will help achieve their strategic goals without taking too many risks or exhausting too many resources. When a multinational firm targets market entry or attaining country-specific knowledge, a lower percentage of equity ownership may be acceptable. At the early stage of market penetration, since the firm faces an unfamiliar environment, it tends to avoid significant, risky equity investment. On the other hand, if the firm aims at acquiring country-specific knowledge, it may be either lacking the relatively bargaining power in negotiating for a majority ownership or reluctant to take a majority position in the venture because of its lack of knowledge about the host country. Similarly, if a joint venture is designed to share financial risks and operational uncertainties with other firms, the foreign firm will more likely opt for a low level of equity. By so doing, the firm not only lowers its commitment and contribution, thus diversifying more risks, but also creates better ties with its partner, thus mitigating opportunism. By contrast, if a multinational firm is interested in pursuing sustained profitability and growth by most efficiently utilizing its tacit knowledge and distinctive resources, ownership control is critical unless it has nonequity-related bargaining power derived from proprietary competencies. Overall, the greater the strategic importance of local operations to a partner, the greater the need for higher equity ownership from this partner's perspective.

Investment Commitment

Expected investment commitment is often manifested in investment size, venture turnover or duration, and capital requirements. When the required commitment is high, the firm is inevitably engaged in greater financial risk and economic exposure. In these circumstances, the foreign company may be more circumspect with respect to equity contribution. Unless the company aims to launch the project at whatever costs (e.g., as in pioneering in the market as the first mover), the firm will usually opt for a low percentage of equity status when the joint venture project is extremely large, has a high capital requirement, or has a long investment turnover. This arrangement decreases the firm's resource commitment, thus reducing its financial risks and operational variability. Further, the focal firm's lower equity ownership may make the majority partner more cooperative and dedicated to the venture, as the partner has a bigger stake in the joint project.

Knowledge Protection

Protecting a firm's proprietary competencies (e.g., technologies, know-how, brand names, trademarks, copyrights, patents) without leakage to the partner or other local businesses constitutes one of the predominant managerial tasks for venture success. This is particularly true in developing or emerging economies where appropriate legal systems for protecting proprietary rights are lacking or entirely missing. Sharing arrangements serve as one of the major control mechanisms safeguarding a firm's proprietary assets. Everything else being constant, a stronger equity ownership position or dominant ownership control will better protect a firm's tacit knowledge and strategic resources (Blodgett 1991). The level of equity status is therefore an increasing function of the necessity for protection of such resources and knowledge.

Global Integration

Ownership status must be subordinated to creating an optimal balance between global integration and local responsiveness. Any investment decisions involving a foreign market must be viewed as an integral part of the multinational firm's entire global network. Equity control serves as one of the important tools used in implementing the firm's transnational strategy. When a tighter global integration is required, greater equity ownership in a particular joint venture becomes necessary, *ceteris paribus*. This sharing strategy gives the firm better control over the venture, thereby better internalizing operations and activities taking place in various nations within an integrated network. From corporate consolidation point of view, majority holdings in international joint ventures are certainly desirable. However, if the requirement for global integration is low while local responsiveness is high (e.g., in a multidomestic structure), the ownership level of a particular joint venture in a particular host country probably will not impose significant effect on the firm's overall business strategy. In this case, a low level of equity status may be acceptable.

Ownership Structure and Control

According to the economics literature, ownership serves as a mechanism to claim "residual rights of control"—the rights to make decisions concerning an asset's use that is not explicitly stipulated by law or contract (Milgrom and Roberts 1992). This literature suggests that decisions regarding the choice of ownership position depend on the relative importance of the investment of the firm to that of the other firm in gaining an ex post return for the investment. Anderson and Gatignon (1986) share a similar view. Drawing on transaction cost theory, they argue that the choice of a desired ownership level reflects the interplay between the firm's desire to secure control and its attitudes towards investment risks. As we stated earlier, although the exercise of managerial control over a joint venture can be gained also through non-equity-based mechanisms, ownership control remains the most significant determinant of management control (Lecraw 1984; Yan 1993).

As an institutional mechanism in the joint venture's governance, ownership control is imperative, given the potential for interpartner conflict during the formation and operation stages. During the formation stage, goal heterogeneity, low trust, resource homogeneity, and ambiguous contracts are endogenous factors driving up subsequent interfirm conflict. During the operation stage, opportunistic behavior, difference in operational policies, emergence of local contingencies, and changes in strategic goals and plans can result in conflict that may impair the creation of expected synergies. Increasing formalization and monitoring of interpartner relations can also lead to dissent between parties struggling to maintain organizational autonomy in the face of growing interdependence. Moreover, the increase in resource transactions between partners over time implies that their domains will shift from being complementary to being more similar. This increases the likelihood of territorial disputes and competition. Cooperation and stability within a joint venture require some form of institutionalized mechanisms to control opportunism and guarantee the fair sharing of rewards. The vulnerability of joint ventures to external hazards requires special bonds between the parties if stable and honest transactions are to be sustained. Joint venture management needs to develop institutional control mechanisms because the norms of reciprocity and trust are likely to be insufficient. For instance, Ameritech pulled out of Poland in January 1997, selling its 24.5 stake in cellular carrier Centertel to partners Telekomunikacja Polska and France Telecom. The withdrawal happened after Ameritech realized its inability to maintain either equity or institutional control over joint venture operations.

When firms expand overseas, increasing in both complexity and diversity, the demand for monitoring, coordinating, and integrating their activities and resources increases. When operating in a highly complex, dynamic environment, an interfirm network tends to be more vulnerable to environmental changes and conflict between parties. Environmental change and uncertainty become a serious external threat to the venture. For instance, in one of the first joint ventures between an outsourcer and its client, AT&T and Delta Air Lines announced a fifty-year joint venture in applications development, associated with a ten-year, $2.8 billion outsourcing contract. The joint venture, TransQuest, was launched in 1995 and folded, along with the outsourcing contract, a year later with AT&T's decision to spin off NCR and Lucent Technologies. Even when businesses are stable, it may still take time to discover the right proportions of ownership structure. In early 1997, Perot Systems Corp. and Swiss Bank Corp. renegotiated their landmark partnerships when both feared losing control of IT operations. The original deal, a twenty-five-year, $6.25 billion contract awarded in 1995 to Perot Systems, had Swiss Bank taking a 24.9 percent stake in Perot. The new terms whittled the contract down to ten years and $2.5 billion, with Swiss Bank's stake in Perot Systems dropping to 15 percent.

In addition, as we briefly discussed earlier in the chapter, resource-based joint venture theory suggests that a parent firm can use ownership as a leverage to protect its firm-specific capabilities. Because these capabilities are often intangible, a crucial factor determining the returns a parent can expect is its degree of control over the venture's operation. Controlling resource applications may determine actual rent extractions, and controlling the leakage of proprietary knowledge prevents uncompensated transfer of capabilities. Insufficient or ineffective control can limit the parent firm's ability to effectively coordinate activities, utilize resources, and implement strategies. For example, the Spanish confectionery giant, Agrolimen, has recently taken full control of GCIL (General de Confiteria India Ltd.), previously a 51–49 joint venture with Dabur India Ltd., by buying out the equity shares held by the India firm. This joint venture was incorporated in December 1993 and was engaged in the manufacture and marketing of leading confectionery brands such as Boomer, Bonkers, and Donald. The major reason underlying this change in equity control is that the Spanish parent strategically attempted to control and integrate its global businesses in confectionery products under one umbrella by renaming itself Joyco Group. It is planning to launch numerous new joint ventures producing localized brands around the world. Ta-Ta, for instance, a bubble gum brand developed specifically for the Chinese market, has done extremely well. The company's latest lollipop, Pim Pom, has also emerged one of the leading brands in China.

However, the effect of ownership on managerial control is more complex and thus should not be oversimplified. The effect of ownership on managerial control can be easily exaggerated. Previous empirical evidence suggests that while a partner's equity contribution serves as a principal contributor to managerial control, it is only one of potentially many factors in the venture's control structure. For example, Yan and Gray (1994) reported that contribution of nonequity resources, such as proprietary technology and know-how, management expertise, international marketing networks, and information systems, gained joint venture partners a significant competitive edge in exercising control over the joint venture's decisions. More important, these authors found that only nonequity resources lead to control over the venture's routine operations, while equity structure does not affect control at the operational level. Particularly, only the tacit, irreplaceable, nonequity resources can gain a competitive advantage that is sustainable. In contrast, the partner that lacks critical nonequity resources, although it may be an equal or even a majority owner of the venture, will conceivably be in a subordinate position in controlling the venture's routine operations.

Equity ownership is an important determinant of managerial control yet not the only one. In chapters 5 and 9, we will further discuss this subject in the context of managerial control structure, partner bargaining power, interpartner working relationship, and joint venture performance.

A Mini-Case Example

Esquel Group's Joint Venture in China

Founded in 1978, the Esquel Group today is one of the world's largest cotton apparel manufacturers. The company, headquartered in Hong Kong with more than twenty factories in Malaysia, Singapore, China, Jamaica, and Mauritius, hires more than 30,000 employees. It annually produces more than 4 million dozen garments and 24 million yards of woven and knit fabric. The company's product range features a wide variety of men's and ladies' pure cotton and high-quality cotton apparel. Strategic integration in the areas of cotton farming, spinning, weaving, knitting, dyeing, finishing, and accessory manufacturing has enabled the company to employ strict quality control at every stage of production and to respond quickly to changes in the market. The company's customers include world-class fashion brands such as Polo Ralph Lauren, Tommy Hilfiger, Nordstrom, Marks & Spencer, and Fila in the U.S., Japan, and European markets.

The Esquel group began investment in China in 1978, gradually increasing its holdings in the cotton textiles and manufacturing sector to its current portfolio of twelve factories, located primarily in the Guangdong, Jiangsu, Zhejiang, and Xinjiang provinces. Annual output has exceeded 1 million dozen garments and 24 million yards of quality cotton fabrics.

Of its six main manufacturing factories in China, the Esquel Group wholly owns three joint ventures and has controlling stakes in three others. Of the three wholly owned factories, one supplies the whole group with high-quality cotton yarn, using the world-famous raw cotton material from Xinjiang. The other two plants produce all the woven and knitted fabric needed by the garment factories. One factory, Golden Field United Textiles Ltd., also produces garments mainly exported to the Japanese market where there is no quota on textile products from China. Golden Field, which was started earliest, was initially a three-way joint venture among Esquel, a small Chinese cotton mill in Guangdong, and a Japanese textile company. This format lowered the company's risk in investment in mainland China when the Chinese government's policy was not yet stable. As it gained confidence in long-term investment in China, the company bought out the other two partners' interests one year and five years later respectively, in order to obtain full control over production. Except for the three garment factories in Jiangsu and Zhejiang provinces in which the company used the joint venture format in order to get enough export quota from its Chinese partners, the company wholly owns all its manufacturing factories. This ensures that high-quality products can serve the high price segment of Western apparel retailers.

The company started cooperation with China immediately after it was founded in 1978, just as China implemented its open door policy to encourage foreign investment. At that time, the company's factories in Malaysia and Singapore were suffering from increasing labor costs. In order to avoid risks associated with being a first mover, Esquel first started its nonequity, contracted manufacturing arrangement with the No. 1 Garment Manufacturing Co. in Changzhou, Jiangsu Province, in which it transported fabric and accessories for processing. Having gained more confidence in the Chinese government's policy, the company converted the nonequity partnership into a shared equity joint venture in 1995. It later injected more capital to gain full control over the production.

The city of Changzhou, 165 km from Shanghai, China's largest international business center and harbor, is an important industrial base in Jiangsu province. The city had experienced high economic growth, averaging 30 percent in the 1980s and early 1990s, and had developed a strong and competent infrastructure. Jiangsu province is one of the more economically developed provinces in China, and is particularly famous for its advanced textile industry. This gives the joint venture company easy access to the high-quality fabric and accessories in the area. In addition, the No. 1 Garment Manufacturing Co., the local partner, already built a solid manufacturing facility even before the joint venture project.

The other two partners in the joint venture are Jiangsu Garment Import and Export Co. and Jiangsu Knitting Textiles Import and Export Co. With these two quasi-governmental partners, the joint venture was able to get much cheaper quotas for export to the U.S. market. Since the Esquel group held 51 percent in each of the two projects, and later increased its ownership by injecting further capital, it was able to achieve control over production and low sales costs simultaneously.

For a long time after the Esquel's initial investment in China, all its products manufactured in China were exported to Western countries. The operations in China served only as a manufacturing base. Starting from 1995, Esquel decided to set up its own fashion brand, aiming at the huge market of 1.2 billion local Chinese consumers. Initially named "Shirt Stop" and later changed to "PYE," the new brand was designed to take advantage of the company's strong production facilities and experience in style design gained through serving the big U.S. and European fashion companies. The company used the franchise format to set up specialty stores selling pure cotton apparel under the new brand name. Within two years, there were more than 100 PYE stores in Beijing, Shanghai, Guangzhou, Dalian, and other major Chinese cities. However, rapid expansion prompted problems such as lack of retail experience, especially in marketing and inventory management. The company started suffering from heavy losses.

In analyzing its strategy, Esquel found that the fashion market project does have its attractions in China. Compared with Esquel's cotton apparel, most Chinese products are of much lower quality and unattractive design. With the emergence of richer consumers in China, more people are able to afford the company's higher-priced products, which are still cheaper than most famous foreign name brands. With production facilities and offices in China, the company can react fast to changes in the local market and can take advantage of cheap costs in transportation and management. In spite of its present loss, the company was still confident in realizing long-term profitability in apparel retail in China. As a result, it planned to open more stores in the near future.

The chairman of the Esquel Group, Margie Yang, clearly knew the importance of the *guanxi* network to conducting businesses in China. Esquel has participated actively in events supporting China's economic development and educational projects. For example, the company donated RMB 1 million to the Chinese government for irrigation projects in Xinjiang and another million to found a high school in Guangdong province. In August 1996, the company donated RMB 300,000 to the provincial government of Xinjiang to support education programs, and RMB 500,000 to help provide electricity to a county where the company was expecting to start another cotton-spinning project. In addition to these generous donations and active cooperation with local governments, the company invited Chinese government officials to visit their factories and to sample their products. All these efforts have set up a close relationship between the company and the government, which in turn has further facilitated the company's business growth in China.

——— 5 ———

Structure of Parent Control

As joint venture partners come together to form a separate organization with shared ownership, how do they exercise control over the venture's strategic and operational activities? The exercise of management control in joint ventures is far more complex than controlling stand-alone companies and has received considerable attention by joint venture researchers and practitioners alike. In this chapter, we discuss the conceptualization and significance of parent control, different types and dimensions of control, the performance implications of management control, and factors that influence the choice of a particular control structure. These analyses formed the theoretical background of the empirical studies of management control reported later in the book.

The Concept of Management Control

In the previous chapter we discussed the structure of ownership of joint ventures among their sponsors. We stated that the structure in which the partners pool their capital and financial assets and thus share the ownership of the partnership might have significant implications on the structure of management control exercised by the partners over the venture's operation. In practice, many international companies consider the partners' respective equity shares in a joint venture as a critical mechanism of exercising management control. It is frequently observed that the ownership structure for a proposed joint venture stands out as a central issue on which potential partners bargain really hard and even fall into deadlocks during the venture's founding negotiations. In many cases of joint venture negotiations, ownership structure may serve as a threshold: If an agreement is reached, negotiation will continue; if not, nothing is going to happen (Yan and Gray 1994). Clearly, the underlying assumption many companies hold in joint venturing is that one has to rely on majority ownership to gain the right for operating and managing the joint venture. Therefore, some firms were found striving for management control by investing a symbolic majority of capital (Harrigan 1986).

Similarly, earlier joint venture researchers did not distinguish ownership control and management control. For example, Darrough and Stroughton (1989, 237) consider that, by definition, a joint venture is jointly owned and jointly controlled by both parents. Other researchers conceptually note the differences between asset (ownership) control and management control, but blur the two concepts in operationalization by using the former as a proxy for the latter (Stopford and Wells 1972; Fagre and Wells 1982; Blodgett 1991).

However, the relationship between ownership control and management control is not as straightforward as one might expect. For example, many multinational companies found that the specific ownership structure for a joint venture is far from a "decision variable" free for a company's strategic choice or even for interfirm bargaining. Rather, it is a "constant" set by the local government not at all subject to negotiation. Particularly in joint ventures in developing countries, multinational firms often fail to gain control by solely relying on ownership because attaining a majority holding in a joint venture may be simply impossible (Moxon and Geringer 1985; Contractor 1990). Killing (1983) first challenged the ownership–management control assumption by showing that one-parent dominance can occur in international joint ventures whose ownership is evenly shared between the partners. Similarly, partners can equally share management control over a joint venture in which ownership is unequally distributed. Although researchers have reported a high statistical correlation between ownership and management control—for example, 0.57 in Lecraw (1984) and 0.60 in Yan (1993)—they were far from a 1-to-1 correspondence. Researchers further noted that the combination of partner contributions in managerial skills and knowledge could affect the venture's structural configurations with respect to parent control. For example, in joint ventures with a 50–50 ownership structure, the partner that contributed to the partnership the most advanced and competitive technology may exercise dominant control over the venture's strategic and operational decisions (Mjoen and Tallman 1997; Yan and Gray 1994).

In this book, we treat ownership control and management control as two different concepts. While ownership split represents a static decision reached between the partners in the founding negotiations, management control is both a structure and a process depending largely on interpartner interactions in the venture's decision making. Since we discussed ownership structures in the previous chapter, in this chapter we focus only on the structure of management control.

Control in organizations is an important but sometimes neglected facet of organizational structure (Eisenhardt 1985). A variety of definitions of control exist in the organizational theory literature. Traditionally, control was defined as a process by which the organization verifies the conformity of its actions to plans and directions (Fayol 1949). From an economic point of view, Arrow (1974) defines control as activities of choosing operating and enforcement rules to maximize the organization's objective function. Tannenbaum (1968) discusses control in terms of the activities in which one individual engages so as to influence others' behavior. Consistent with cybernetics theory (Weiner 1954), from which the term control was initially adopted, modern organization theorists tend to agree that control is a purposely designed and implemented process by which the organization achieves its goals. This is exemplified by Flamholtz, Das, and Tsui's (1985, 38) definition: Control is a process by which an organization influences its subunits and members to behave in ways that lead to the achievement of organizational objectives. In the case of international joint ventures, we define management control as the mechanisms and process in which the foreign and local sponsoring organizations as well as the venture management influence the venture's strategic and operational decisions and regulate its business activities in order to meet the parents' strategic expectations.

Why Control?

Partners forming international joint ventures are engaged in mixed-motive games in which cooperative and competitive dynamics occur simultaneously (Lax and Sebenius 1986; Hamel, Doz, and Prahalad 1989). On the one hand, the symbiotic dependence drives the partners to collaborate so that they are able to gain benefits derived from the venture that would not be available if each acted on its own. On the other hand, the competitive interdependence between the partners provides incentives for them to compete with each other to gain bargaining advantages. Whenever possible, the self-interests of the partners motivate them to achieve benefits from a collaboration beyond the level mutually agreed upon or in the areas where the alliance's contract is incomplete (Fama 1980; Williamson 1981). The major theme of the mixed-motive game between the joint venture partners is simply stated by Hamel et al. (1989, 133) in the title of their article: "Collaborate with Your Competitors—and Win!"

Partner desire and competition for management control over the joint venture are originated in the partners' general fear of uncertainty. Joint ventures represent a tightly coupled form of interorganizational arrangements (Astley and Fombrun 1983). Not only do they involve joint ownership and quasi-hierarchical control mechanisms, but also they are expected to have a longer duration than other types of cooperative alliances (e.g., technology transfer agreements). In addition, unlike other forms of bargaining and negotiation (e.g., labor-management bargaining or arm's-length trade negotiations) in which outcomes are largely derived during the bargaining process and readily observable immediately after the bargaining is over, joint venture negotiations in the formation stage only result in an agreement of association. The expected outcomes for each partner with respect to the cooperation (i.e., the "pie," in the economist's term) are not yet available for distribution when the contract is signed, but need to be created down the road through the venture's operation. Frequently, it takes quite a while for the partners to achieve their goals. Therefore, the partners in a joint venture foresee a high level of uncertainty with respect to whether their expectations will be fulfilled. Particularly when joint ventures operate in a cross-country and cross-cultural environment, one can imagine that the level of uncertainty and unpredictability to be experienced by the partners is significantly higher than in a domestic environment.

A specific type of uncertainty that a joint venture sponsor can experience is partner opportunism. Most joint ventures are created between partners who do not have substantial information about each other; therefore, the initial interpartner relationships resemble arm's-length market transactions, in which competition is the norm (Williamson 1991) and relative power and bargaining are inherent features (Newman 1992, 75). Similarly, in the early stages of the venture, the future of the prospective joint venture remains largely uncertain to the partners. Therefore, the potential for opportunistic behavior exists until the partners develop a reputation of trustworthiness (Parkhe 1993b). Interpartner trust, however, emerges only gradually and over a long period of time. While not all partners will behave opportunistically, "it is costly to sort out those who are opportunistic from those who are not" (Williamson and Ouchi 1981, 351). Therefore, for each partner, achieving and exercising control by influencing the joint venture's strategic decisions can be viewed as a defensive strategy against potential opportunism by the other partner.

Meanwhile, however, gaining control over the venture's management can serve as a proactive strategy for the partners. As Schaan (1983, 57) argues, by definition, parent control is the process through which a parent company ensures that the way a joint venture is managed conforms to its own interest. This is particularly true when the partners have differing agendas for forming the joint venture and their strategic objectives are not perfectly compatible. In this case, the venture's efforts and outcomes valued by one partner are not necessarily appreciated by the other. Therefore, for each partner, achieving hands-on management control over the venture's operation can enable itself to gain the right of participation in the venture's decision making, through which this partner is ensured that its strategic goals will be vigorously pursued by the venture management. The strategic direction in which the joint venture moves and the ways in which the pooled resources are allocated and utilized will have direct and critical impact on the venture's outcomes.

Competition for management control between joint venture partners can also be explained from the perspective of control mechanisms by which organizations exercise control. In organization theory two alternative mechanisms are available: outcome control and behavioral or process control (Eisenhardt 1989). Outcome control is exercised by measuring and regulating the organization's eventual outcomes (e.g., the quality and quantity of products or services delivered during a period of time, profitability, and growth rates). Behavioral control, however, focuses on monitoring, influencing, and changing, if necessary, the operational process and activities through which organizational outputs are generated. Since payoffs from joint ventures are frequently deferred for several years and the venture's operation is subject to unpredictable contingencies, the exercise of outcome control is unreliable, if not impossible. As a result, the partners must resort to behavioral or process controls in order to protect their investment and achieve their desired outcomes. By securing management control over the joint venture's operation (through selection of personnel, shaping the organizational structure, quality control, etc.), partners exercise their influence over behavioral aspects of the venture.

Parent Control Structures

Organizational structure refers to an organization's basic design and the management processes used to coordinate and control operations

(Hrebiniak, Joyce, and Snow 1989). Discussions of structure usually include variables such as functional forms, governance and coordination mechanisms, decision making systems, and degree of autonomy (Andrews 1987). We define the structure of parent control in international joint ventures as the ways in which the joint venture parent firms and the venture management divide their control over the joint venture's strategic and operational management. From the joint venture's perspective, its structure reflects the degree of control exercised by each parent, the extent and scope in which strategic information is exchanged with the parents, and the degree of autonomy relegated to the venture's management personnel. Among the multiple relationships in a joint venture, how the venture is managed with respect to each of its parents is particularly critical.

Building on and extending the pioneering work by Killing (1983, 1988), below we specify five distinct types of international joint ventures with respect to parent control structure. They are (1) dominant control, (2) shared control, (3) split control, (4) rotating management, and (5) independent joint ventures.

Dominant Control

International joint ventures with a dominant control structure are managed by one of their parents, either the foreign or the local parent, virtually as if they were wholly owned subsidiaries of that parent. The other sponsors of the venture, as silent partners, however, forgo direct control over the venture's operations. Although maintaining various degrees of influence at the venture's board of directors level, these passive partners are not engaged in active and significant participation in the venture's ongoing decision making. In most dominant control joint ventures, the venture's management system is a coherent part of the organizational hierarchy of the dominant parent firm, in which the functional departments of the venture maintain a reporting relationship to their corresponding counterparts in this parent's organizational structure. Dominant control structure can be observed in a variety of international joint ventures regardless of ownership splits or industry differences. For example, many U.S.-Japanese partnerships adopted such a structure, in which the venture's daily operations are controlled by Japanese managers using Japanese management methods and practices (e.g., NUMMI and Diamond-Star in the automobile industry and Fuji Xerox in copier manufacturing). However, it seems that dominant control is more popular a structure for joint ventures formed between partners that are all from developed countries, in which each of the participating firms likely possesses the necessary managerial competencies to run the venture. In addition, the partners from developed countries tend to share common interests that are most likely business and financial in nature. Therefore, which partner is in charge of the venture's operation will become politically less important, because when one partner's objectives are achieved, the other's will be achieved automatically. This contrasts joint ventures in developing countries, in which the partners, more often than not, have diverging goals and goals that are noneconomic in nature. Even if business and financial goals might be the same, the time horizon of when to reach them might be different. For example, Chinese firms and Asian companies in general are longer-term oriented, while American businesses usually are dictated by shorter-term (e.g., quarterly or monthly) goals.

Shared Control

Joint ventures have a shared control structure when both parents exercise a high degree of influence on the venture's decisions about its operation. Shared control can be achieved through the installation of a jointly participated board or executive committee that possesses and exercises substantial power over the venture's operational as well as strategic decisions. In most such joint ventures, however, the venture management personnel consist of two groups of managers, one from the foreign partner, the other from the local partner. At the top executive level, one parent nominates the venture's general manager or president, while the other parent matches with a deputy general manager or vice president. Usually, this shared nature of organizational structure is also implemented at the lower levels of management. For example, an expatriate financial controller is teamed up with a deputy controller, or a local human resources manager is supported by an expatriate assistant manager. Among the trademark features of shared control joint ventures, both parents are actively involved in the venture's decision making, and a relatively stable balance of control between the partners is maintained over time. The shared control structure is widely observed in joint ventures created between developed country and developing country partners. Since both partners contribute to the venture substantially different, though complementary, types of resource and expertise, effective management of these resources likely requires both partners' participation. Moreover, because, more often than not, partners of this type of joint venture do not share a set of common objectives, all have a strong desire to exercise process control over the venture's daily management, as we argued earlier in the chapter.

Split Control

In a split control joint venture, each parent plays a functionally distinct and separate role in the venture's management by exercising control along different functional lines. For example, as frequently observed in joint ventures in developing countries, the multinational partner brings to the joint venture advanced technology and know-how, while the local partner contributes expertise in marketing, human resources management, and government relations. From the point of view of both expertise utilization and opportunism protection, the foreign partner tends to take positions in such functional areas as product development, engineering, manufacturing, and quality control, whereas the local partner is likely to hold positions in marketing, sales, human resources, and public relations.

   Split control can be considered as a hybrid structure between shared control and dominant control. At the venture's top and overall management level, control is shared between the partners. However, the structure is different from a shared control structure in that sharing of control does not occur at the functional management level. In fact, at the functional management level, the split control structure is quite similar to the structure of dominant control. As shown in the above example, management of the joint venture's technology and production functions is dominated by the foreign partner, while the local partner takes primary responsibility for managing the marketing and human resource functions.

Rotating Control

In this type of joint venture, the venture's management team consists of two groups of executives, one from each parent, who shift roles periodically according to a pre-agreed term of two or three years. In each term, one group of executives takes the "principal" managerial positions, while the other group of managers serves the deputy or assistant positions. This arrangement applies to both the top management (e.g., general manager, controller, and chief engineer) and the middle functional management (e.g., marketing manager, sales manager, etc.) levels. In the next term, the roles are reversed. This structure, observed frequently in international ventures between developed and developing countries, is adopted to ensure that managerial expertise is transferred to the developing country partner, or as a temporary mechanism when the level of understanding and trust between partners are low. For example, both of these reasons are quite evident in the Chinese government's recommendation of this rotating management structure for international joint ventures in China in the early years of the "open door" policy (Liu 1980).

Similar to the split control structure, the structure of rotating control represents a hybrid form of governance. Considering the venture's operation over a long period of time, control is shared because both partners have the opportunity to nominate the venture's key executives. During each period of time, however, the structure of rotating management resembles the dominant control structure, because all principal managerial positions of the venture are filled with nominees from only one partner. Like dominant control, this structure can effectively reduce the transaction costs associated with resolving interpartner conflict, building consensus, and addressing demands for coordination and integration at all management levels that are necessary for shared control joint ventures. Like the shared control structure, rotating control can balance the desire of the partners for participating in the venture's decision making. However, a key liability of the rotating control structure is the loss of continuity of the venture's management team.

Independent Joint Ventures

In an independent management structure, neither of the parents is actively involved in the joint venture's operational management. The managers of the venture are authorized to exercise full control over operating decisions. The top management team of the joint venture, either hired from a neutral market or dispatched by a third party on a subcontracting agreement, is granted a great deal of autonomy, while the venture's board of directors largely plays a nominal role. In fact, independent management ventures function as separate and freestanding companies in parallel with their parent organizations.

Each of the five control structures described above possesses distinctive characteristics. However, it is important to note that they are not necessarily mutually exclusive. First, different structures may share some common features. For example, consider the two hybrid structures: split control and rotating control. They can be considered as different formats of shared control, yet they also show important similarities to the dominant control structure. Second, one-partner dominance, shared control, and independence are all a question of degree. They should be considered as continuous, rather than absolute or dichotomous, variables. For example, in shared control joint ventures, the extent to which the partners actually divide control may vary significantly from one venture to another. Similarly, in an independent joint venture, while the venture management may remain highly independent when the venture is performing well, parent intervention may significantly increase when performance goes on a downturn (Killing 1983). Third and finally, the structure of control in joint ventures does not stay unchanged forever. Under the influence of environmental, interorganizational, and internal forces, the control structure established at the venture's founding may be subject to reconfiguration, significant change, or overhaul. We will pick up this subject later in the book when we address the evolution of joint ventures over time.

Dimensions of Control

Management control in joint ventures is a multidimensional phenomenon. Although exercising control in joint ventures has no fundamental conceptual differences from controlling in single stand-alone companies, both the intra- and interorganizational nature of the parent-venture and parent-parent relationships have made control in joint ventures a significantly more complex and challenging task. Therefore, a more fine-tuned approach to control in joint ventures is warranted. Geringer and Hebert (1989) made an important contribution by synthesizing the research literature on control and characterizing parent control in international joint ventures as composed of three major dimensions: the scope, extent, and mechanisms of control.

Scope of Control

The scope or focus of control specifies the areas of the joint venture's operations in which control is exercised. This line of research was originated in Killing's (1983) specification of "locus of decision making," in which, based on interview data, nine specific areas in which decision making is called upon were identified. These decision areas include: pricing policy, product design, production scheduling, manufacturing process, quality control, replacement of managers, sales targets, cost budgeting, and capital expenditures. Killing's work was subsequently examined by Schaan (1983) in his dissertation study of ten international joint ventures in Mexico. Among the most important findings, Schaan found that joint venture parents did not strive for control over all and every area of decision making. Rather, they chose to exercise control selectively—over only a relatively narrow scope of the venture's activities and in the areas they deemed critically important. These findings support the notion that control is not free—the exercise of control costs critical organizational resources (e.g., executive time, budget, and expatriation of managers). In fact, the tendency of parent firms to control their joint ventures parsimoniously and on a contingent basis was argued to be a major reason why a split control structure is preferred by many joint venture sponsors.

Extent of Control

The extent of control, frequently measured on an interpartner or parent-venture comparative basis, refers to the degree to which each party in the venture exercises control. Originally, the notion of the extent of control was examined in the context of the relationships between a multinational firm and its international subsidiaries, wholly owned units or joint ventures alike. The focus, however, was placed on the "right" amount of autonomy that the parent company should grant the subsidiary in the former's attempt to centralize or decentralize the organization. For example, Dang (1977) defined control as the operational autonomy enjoyed by an international subsidiary and measured the construct using a "decentralization index" based on seventeen key decisions. Again, it was Killing (1983) who extended the notion of extent of control to the interpartner and the parent-venture comparative levels. In each of the nine decision-making areas (as listed above in our discussion of the scope of control), he asked his informants to identify the relevant decision agents and to classify decisions into several different scenarios: decisions made (1) by the venture general manager alone, (2) by the local parent alone, (3) by the foreign parent alone, (4) by the venture management with input from the local parent, (5) from the foreign parent, or (6) from both parents. Using this classification, Killing was able to assess the degree of influence each party exercised on the venture's decision making. For example, in a shared control joint venture, most strategic decisions were made with the active participation by, or significant inputs from, both the foreign and the local partners. Killing's pioneering work on the extent of control has been followed by a series of new studies over the past one and a half decades (e.g., Beemish 1984; Child et al. 1997; Lecraw 1984; Schaan 1983; Yan 1993; Yan and Gray 1994). This line of research has shifted the focus of control in joint ventures from the multinational parent-venture relationship to the foreign-local partner interorganizational dynamics.

Mechanisms of Control

The mechanisms of control refer to the means by which parent control is exercised. As we discussed earlier in this chapter, many international firms frequently relied on majority ownership as a primary means to achieve management control. However, although a majority position in equity holdings could ensure some degree of control over the venture, the same argument might not be valid for international joint ventures where the equity is equally divided between parents or in which a firm is legally allowed only a minority participation role (Geringer and Hebert 1989). In practice, many firms were found to explore alternative mechanisms to exercise management control. Previous research has documented a variety of control mechanisms in addition to equity ownership, such as right of veto power, representation in the venture's management team, technology or management licensing agreements, or leverage of superior technical or managerial expertise. For example, in his in-depth study of Mexican joint ventures, Schaan (1983) was able to identify a wide range of control mechanisms available to parent firms, including the venture's board of directors, formal agreements, the appointment of key personnel, the venture's planning process, and the reporting relationships. A variety of informal mechanisms were also found effective for exercising parent control, such as setting up integrative structures between the venture and the parent, running training programs for the venture's personnel, and inviting the venture's managers to attend the parent's corporate business meetings.

The multidimensional approach has contributed to a more comprehensive understanding of how parent control is exercised in joint ventures. It also provides useful implications for practitioners in terms of how to strategically select the focus, the magnitude, and mechanisms of control. However, a multidimensional examination of control has also increased difficulties and challenges for joint venture researchers. Since individual studies usually focus on different dimensions of control—for example, Killing (1983), Lecraw (1984), Yan and Gray (1994) on extent; Child et al. (1997), Geringer (1986), Hebert (1994) on scope—and Schaan (1983, 1988) and Yan (1993) on means and mechanisms—the results of previous studies have been hardly comparable.

Performance Implications

The study of management control in joint ventures is not an end in itself. Of particular interest to joint venture researchers and practitioners alike has been the effect of control on performance. Beamish (1984, 45) argues that parent control is "the most common variable discussed in conjunction with performance" in the international joint venture literature. How does the exercise of management control affect performance? This question has been a focus of inquiry among joint venture researchers for more than a decade. Its pursuit, however, has generated ambiguous and perplexing results (Geringer and Hebert 1989).

Tomlinson's (1970) study of U.K. joint ventures in India and Pakistan is often cited as the first attempt to understand the control-performance relationship. The variable for parent control in this study, however, was the "attitude toward control" of the multinational U.K. parent firm, rather than control actually exercised. Using a sample containing seventy-one joint ventures, the study found that higher performance (as measured in profitability) occurred when the multinational parents assumed a more relaxed attitude toward control. When the foreign partner's control was tight, the venture's performance suffered. Another quite influential study of the control-performance relationship was conducted by Franko (1971). Focusing on the multinational firm's strategy, this study examined the relationship between firm strategy and performance (as measured in venture stability). Among his findings was that joint ventures were more stable when the multinational parent adopted a product-diversification strategy. In contrast, high instability occurred as the parent followed a product-concentration strategy. Since each of these strategies is frequently associated with a distinct type of structure (according to the "structure follows strategy" argument), an indirect relationship was established between parent control, as a structural variable, and performance. For example, subsidiaries usually enjoy a high level of autonomy under a product-diversification strategy, whereas centralized control is often associated with a product-concentration strategy.

Research on a direct relationship between parent control and performance can be traced back to the milestone work by Killing (1983). In this in-depth study of thirty-seven joint ventures in developed countries, control was measured in terms of aggregated involvement of the parents in the venture's decision making, while performance was indicated by liquidation, reorganization, and management-perceived success. The study found that independent joint ventures and ventures with a dominant control structure outperformed those in which management control was equally shared between partners. Killing's data also led him to conclude that among the shared control joint ventures, "the more equally the parents share the management of a venture, the worse it will perform" (p. 23). Conceptually, Killing argues that the exercise of control by two or more parents simultaneously creates interpartner misunderstanding, conflict, and politics, therefore making the venture's management extremely difficult. In contrast, the unity of command in dominant control and independent joint ventures simplifies the management tasks and enables prompt decision making, thus, contributing to performance.

Recent empirical studies have generated fresh evidence for a positive relationship between parent control and joint venture performance. Using international joint ventures located in different parts of the world (e.g., China, Europe, and North America), several studies have consistently shown that management control over a joint venture's daily operations exerts a strong positive effect on performance (Child et al. 1997; Hebert 1994; Mjoen and Tallman 1997; Yan 1993). Meanwhile, however, these studies also pointed out that the linkage between the two constructs is far from a simple, linear relationship. Yan and Gray (1994) found that interpartner working relationship and trust, common goals shared between the partners, and formally contracted partner objectives served as moderators of the control-performance relationship such that when these factors are present, the division of parent control becomes less predictive of venture performance. Hebert's (1994) dissertation research reported similar results: In addition to a direct relationship between the level of control exercised by a parent and performance from this partner's assessment, interpartner dynamics variables such as trust, mutual commitment, and conflict moderated the control-performance relationship.

The inconsistent previous research results in the literature are not surprising. A key factor in the empirical inconsistency is the lack of well developed theories for the control-performance relationship (Yan and Gray 1994). While the effect of control on performance is assumed to exist or is taken for granted, convincing theoretical explanations have yet to develop. Among the scattered theoretical attempts, Killing's (1983) explanation for the poor performance of shared control joint ventures was based on interpartner conflict and autonomy of decision making in joint ventures. The same phenomenon was explained by Geringer and Hebert (1989) as increased transaction costs in such ventures. From a strategy-structure fit perspective, several researchers argued that parent control over a joint venture, as a structural variable, has to be examined in parallel with the parent's strategy so that the coalignment between the two would lead to performance (Geringer and Hebert 1989; Janger 1980; Schaan 1983).

Finally, Yan (1993) explained the relationship between control and performance from both a transaction costs and agency theory perspectives. In his argument, however, venture performance was assessed in terms of the achievement of partner objectives, particularly at an interpartner comparative level. From the transaction costs perspective, exercise of management control can enable a joint venture partner not only to minimize potential opportunism of other partners, but also to utilize the venture's common stock of resources to pursue its own strategic interests. As a result, the achievement of this partner's strategic objectives should be enhanced.

Consistent with the transaction costs argument, another economic theory, "agency theory," may shed additional light on the control-performance relationship. Agency theory focuses on two parties in a cooperative relationship in which one party (the principal) authorizes the other (the agent) to act on the principal's behalf (Eisenhardt 1989; Fox 1984). Because of the inherent conflict between the self-interests of the principal and the agent, agency cost occurs when the agent does not act in the best interest of the principal (Jensen and Meckling 1976). At the more general level, agency problems are "metering problems" (Alchian and Demsetz 1972), which occur when two economic entities, as a team, jointly produce output. Unless monitoring occurs, each team member will not necessarily pursue the best interests of the other member or those of the team as a whole, but will act opportunistically to pursue its own strategic interests (Moe 1984).

It is arguable that international joint ventures resemble such a team in agency theory—"A team whose members act from self-interest but realize that their destinies depend to some extent on the survival of the team in its competition with other teams" (Fama 1980, 289). The agency problem in joint ventures is rooted in the divergent self-interests of the partners and their objectives for the venture's operation. Each partner has strategic interests and objectives that are not salient for the other and must rely on the other to achieve. Therefore, each partner (the hypothetical principal) gives the other or the other's management nominees to the venture (the hypothetical agent) authority to act on the former's behalf (Fox 1984). As a result, agency costs incurred in the interpartner relationship reduce the venture's performance.

Both transaction costs theory and agency theory predict that the partner with greater control of the joint venture will use the common pool of resources to pursue its own interests rather than those of its partner, or the best interest of the joint venture overall. Therefore, in effect, the management control structure becomes a critical vehicle through which decisions about whose objectives to pursue are made. As a result, venture partners with greater control will satisfy more of their objectives than will partners who exercise less control. By the same logic, in a joint venture in which control is relatively equal, both partners should achieve a relatively equal proportion of their strategic objectives.

Determinants of Control

Envisioning the performance implications of parent control, a question arises for joint venture scholars and practitioners: What are the determining factors in the choice of a particular structure of parent control? From a practitioner's point of view in particular, the pursuit of this question has significant practical values, because structuring an organization under multiple command systems is never an easy task. Below, we present two contrasting perspectives on the determinants of control in joint ventures.

A Strategic Choice Perspective

In practice, many multinational companies were found applying exactly the same criteria and practices that they use in managing wholly owned divisions to the management of their shared-ownership international ventures, because doing so is a straightforward business practice and most likely receives institutional support (Anderson 1990). Similarly, previous research has been dominated by a perspective rooted in strategic choice theory (Child 1972) by considering only the role played by the multinational partner in designing the venture's management control structure. This "strategic intent" perspective (Geringer and Hebert 1989; Tomlinson 1970) usually does not take into consideration the local partner's influence on control and, more importantly, the negotiated nature of structural decisions between the partners. Following this perspective, control in international joint ventures has been studied over a long period of time as an issue of trade-off between the multinational firm's corporate centralized control and the magnitude of autonomy granted to the joint venture management (Geringer and Hebert 1989). To a large extent, control in joint ventures was considered not as an interorganizational phenomenon, but as an endogenous, intra-organizational variable subject solely to the multinational firm's strategic choice. For example, Franko (1971) recommended that the multinational firm create and maintain a fit between its structure and strategy with respect to the joint venture to enhance performance. Similarly, Geringer and Hebert (1989) propose a strategy-structure fit model in which the joint venture's control structure is designed in such a way that it co-aligns with the multinational firm's overall international strategy.

Parent control has also been discussed as a central issue in the context of entry modal choices, ranging from exporting to licensing and franchising, nonequity cooperation, equity joint ventures, and wholly owned options. A dominant theoretical framework in analyzing the different governance structures in an international entry decision has been transaction costs theory. This theory argues that firms choose different governance structure based on the efficiency criterion, that is, minimization of transaction costs. Once again, the level of analysis is focused on the multinational firm, and the relationship between the firm and its joint venture is treated as a relationship between the company's headquarters and a business unit not fundamentally different from a wholly owned affiliate. From this perspective, the structure of control in a joint venture is largely dependent on the multinational firm's strategic intent.

A Negotiations Perspective

Characterizing joint ventures as primarily interfirm arrangements, a negotiations perspective (Gray and Yan 1997; Yan and Gray 1994) was developed to explain the determinants of parent control. This perspective, rooted in the literature on interorganizational relations and power dependence and resource dependence theories in particular, stresses the interdependence between joint venture partners in forming and managing the cooperative relationship and the venture's external environment at large. The key argument of this perspective is that management control exercised by a joint venture participant is dependent upon its bargaining power relative to the venture's other participants.

Initiated by Emerson (1962), power dependence theory argues that bargaining power rests on the exchange relationship between two actors (individuals, units, or organizations). One actor's power resides in another's dependency. More specifically, actor A's dependence on actor B is "directly proportional to A's motivational investment in goals mediated by B, and inversely proportional to the availability of those goals to A outside of the A-B relation" (Emerson 1962, 32). Therefore, an actor involved in an exchange transaction (such as a joint venture negotiation) can gain bargaining power by decreasing its dependence on its partner, by increasing the number of alternatives that it can substitute for its relationship with this partner, by cultivating the dependence of the partner on the focal actor, or by reducing the partner's viable alternatives (Bacharach and Lawler 1984; Cook 1977). From this perspective, bargaining power is defined as the capability of the bargainers to favorably reframe or change the bargaining relationships (Lax and Sebenius 1986), to win accommodations from the other (Dwyer and Walker 1981; Tung 1988), and to influence the outcome of a negotiation (Schelling 1956).

Harrigan (1984) and later Harrigan and Newman (1990) analyzed joint ventures within a general framework in which a venture's structural configuration is determined by the bargaining power of its parents. Yan and Gray in their different publications (1994; 1995) systematically extended the bargaining power framework to consider two parallel derivatives of power dependence theory, each focusing on a different aspect of the interdependence between the parties involved.

Context-Based Bargaining Power

The first derivative of power dependence theory stresses the context-dependent relationships between the bargaining parties. It argues that the relative bargaining power of a party depends upon the mutual dependence of the partners, in particular, the exclusivity of the dependence (Blau 1964; Emerson 1962; Thompson 1967); and this power is determined by the alternatives available to it and the significance of the stakes it has in the current relationship, and in the potential outcomes of bargaining (Bacharach and Lawler 1984; Cook 1977). In joint ventures, this context-based bargaining power is rooted in the viable alternatives available to each sponsor and by the strategic importance of the venture to each of the sponsors. First, the party having more potential partners or alternative modal choices for entering a market has greater bargaining power because it can threaten to walk away from the current negotiation and to exercise its best alternative to a negotiated agreement (BATNA) (Fisher and Ury 1981). Second, joint venture sponsors do not always deem the partnership equally important in their overall strategic portfolio (Bartlett and Ghoshal 1986). Therefore, the partner with greater stakes (i.e., for which the venture is of greater strategic importance) has greater dependence and therefore less bargaining power than the partner with a lesser stake.

Resource-Based Bargaining Power

The second derivative of the power dependence perspective, represented by resource dependence theory, focuses on the resource-dependent relationships between the parties. It argues that bargaining power in interorganizational settings derives from the possession or control of critical resources (Aldrich 1977; Pfeffer and Nowak 1976; Pfeffer and Salancik 1978). According to Pfeffer and Salancik (1978, 27), "one of the inducements received for contributing the most critical resources is the ability to control and direct organizational action." Thus, a partner's contribution in critical resources will enhance its management control (Harrigan 1986; Harrigan and Newman 1990; Root 1988).

To further specify bargaining power gained by contributing critical resources to the venture (e.g., financial capital, technology, market access, and managerial knowledge), Yan and Gray (1994) differentiate between capital resource–based and noncapital resource–based power. Capital resource–based power is derived from contribution of financial resources or their equivalent in physical or proprietary properties. In contrast, noncapital-based bargaining power consists of contributions of critical tacit resources (Chi 1994) such as technology, know-how, managerial expertise, marketing channels, and political networks.

Regardless of its sophisticated theoretical grounds, the fundamental tenet of the negotiations perspective is rather straightforward: The less dependent a joint venture partner, the more powerful it is, and the higher the level of management control this partner is able to exercise. Practically, this perspective not only echoes well the common sense wisdom—in business dealings, one doesn't get what one wants or even what one deserves, one only gets what one negotiates—but it is also evident in real-world observations. For example, upon his in-depth observation of the Nantong Cellulose Fibers Company, a joint venture between Celanese Fibers Operations (a large U.S. division of what is now Hoechst/Celanese Corporation) and the China National Tobacco Corporation, Newman notes (1992, 78),

> Finding a win-win concept for the joint venture usually involves some bargaining. Each potential partner, thinking about its own wants and resources, would like the lion's share of the benefits of the cooperative activity. Relative power comes into play. Although recognizing that each partner must benefit, discussions usually have the tone of two parties making a deal.

An Integrative Perspective

Each of the two perspectives has its own limitations, as well as strengths. Although the strategic choice or strategy-structure fit perspective might make perfect sense in the setting of wholly owned international operations, its explanatory power for control in joint ventures is limited. This perspective neglects the interfirm nature of joint ventures and oversimplifies the more complex and dynamic interactions between the partners jointly owning and, most times, jointly operating the partnership. In particular, this perspective is unable to predict the control structure when both partners have the same strategic intent or both choose to exercise control in the same areas of the joint venture's operation.

In contrast, the negotiations perspective on control characterizes joint ventures as an arena in which the partners interact, and considers both partners' roles in determining the venture's control structure. Drawing heavily on the interorganizational relations literature, this perspective treats both bargaining power and control as relational concepts to be analyzed from an interpartner comparative basis. As Galaskiewicz (1985) notes, "In the literature on interorganizational relations, power has always been conceived in relational terms and, more specifically, within a social exchange framework" (p. 283). The negotiations perspective also has weaknesses, however. For example, without considering strategic intent, a partner would get lost in the negotiations by not knowing where to compromise and where to insist, which may leave the control structure completely undeterministic. In addition, both perspectives tend to focus on the organizational or interorganizational dynamics while downplaying the role of the external environmental forces in shaping a joint venture's control structure.

A complete explanation for the determinants of control in joint ventures rests on the strategic intent and the bargaining power perspectives. As recent research (Blodgett 1991; Tallman and Shenkar 1994) suggests, the division of control among joint venture partners is the result of the interaction between two sets of factors: first, what the partner wants, which is related to its strategic intent; and second, what the partners can obtain, which is essentially linked to its bargaining power. Thus, a parent's control position in the venture can be seen as a compromise between its "wants" and its "cans." Longitudinally, we expect that the two perspectives converge: A partner can increase its bargaining power to achieve its unmatched strategic intent over time, whereas the formulation of new strategic intent can only be realistically done in the context of the current balance of bargaining power between the partners.

To conclude this chapter, we hope that we have made it conceptually clear that exercising management control in international joint ventures is a critical task for venture partners. Moreover, due to the unique features of joint ventures as an interfirm cooperative arrangement, control in such partnerships deserves special and separate attention. In fact, as we will illustrate in chapter 7, management practices that do not differentiate joint ventures from wholly owned business units can lead to serious business as well as managerial problems. To stress the importance of the subject, we will report in chapter 9 two systematic empirical studies of parent control and performance.

A Mini-Case Example

Iveco-Ford

Iveco-Ford, a joint venture between Ford Motors and Iveco, the truck group of Fiat, began operation in the United Kingdom in January 1986.

Although the venture was created as an equally owned partnership, Iveco took the lead in operational control; therefore, the venture was managed on a daily basis as if it were a wholly owned division of Iveco. Meetings three times a year, the joint venture's board of directors is not involved in the venture's day-to-day operations. However, the Board's unanimous approval is required when major decisions are made, such as capital reinvestment, market withdrawal, or changes in key products. Theoretically, major operational decisions are subject to the board's "majority approval." However, since Iveco controls the majority of the board, it also controls the decisions. As a dominant partner exercising operational control, the venture's board and the executive committee do not hold an independent structure.

The venture's board consists of the following individuals: the directors in human resources, manufacturing and sales were named from the United Kingdom, the chairman and the financial and marketing directors were appointed from the Italian side. The local market knowledge was represented on the board, while effective and rapid decision making was facilitated between the venture's management and Iveco.

The board plays an important role in the venture's strategic goal setting and budgeting. In particular, it has to reconcile the differences between the partners with respect to issues of strategic importance. Although Iveco as a dominant partner is entitled to make operational decisions without Ford's full agreement, substantial information sharing at an informal level occurs between the partners to avoid surprises that might break down confidence or hinder the relationship between the partners.

(Adapted from The Conference Board, Report Number 1028: *Strategic Alliances: Guidelines for Successful Management*, p. 20. This case summary was based on the *Iveco-Ford* case described in Jordan D. Lewis, 1990. *Partnerships for Profit: Structuring Alliances*. New York: Free Press, pp. 169–172. Permissions from both sources are available.)

Part III

Managing International Joint Ventures

6

Interpartner Learning and Knowledge Transfers

As a result of increasing global competition and unabated technological advancement, many cross-border joint ventures are created by partners intending to access knowledge, skills, and resources that cannot be internally produced in a timely or cost-effective fashion. This chapter articulates both opportunities and challenges derived from interpartner learning and knowledge transfer. It delineates major steps in knowledge transfer between cross-border partners and illuminates how to benefit from learning opportunities while mitigating challenges. Specifically, we suggest the following measures for creating greater payoffs from interpartner learning: (1) scrutinizing partner commitment; (2) improving knowledge flow; (3) aligning with different cultures; (4) building interpartner trust; (5) integrating acquired knowledge; (6) preventing knowledge leakage; (7) avoiding undue dependence on joint ventures; (8) establishing reward systems; and (9) institutionalizing acquired knowledge.

Interpartner Learning in Joint Ventures

The Importance of Learning

A key asset of the multinational corporation is the diversity of environments in which it operates. This diversity exposes the firm to multiple stimuli, allows it to develop a wide range of abilities, and provides it with broader learning opportunities than are available to a purely domestic firm. The enhanced organizational learning resulting from internalized diversity can explain a firm's ongoing growth, while its initial stock of knowledge may be the strength that allows it to create such organizational diversity in the first place. To exploit such a potential, the firm must treat learning as an explicit objective of international cooperative arrangements and create mechanisms and systems by which such learning can take place.

Organizational learning has long been considered a key building block and a major source of competitive advantage. Sustainable competitive advantages are only possible when firms continuously reinvest in building resources. New inputs to a firm's resource base are imperative for developing a resource pool. Thus, both a dynamic resource mix and organizational learning are crucial to firm growth. The necessity for dynamic learning is magnified during international expansion because it helps the firm overcome the liability of foreignness when operating abroad. On the one hand, international expansion provides learning opportunities through exposure to new markets, internalization of new concepts, gleaning new ideas from different cultures, access to new resources, and exposure to new competitors and terms of competition. These opportunities can result in the development of new capabilities that may be applicable to both old and new locations; they thus promote evolution of the firm's strategic configuration.

Learning does not take place in a vacuum, but in specific social and organizational environments. To the multinational partner in a joint venture, host country environments represent both great market opportunities and tremendous uncertainty. Environmental unpredictability forces the foreign firm to learn how to respond to local settings. To the local firm, teaming up with a foreign partner is also associated with uncertainty and anxiety. For example, the general lack of experience in the international markets and the up-to-date technology prompts the local partner in a developing country to desire knowledge acquisitions. Overall, while possession of rent-generating resources is indispensable for firms exploring new opportunities, learning capabilities are critical to these firms to reduce vulnerability and to gain a competitive edge.

Interfirm learning is an important source of knowledge acquisition during international expansion. Firms expand internationally in order to acquire distinctive skills critical to global success, which are only available from foreign businesses or rivals. Global competitiveness is largely a function of the firm's pace, efficiency, and extent of knowledge accumulation. Core competencies and value-creating disciplines are not distributed equally among international companies. International collaboration can lead to increased knowledge. A joint venture may be not only a means by which partners trade access to each other's skills (quasi-internalization) but also a mechanism for actually acquiring a partner's skills (de facto internalization). By forming joint ventures, a firm can gain cheap, fast access to new markets by "borrowing" a partner's core competencies, innovative skills, local infrastructure, and country-specific knowledge.

Joint Venturing as a Learning Vehicle

Learning from new opportunities requires participating in them. A wide range of interorganizational linkages, including joint ventures, is therefore critical to knowledge diffusion, learning, and acquisition. As global competition intensifies and technological development accelerates, research breakthroughs are so broadly distributed that no single firm has all the internal capabilities necessary for success. Many competitors are likely to be working on the same targets; the rewards go only to those that act most swiftly. Thus, new technology is both a stimulus to and a focus of cooperative effort that seeks to reduce the inherent uncertainty associated with novel products or markets. It is a widely accepted view that collaboration enhances organizational learning (Hamel 1991; Powell 1990).

The establishment of international joint ventures provides a promising vehicle for interorganizational learning. Multinational firms turn to international joint ventures to acquire resources and skills they cannot produce internally, when the hazards of cross-border cooperation can be held to a tolerable level (Pisano 1989). In bringing together firms with different skills, knowledge bases, and organizational cultures, international joint ventures create unique learning opportunities for the partner firms. By definition, joint ventures involve a shared access to each other's resources. This access can be a powerful source of new knowledge, which would not be possible without the formal structure of an international joint venture. Partner firms that use this access as the basis for learning have the opportunity to acquire knowledge that can be used to enhance partner strategy and operations. Therefore, for many multinational firms, international joint ventures are no longer a peripheral activity but a mainstay of competitive strategy. Particularly in technologically intensive industries, where there are large gains from innovation and steep losses from obsolescence, competition is best regarded as a learning race.

Knowledge Transfer Between Joint Venture Partners

A direct consequence of interpartner learning in joint ventures is knowledge transfer between the partner firms. Knowledge to be transferred between partners in an international joint venture can be characterized from different angles. First, considering the nature of knowledge, some knowledge is tacit while other is explicit. In general, creation of organizational knowledge involves a continuous interplay between tacit and explicit knowledge. Unlike explicit knowledge, which is often tradable and accessible from the open market (e.g., through licensing or franchising), tacit knowledge is organizationally or individually embedded and thus nontradable. Because of this, interpartner collaboration in which two or more firms contribute complementary resources including tacit knowledge (such as know-how or managerial skills) is an ideal choice for acquiring tacit knowledge. Tacit knowledge normally generates more of a sustained competitive advantage than does explicit knowledge. At the same time, however, tacit knowledge is hard to formalize, making it more difficult to communicate or share with others than explicit knowledge.

Second, for each partner, knowledge acquired via international joint venture can fall into several categories: (1) knowledge about how to design and manage international joint ventures, (2) access to the partner's knowledge without internalizing it in one's own operations, and (3) using a partner's knowledge to enhance one's own strategy and operations at home or in the global marketplace. Although many firms seek to integrate acquired knowledge with their own operations, not every kind of knowledge sought by a joint venture partner needs to be internalized in the entire network operations of a multinational firm. For instance, an international distributor may form a joint venture with an overseas manufacturer to ensure a stable product supply and thereby gain access to manufacturing skills. If the distributor has no intention to acquire such skills, the manufacturing knowledge embodied in the international joint venture output will have limited value to this partner.

Third, considering the function of knowledge, partner knowledge can be broadly categorized as either operational or managerial. Operational knowledge includes knowledge about technology, production processes (e.g., quality control), marketing skills, and other expertise (e.g., public relationship building). Managerial knowledge is composed of organizational and managerial skills (e.g., leadership, human resource management, organizational structure, managerial efficiency, and employee participation), marketing expertise (in international and host country markets), industrial and collaborative experience, and financial management (e.g., cost control, taxation, capital utilization, financing, risk reduction, resource deployment, and asset management).

Lastly, parental origin, whether foreign or local, provides different perspectives on international joint venture knowledge. While joint venture partners may share the same interest in acquiring each other's knowledge, they are likely to differ in terms of their foci with respect to learning. Foreign investors may seek experiential knowledge about the host-country market from local partners. Such knowledge may include host-country culture and business practices, the cultivation of relationships with the business community and governmental agencies, culture-specific managerial expertise, and unique marketing and promotional skills. Local investors, on the other hand, may be more interested in obtaining cutting-edge technology and innovations or international business experience from their foreign counterparts. Such reciprocity in learning is heavily based on the partners' resource complementarity, which, ironically, tends to diminish over time as a result of learning.

In summary, the use of international joint ventures has been seen to dramatically shape knowledge transfer patterns. International joint ventures not only change how knowledge flows within and across formally linked organizations, they also affect how individual organizations conduct business. International joint ventures involve not only learning by individual joint venture partner firms, but also interpartner joint learning. Joint ventures forge new knowledge transfer pathways, across both technologically and traditionally linked positions. Therefore, learning and knowledge transfer in joint ventures should be assessed from multiple perspectives.

Challenges of Learning

International joint ventures enable the partner firms more learning opportunities. However, joint venturing also entails tremendous challenges and complexity as knowledge is acquired and institutionalized in a cross-firm and cross-cultural setting, which deserves serious attention by international managers.

International joint ventures are not simply a means for compensating for a lack of internal skills. Using and relying on external learning and knowledge transfer is challenging, uncertain, and complex. The choice to pool resources with another organization depends on calculations involving risk versus return. A lack of trust between parties, difficulty in relinquishing control, the complexity of a joint project, and differential ability in learning new skills are all barriers to effective collaboration. Moreover, in those industries in which interfirm agreements are relatively frequent, there can be confusion about which firms are allies and which are not. The partnering decision depends on each partner's size and position in the value chain, levels of technological sophistication, resource constraints, and prior experience with joint ventures.

There are several fundamental impediments to interpartner learning and knowledge transfer. The first originates in the socially embedded nature of knowledge. Many of the difficulties encountered in the learning process cannot be easily resolved through governance structures since they do not lie in structural barriers alone. In contrast to codified, explicit knowledge, which is generally transparent, readily accessible, and thus inherently diffusible, most knowledge transferred between joint venture partners is tacit, context-specific, and socially or organizationally embedded. As we discussed earlier in this chapter, such tacit knowledge is generated and stored in organizational relationships; the mode of coordination is based on a human network. This type of knowledge is therefore not amenable to systematic codification (Kogut and Zander 1992). In organizations, tacit knowledge involves intangible factors embedded in personal beliefs, experiences, and values. When knowledge supporting an organizational or operational process is extremely tacit, it is difficult to describe and articulate the process.

Studies on organizational learning argue that a large part of human knowledge is contextual, firm-specific, and tacit in nature (Nelson and Winter 1982). There are limits to its ability to be effectively articulated and transferred. Badaracco (1991) used the term "embedded knowledge" to denote the fact that some of the knowledge being created around the world is not transferable because it is deeply embedded in complex social interactions. Unlike knowledge that can be encapsulated in formulas, manuals, and blueprints, embedded knowledge is "sticky" and moves very slowly. Granovetter (1985) depicts organizations as bundles of embodied knowledge, including technology, procedures, organizational structures, and hierarchical relationships. Analysis suggests that the knowledge of an organization has its own systematic structure; and differences in the knowledge architecture of an organization can inhibit knowledge transfer. The problems of knowledge sharing within international joint ventures are magnified because of their greater diversity of knowledge and organizational systems. Incompatibility of knowledge structures and work systems between partner firms can generate many conflicts. Different degrees of tacitness of knowledge can also create interpartner asymmetry in knowledge transfer. Such asymmetry is likely to obstruct interpartner learning and knowledge exchange.

A second problem with knowledge transfer concerns partner incentives for knowledge sharing and protection against knowledge leakage. Naturally, each party wants to protect its knowledge from uncompensated leakage to the other or any third party. Because of interpartner asymmetry of knowledge demand and supply, it is expected that partner protectiveness and accessibility to its knowledge will be correspondingly asymmetrical. In general, international joint venture partners are likely to be more protective of their knowledge resources when their competitive advantages rely more on them. In a situation of high competitive overlap between partners, the firms may be reluctant to share knowledge and will strive to prevent knowledge leakage to partners because of the risk of knowledge spillover. Therefore, if international joint venture partners are rivals or potential rivals, it is reasonable to predict that they will have a limited incentive to share knowledge. In fact, a firm may have little incentive to form international joint ventures, let alone could knowledge sharing potentially lead to the creation of a competitor (Hamel 1991; Inkpen 1998).

A factor influencing partner willingness or reluctance to share knowledge is the extent to which the knowledge possessed by the partners is mutually complementary. Knowledge complementarity stimulates interpartner learning and leads to knowledge transfer. First, a reciprocal need for each other's knowledge serves as a solid basis for collaboration. Meanwhile, high complementarity increases both incentives for knowledge transfer and accessibility to partner knowledge. In a two-partner joint venture, accessibility to partner A's knowledge by partner B depends upon the extent to which partner B is open with its own knowledge to partner A. Similarly, a reciprocal need for each other's proprietary knowledge boosts knowledge exchange between partners and ensures resource accessibility. Ideally, partner protectiveness will be minimal when an international joint venture is designed by both parties to facilitate knowledge transfer.

Third and finally, the extent to which one partner's knowledge is accessible to the other depends on interpartner trust. Increasing trust between international joint venture partners may mitigate partner protectiveness. When a new venture is formed between unfamiliar parties who have no prior collaboration, the partners will often hesitate to share knowledge. If the venture is able to survive the honeymoon period, deeper ties between partners are likely to become the norm. In many cases, ties develop between the managers involved in the international joint venture. After a relationship is formed and a pattern of interactions develops, partner firms may decrease their efforts to protect knowledge spillover. Specifically, as interpartner trust increases and mutual understanding develops, access to each other's knowledge base will become less problematic.

Steps in Knowledge Transfer

Organizational learning is a collective learning process by all members of an organization. Learning in international joint ventures includes three sequential steps: (1) perception, (2) internalization, and (3) abstraction. In the perception stage, the product and market know-how of the partners is transferred to the joint venture organization. When one parent firm transfers its knowledge to the venture, the joint venture employees hired from the other parent gain experience about this knowledge and thus enrich their knowledge base. However, there has been no knowledge transfer across the organizational boundaries in this stage because the learning has occurred and will be contained only within the joint venture's boundaries.

During the internalization stage, one partner actively extracts knowledge from its partner and transfers the knowledge to its own organization. As such, the learning firm seizes possession of knowledge from its joint venture partner. Richter and Vettel (1995) provide an example to illustrate how Bosch, a German car supplier and electronic company, internalized its Japanese partner's knowledge resources. In Bosch's five joint ventures in Japan, it established "strategy meetings" focusing on directing the regional flow of knowledge. These meetings promoted an intense exchange of technicians, who helped to establish a worldwide "Bosch standard." Bosch sent trained German technicians to the Japanese joint ventures to guarantee an effective transfer of technology and to maintain the company's high-quality standards. A further incentive for Bosch was to get in-depth information on culture-based knowledge created in the joint ventures and to transfer that experience to German headquarters. The resulting knowledge benefited all members of the Bosch group in an effort to access their Japanese clients worldwide.

After a successful knowledge transfer, the partner's knowledge is analyzed to define underlying culture-bound values and assumptions. By this process, pragmatic changes are undertaken, and internal knowledge is altered on many dimensions. Management processes are reorganized based on the tacit knowledge gained. The company may even alter the internal procedures related to tangible knowledge. In this way, abstract learning can consequently change the internal capability for knowledge generation within the organization. For example, Bosch's increased business activities in Japan were aimed at compensating for its potential loss of market share in Europe. By gaining access to Japanese carmakers, Bosch acquired supply contracts for its European plants. By becoming familiar with the culture of its Japanese partners, Bosch was able to anticipate its partner's technological and organizational development and to react to it accordingly. Its activities in Japan consequently have served as a sensor monitoring changes in the Japanese market. Thus, Japan functioned as a training ground for Bosch, which internalized Japanese knowledge and learned to anticipate competitor moves.

Taking Opportunities and Avoiding Challenges

Interpartner learning and knowledge transfer can provide a significant payoff. Formed among firms with unique skills and capabilities, international joint ventures can create powerful learning opportunities. However, without effective management of the learning process, many of these opportunities will remain unexploited. Multinational firms should institute policies, structures, and processes to spur learning and knowledge transfer. Forming an international joint venture does not alone ensure that learning potential will be realized. As March (1991) and Pisano (1989) suggested, organizational learning is a systems-level concept that becomes useful only when its component parts are thoroughly understood down to the operational level. Organizations cannot create knowledge without individuals. Unless individual knowledge is shared with other individuals and groups, knowledge will have a limited impact on organizational effectiveness. Thus, organizational knowledge creation should be viewed as a process whereby the knowledge held by individuals is amplified and internalized as part of an organization's knowledge base. Clearly, knowledge creation and utilization are closely linked. As individual knowledge becomes accepted by other organization members and is utilized in organizational processes, the knowledge-creation process moves beyond individual perspectives.

By focusing on international joint venture knowledge management, below we develop a framework of collaborative learning that should prove instructive for managers aiming to exploit international joint venture learning opportunities. In this framework, we suggest the following measures for creating payoffs from interpartner learning: (1) scrutinizing partner commitment, (2) improving knowledge flow, (3) aligning with different cultures, (4) building interpartner trust, (5) integrating acquired knowledge, (6) preventing knowledge leakage, (7) avoiding dependence on international joint ventures, (8) establishing reward systems, and (9) institutionalizing acquired knowledge.

Scrutinizing Partner Commitment

By determining a prospective partner's intentions, values, level of commitment, and capabilities, a focal firm can find out how serious the partner is about the international joint venture and what caliber of personnel, resources, and knowledge it is likely to commit. With this information, it will be better able to design its own strategies with respect to learning and knowledge transfer. Working with a prospective partner on a small preliminary project is often a safe way to get a clearer sense of the other party's culture and capabilities before creating a full-scale international joint venture. In the end, a promising ally should show depth of capabilities and commitment, not just capital or the capacity to produce a single product cheaply. With such an ally, the firm will be able to adapt to changes in technology, exchange rates, markets, and government policies.

Examining partner commitment is also an important prerequisite for verifying whether both partners have complementary knowledge. Learning is generally more effective when one partner provides what the other party wants and vice versa. For any firm pursuing knowledge transfer from its joint venture partners, it is critical to diagnose what knowledge the partner firm can contribute to the venture, how much commitment the partner will make over time as the venture evolves, what strategic motives underlie the partner's participation, and whether the partner's contributed knowledge will align with the focal company's own needs.

Improving Knowledge Flow

The creation of organizational knowledge requires dissemination of individual experiences within a multinational network. As one organizational unit is engaged in a knowledge transfer arrangement with another firm, other units within the same organization will be in a position to amplify, modify, and clarify such knowledge. For knowledge in an international joint venture to migrate to a parent firm, there must be a well-established system of knowledge flow from the venture to its sister subsidiaries within the multinational firm's network as well as to the parent's headquarters. The linkage between the newly acquired knowledge and the firm's existing knowledge base should be discussed, verified, and integrated. With knowledge connections in place, new knowledge has a higher probability of survival and integration into the firm's globally coordinated knowledge base. When knowledge flow is consciously managed between the joint venture and the firm's network, the effectiveness of knowledge sharing and dissemination among various units is significantly enhanced.

Any subsidiary in a multinational network can be arrayed along two dimensions of knowledge flow, that is, the extent to which a subsidiary receives knowledge inflow from the rest of the network and the extent to which the subsidiary provides knowledge outflow to the rest of the corporation. A well-constructed knowledge flow infrastructure should be able to improve the firm's overall input, throughput, and output process. It drives up overall integration because it enhances transaction cost economies for the system as a whole, promotes information exchange, and yields more revenues from the cross-border value chain.

Firms must establish an effective information flow system to ensure that knowledge flow is properly monitored and adjusted within a portfolio network. Information system transparency forces conflicts in the knowledge flow process to be resolved on the basis of improved problem definition, rather than smoothed over or decided upon on the basis of organizational formal authority or political maneuvers.

Aligning with Different Cultures

Interpartner cultural difference, whether at the national, industrial, or organizational level, can hinder interfirm learning and knowledge transfer in international joint ventures. Firms with open cultures that view change as positive can facilitate learning. In contrast, cultures that view stability as a key value present barriers to learning. Awareness of normal cultural interactions, as well as degree of institutionalization and change over time, makes a difference in both understanding and implementing learning. Sending expatriate managers familiar with the host country culture to international joint ventures helps mitigate problems arising from cultural difference. Similarly, working with local partners with previous collaborative experience also reduces cross-cultural problems. More importantly, managers in international joint ventures should be well versed with adapting to different cultural environments and learning orientations. To make knowledge transfer between the venture and its parents effective, the joint venture managers and the managers at the parent firms have to work closely to remove the stigma of us versus them (Inkpen 1998). If managers don't trust each other or they harbor suspicions of each other's motives, effective organizational learning can hardly occur.

Building Interpartner Trust

Openness is crucial to interpartner learning: Much of what the parties are trying to learn from each other is oftentimes difficult to articulate or communicate. It is often embedded in a firm's practices and culture, and it can only be learned through working relationships that are not hampered by constraints. In order to enhance interpartner trust, commitment from each party is necessary. For instance, GM stationed personnel in Tokyo to facilitate its Japanese partners, Isuzu and Suzuki, in their dealings with Chevrolet back in United States. These managers on expatriation include marketing, manufacturing, and engineering consultants, as well as planners, procurement and distribution managers, and industrial analysts. Similarly at Daewoo, GM was represented by a career executive who lived in Korea and served as executive president of the Daewoo Motor Company and its joint representative director.

Integrating Acquired Knowledge

Internal capability building and external acquisition of knowledge are mutually enhancing. A firm cannot build a competitive and sustainable knowledge base by solely and passively receiving new knowledge from its cooperation with other firms. By using international joint ventures as a sole source of knowledge, the firm cannot build its own. This creates heavy dependence on its international partners. Once turbulence occurs—for example, joint venture termination—the firm's knowledge base will erode. Therefore, particularly in industries in which know-how is critical, companies must be expert at building both internal and external knowledge bases. A firm with a greater absorptive and integrative capacity is able to contribute more to a partnership and meanwhile learn more extensively from the cooperation. Overall, internal capability is indispensable in evaluating outside research, while external collaboration provides access to new ideas and resources that cannot be generated internally. A dynamic network can serve double functions by acquiring knowledge and resources that are otherwise unavailable, and testing and utilizing internally generated knowledge and capabilities (Powell 1990).

Preventing Knowledge Leakage

The risks of opportunism and knowledge leaks are particularly pressing when partners want to create new knowledge and capabilities. Partnerships between firms engaged in knowledge-intensive competition are unlikely to be guided solely by harmony and goodwill. Joint venture knowledge links create the risk that core knowledge and capabilities will flow to partners in unintended and harmful ways through the actions of the venture's employees. In most cases, core knowledge does migrate, but not because a firm's partners are devious or predatory. Rather, many relationships have been created expressly to combine the capabilities and knowledge of two firms. This implies that each partner is expected to learn a certain amount about the other's capabilities and that channels of communication have been opened. This risk, however, is not a reason to shun international joint ventures. As with any business risk, the key questions are whether it has been assessed accurately, is justified by the possible benefits, or can be effectively controlled.

There are several ways to protect core knowledge from uncompensated leakage to partner firms. First, the design, development, manufacture, and service of a product manufactured by an international joint venture may be structured so as to wall off the most sensitive technologies. For example, in the international joint venture between GE and Snecma that builds commercial aircraft engines, GE tried to reduce the risk of excess transfer of knowledge by keeping certain sections of the production process secret, while permitting Snecma access only to final assembly. This modularization cut off the transfer of what GE felt was key competitive technology. Similarly, in Boeing's joint venture in Japan that builds the 767s, Boeing walled off research, design, and marketing functions, considered more central to Boeing's competitive position, but allowed its Japanese partner to share production technology. Boeing also effectively separated out technologies not required for 767 production.

Second, contractual safeguards can be written into an international joint venture agreement. For example, TRW Inc. has three strategic alliances with large Japanese auto component suppliers to produce seat belts, engine valves, and steering gears for sale to Japanese-owned auto assembly plants in the United States. TRW has clauses in each of its joint venture contracts that bar the Japanese companies from competing by developing component parts. These contractual items have prevented the Japanese firms from gaining access to TRW's home market as direct competitors.

Third, both parties to an international joint venture can agree in advance to exchange specific skills and technologies that ensure a chance for equitable gain. Cross-licensing agreements are one way of achieving this goal. For example, in the alliance between Motorola and Toshiba, Motorola licensed some of its microprocessor technology to Toshiba, and in return Toshiba licensed some of its memory chip technology to Motorola.

Fourth, the risk of opportunism by a joint venture partner can be reduced if the company extracts in advance a credible commitment from its partner. Although in many cases such commitment per se is not legally binding, good will embedded in a long-term alliance can make such commitment reasonably reliable. The long-lived 50–50 joint venture between Xerox and Fuji illustrates such a commitment. Aimed at the photocopiers market in Asia, Xerox and Fuji invest heavily in people, equipment, and facilities. Fuji, from the very outset, was committed to making the joint venture a profitable and long-term partnership between the two companies.

Avoiding Undue Dependence on a Partnership

As noted above, international joint ventures can be used for supplementing and improving a firm's embedded knowledge, yet not for substituting for internal development. Joint venture sponsoring firms can reduce dependence on their partners by being extremely cautious about establishing joint ventures with competitors or involving their core knowledge in a partnership. GM limited its dependence on its Asian allies in its Saturn project in an attempt to independently replenish the knowledge critical to its business. Similarly, none of IBM's global partnerships involved the manufacturing, design, or sales of mainframe computers, which are core skills of the company. When IBM seeks to link its personal computers with other computers and mainframes in large networks, it reduces its dependence on outside suppliers of parts and components.

When international joint ventures do involve core knowledge, firms must guard against shifts in the balance of bargaining power, maneuvering by other parties, and expropriation of the knowledge. A firm can reduce dependence on a particular joint venture by creating multiple ventures to form a spider's web or by seeking a senior partner status in each relationship. For instance, Toyota exercises a hegemonic influence over its alliances with its suppliers by being a predominant purchaser, helping to finance them, and offering equipment and managerial supports.

Establishing Reward Systems

A reward system can exert a strong influence on a firm's learning effectiveness. It exercises a direct impact on managerial behavior and nourishes knowledge transfer between international joint venture partners.

To routinize and institutionalize new knowledge, appropriate reward systems should exist within the international joint venture and its participating organizations. Lei, Slocum, and Pitts (1997) identify two primary types of reward systems, hierarchy-based and performance-based, to facilitate learning in international joint ventures. A hierarchy-based system creates a strong bond between the firm and its people by building formal organizational boundaries. Alternatively, performance-based reward systems place a premium on quantitative measures of performance. While joint venture managers are encouraged to get results quickly, a performance-based system discourages team-based and cross-unit activities. Well established reward systems and incentive structures increase learning effectiveness and encourage overseas managers to acquire individually embedded knowledge, which later can become firm-specific knowledge. It is important to emphasize that these processes are nonlinear. Complex interactions involving culture, history, technology, structural patterns, work systems, and a host of other related factors come into play.

Institutionalizing Acquired Knowledge

As more firms rely on external relationships for knowledge, the abilities to process, transfer, and transmit knowledge gained in one context to other become critical. Organizational routines for learning must be robust, flexible, and durable. Institutionalizing new knowledge involves making the leaps from information to knowledge and from individual learning to organizational learning. Thus, institutionalization of learning includes both the information-knowledge and individual-organization transformations.

However, developing routines for the transmission of information and experience does not necessarily entail formalization. Information can be conveyed routinely through informal means.

It must be noted that developing routines for knowledge dissemination has to deal with a dilemma: Informal mechanisms may preclude wide dissemination, while formal procedures can inhibit learning. The challenge is to develop regular venues for informal transmission channels, such that the process itself becomes tied to knowledge seeking and creation. As firms vary in their abilities to access and acquire knowledge beyond their boundaries, they should develop different profiles for collaboration, turning to partners for divergent combinations of skills, funding, experience, access, and status. The pharmaceutical industry provides a case in point. A San Francisco–based company, namely, Recombinant Capital, poured $4.5 billion into deals with biotech companies in 1996 with the objective of capitalizing on promising technology and the skills of nimbler small companies in achieving rapid growth. Industrial giant Merck, however, spreads its search efforts globally, working with research institutes in many countries and meanwhile pursuing research partnerships with a limited number of biotech firms. In addition, Merck has entered into many licensing agreements for manufacturing, marketing, and sales.

Mini-Case Examples

Case 1: Fuji-Xerox

Fuji-Xerox is one of the most successful and enduring joint ventures. The two partner companies from different political and business environments have successfully developed the joint venture to its fullest potential. The 50–50 owned joint venture was established in 1962 between Xerox of the United States and Fuji of Japan. With sales reaching nearly $8 billion in 1994, Fuji-Xerox now provides Xerox with over 20 percent of its world revenues. Xerox's success did not come easy, however. In fact, if it were not for this joint venture, Xerox might not have survived the fierce competition in the industry.

Fuji Photo Film is the largest manufacturer of film products in Japan, with $90 million in sales in 1962, at which time it was roughly the size of Xerox. At that time, Fuji was looking to diversify away from photography and had begun experimenting with xerography. It had the finances and name recognition that Xerox was looking for in its partner selection.

The famous Xerox Group was then a maker of photocopiers in the United States. Its revolutionary plain-paper copiers permanently linked the Xerox name with "photocopying." Xerox revenues consistently doubled every ten months between 1960 and 1966. Its success began diminishing, however, as the tremendous competition arose in the Asian market. It needed a way to enter the Asian market and so looked toward Japan.

Unfortunately, establishment of the joint venture with Fuji did not bring Xerox immediate success. It was overcome by the entrance of new rivals from unexpected sources. Over time, however, Xerox learned to use its alliance with Fuji Photo Film to regain its leadership in the industry.

Initially, Fuji-Xerox manufactured and sold large high-volume copiers in the United States. These copiers were sold at premium prices to the high-end market. The joint venture gained a big portion of the American market using this strategy. This in turn aided Xerox in its growth. In Japan, however, Fuji-Xerox lost ground. Competitors such as Canon and Ricoh were producing and selling small, low-volume copiers in the low and mid-price ranges. The copiers produced by Fuji-Xerox also failed to use the Japanese paper standard. In addition, Japanese firms were selling their products in the United States for the same price that Xerox charged for its copiers. It was only then that Xerox noticed it had been virtually ignoring its joint venture with the Fuji Photo Film Company. Both Fuji Photo and Rank Xerox had become passive partners in Fuji-Xerox and slowly discontinued their supply of technology and expertise to this joint venture. Thus, when Fuji-Xerox needed any technology and business advice, it turned to Xerox. Fuji-Xerox benefited from this flow of technology and also enjoyed a high degree of autonomy.

Why did as big a company as Xerox create an international joint venture and then virtually ignore it? Xerox had first intended to enter Japan and the Asian market as a marketing strategy. However, in the early 1960s Japan was still under very tight governmental rule. In fact, the Japanese government denied approval for the original joint venture, which was intended for sales purposes only. The Fuji-Xerox alliance was then revised to give it manufacturing rights, and its management was placed in Japanese hands, although the board of directors consisted of both Japanese and American representatives. Fuji-Xerox developed many strategies and skills aimed at succeeding in the industry, but it was not until the 1980s that it came to the aid of the Xerox Company. Fuji-Xerox had already begun modifying Xerox's designs to suit the Japanese market. In 1978 the joint venture offered to sell low-end copiers to Xerox and Rank Xerox so they could compete with their Japanese competitors. Xerox declined the proposition, but Rank Xerox took it on. Rank Xerox purchased 25,000 machines for sale in Europe and had quite a success with them. Rank Xerox was able to defend its market share while Xerox's market share continued to decline.

The venture eventually began to export the FX2202 and other related machines to the United States. Fuji-Xerox assembled these products for Xerox to sell but, due to U.S. union unrest, actually exported "knockdown" units to Xerox to be assembled. Over a short period of time, Fuji-Xerox played an important role in exporting more and more finished products, kits, and other copier machines to Xerox branches worldwide. In this manner, Fuji-Xerox helped Xerox to advance in the industry. However, Xerox still had not changed how it developed, manufactured, and marketed its products. As Fuji-Xerox began to be seen as a model for quality control, Xerox began to change its own departments. It acquired management ideas, new subcontracting approaches, product development techniques, and competitive data from the once neglected Fuji-Xerox. Although Xerox had initially transferred and licensed its technology and skills to Fuji-Xerox, it was this reverse flow of technology, information, and managerial skills from Fuji-Xerox that enabled Xerox to get back on its feet.

Xerox was able to come out with the 10 series of copiers. Dubbed the "Marathon" family, this line soon became the most popular line in Xerox's history. This success led to a restoration of company morale and finances. Since that time, Xerox has continued to learn from Fuji-Xerox. Most recently, Xerox reduced its supplier base, which enabled it in turn to lower its purchased parts to 45 percent and minimize its manufacturing costs. The most important concept Xerox has learned, however, is to be flexible and adaptive in the new global environment. The U.S. Commerce Department recognized the progress in Xerox's management and presented the Malcolm Baldrige National Quality Award to Xerox.

Case 2: Fujitsu in Spain: Barriers to Knowledge Transfer

During the early 1970s, Japan's Fujitsu was still a computer industry follower with a humble 30 percent market share. It would take significant alterations to meet, let alone overtake, the industry leader, IBM. It wanted to enter new computer markets, but lacked financial backing and assistance. Finally, it decided to enter the computer market in Spain with a twofold manufacturing and sales plan.

In 1973, Fujitsu allied with Spain's largest city bank, Banesto, to create a 50–50 joint venture—FESA (Fujitsu, Espana, S.A.). It proved a mutually beneficial arrangement. Banesto pursued a potentially profitable business venture and Fujitsu used Banesto to satisfy political regulations.

By 1976, Fujitsu was able to separate from Banesto to become a wholly owned subsidiary. Meanwhile, it established a majority ownership in a new company, SECOINSA (Sociedad Espanola de Communicationes de Infomatica, S.A.), partnering with the National Telephone Company of Spain and various Spanish banks. Fujitsu had therefore set up two corporate extensions in Spain, FESA and SECOINSA.

Fujitsu was not able to prevent conflict arising in the real world of joint ventures. The main problem was discussion of terms. Spain had many essential personnel, including engineers, technicians, and research and development people, but communication proved to be a difficulty. Both firms had to rely on English as the common tongue, although it is the second language for both. The actual transfer of knowledge from each party to the other was only effective and efficient when they could work together physically.

Even communication via the written word had its limits, especially for the Japanese, who felt they could not disclose their true feelings in written English. They favored a more interpersonal and fluid rapport that adapted to issues as they arose. They were reluctant to accept binding paper commitments that were not flexible enough to allow for unforeseeable events. For example, the transfer of sophisticated computer technology was a problem. Fujitsu's competitive edge came from its belief that it was producing the highest-quality computers made from the highest-quality components following rigorous Japanese standards. Fujitsu wanted all the components tested in Japan at its facilities, but since manufacturing was to be done in Spain, SECOINSA favored Spanish-made components. SECOINSA suggested that the work could be done in Europe if Fujitsu would supply the specifications, testing, and quality control methods. Fujitsu was willing to provide the needed information, but refused to reveal it to any outside parties and would not pass along any information in writing. This made quality control difficult to ensure.

Fujitsu wanted to maintain stringent control over its products and prevent imitation. It was in favor of redesigning components as needed, but still demanded the same performance and reliability from these altered components. This prevented its Spanish partners from acquiring broad exposure to all segments of the transferred technology. The Japanese also limited the exchange of technological knowledge by disclosing information only as the appropriate project arose.

Cultural differences also played a role in the joint ventures. The Spanish believed the Japanese were too business focused and hidden behind a barrage of company talk that prevented friendships or rapport from developing. They also felt that the Japanese were not well rounded because their at-work and after-work personas merged into one. Spanish people favor a distinct separation between job and leisure. The Japanese feel that the company they work for provides them with identity and status. If Fujitsu is number one, its employees must be careful to adhere to its standards wherever they go and whatever they do. All identities fall into a hierarchical arrangement, regardless of situation. The Japanese rarely adapted to the ways of the Spanish and this in turn made the Spanish believe that the Japanese looked down on local ways. Such misunderstandings on both sides undoubtedly hindered rapport.

Another crucial area of disharmony was in styles of management. The Spanish partners had difficulty understanding why it took so long to make decisions, there were no formal plans of action, and those in positions of authority did not seem to exercise power. Decision making at Fujitsu was through the *ringi-sho* system, in which an idea is documented and distributed to all relevant parties for approval. Weeks later, once finally approved by the president, the idea is quickly implemented. *Ringi-sho* is therefore a conservative approach aimed at minimizing risk to ensure success. The group as a whole is responsible for the outcome, whether failure or success. Any corrective action is taken through another *ringi-sho*, which can draw out the process even longer. Japanese plans of action seem more future-oriented than those of the Spanish.

The Spanish and Japanese also view power differently. The Spanish are more inclined to assume that authority is earned through ability and merit, and that authority automatically leads to power. The Japanese treat age as the determining factor in earning power and authority. They further regard the two as distinct. One can have authority, title, and respect and still not wield any decision-making power. Other people may carry lots of decision-making weight, yet not have obvious authority or titles.

Like other Japanese firms, Fujitsu puts a heavy burden on the shoulders of its employees; middle and lower management levels and laborers have a great role in operating the firm. Because of such widespread involvement, the company has a vision, but reaching its target can take time. The company moves in one direction, then another, always experiencing bumps, turns, or backtracking. It is more important to achieve team effort with total commitment. As this management style was very effective in Japan, Fujitsu saw no reason to alter it for the Spanish market.

International joint ventures consist of more than transfer of knowledge, accumulation of technology, or diversification of risks. There are more complex parameters that affect corporate rapport. Joint ventures need excellent people who are broad-minded and flexible. They need to be flexible and also have a strong will to succeed. There must exist a mutual attitude of open-mindedness and desire to learn between the partners. Traditions and business practices can have an unexpected effect on the success of strategic alliances. A company must be prepared to spend more on improving its human resources through learning new modes of communication.

7

Performance and Performance Assessment

In this chapter, we review the major controversies on performance assessment in international joint ventures with respect to the multiple perspectives on performance held by different parties in the venture, the diverging performance measures, and the effect of timing in measuring performance. Drawing on research on organizational effectiveness, we present an integrative framework in which the goals/objectives of the major strategic constituencies of the venture are used as the foundation of performance measurement. We argue that the achievement of these goals/objectives (both set at founding and emerged or changed over time) is the most realistic and appropriate measure of joint venture success.

Controversies on Joint Venture Performance

Performance has been a central concern of previous research on international joint ventures. The high rates of joint venture failure reported in previous studies have concerned both scholars and practitioners for quite a long time. However, as Beamish and Delios (1997, 105) recently concluded, despite the steady proliferation of joint ventures, venture "performance has not improved substantially in the preceding 25 years." At the very fundamental level, little consensus exists even regarding how performance should be defined. The international joint venture literature reveals a variety of different conceptualizations and measures of performance. Considerable controversy exists among scholars and practitioners alike over how to measure joint venture performance or, more generally, joint venture success (Dymsza 1988; Yan and Gray 1995). As an example, Beamish and Delios (1997, 105) stated: "In a more fine-grained categorization, performance can be defined as the survival, duration, instability, or failure of the (international joint venture); the degree of parental control; the effectiveness of technology transfer; the extent to which financial goals are realized; the degree of managerial satisfaction; and so forth. However, each of these performance measures has limitations."

A careful review of the literature reveals three major areas in which performance assessment is controversial: (1) Whose perspective is used for performance evaluation? (2) What are appropriate performance measures? (3) How are different measures useful in the different stages of the venture's evolution?

From Whose Perspective?

Since joint ventures involve multiple participants, each with distinct expectations, a key issue emerges: From whose perspective should performance be assessed? Reflecting the tradition of international business studies, the dominant approach in previous research is to assess venture performance from the multinational corporation's perspective, while the local partner's and the venture management's perspectives are largely ignored or deemed irrelevant (Yan and Zeng 1999).

Increasingly, empirical scholars have used both partners' viewpoints in assessing performance. Among the studies that measure the level of satisfaction of the parent firms, assessment is usually based on data collected from executives at both parent firms and thereby reflecting the partners' perspectives. For example, Schaan (1983) and Beamish and Banks (1987) consider a joint venture as successful only when both partners are satisfied. "If one or both partners were dissatisfied with the performance, the venture was considered unsuccessful" (Beamish and Banks 1987, 8). This approach was also adopted by Harrigan (1988) in assessing the success of joint ventures. A venture was coded as being a success based on both sponsors' judgment.

Other researchers, however, assess performance/success from the joint venture management's perspective. In an in-depth study of thirty-three joint ventures, Killing (1983) based his measure of performance primarily on the assessment of the venture's top managers. He asked the general manager of each joint venture to assess the venture's success. Yan (1993) used the same approach in his empirical work that tested the effect of management control structure on venture performance. This approach can be supported by the argument that, although jointly formed between firms, joint ventures are economically and legally independent organizational entities (Pfeffer and Nowak 1976). From a methodological point of view, Geringer and Hebert (1991) empirically demonstrated that the joint venture's management is a more reliable source of data for assessing performance than either of the parent firms if only a single source of data is available.

The fact that joint venture performance can be assessed from different viewpoints may have important implications. First, it is possible that for the same joint venture, different parties involved in the partnership can come up with significantly different assessments. With this in mind, researchers on the subject are challenged both conceptually and methodologically that multiple perspectives/multiple sources of data are necessary for an accurate assessment of performance. In case such data are not available, clear specifications and reasoning must be provided in terms of whose perspective is adopted.

What Are Appropriate Performance Measures?

A second controversy in performance measurement stems from the measures themselves. The literature does not distinguish between performance and venture success. Tracking the history of a large sample of international alliances, Franko's study (1971) used changes in the ownership structure among the parent firms as an indicator of success. A joint venture was considered unsuccessful when the percentages of equity holdings changed among the partners, or the venture was acquired by one of its parents or liquidated by mutual consent. Similar to Franko's treatment, Killing (1983) used joint venture survival as a measure of success. A venture was recorded as a "failure" if it had been disbanded through liquidation (e.g., one partner's taking over the venture or its being sold to a third party) or had undergone a major reorganization (e.g., significant changes in management control structure or in key executives). Other scholars used duration of joint ventures as a measure of success (Dymsza 1988; Harrigan 1988). For example, Dymsza (1988) concludes that "successful joint ventures are those that survive over a reasonable period of time, generally over eight years" (p. 403). Still, other researchers adopt some conventional performance measures such as profitability (Tomlinson 1970) and cost efficiency (Rafii 1978).

On the side of practitioners, many firms tend to adopt conventional performance criteria to assess joint venture performance. Using data collected from a Conference Board survey of 168 large firms, Anderson (1990, 20) found, "These firms tend to evaluate the venture much as they do one of their own divisions. Imposing a formidable amount of paperwork on the venture, these parents typically evaluate performance using financial reports, supplemented by whatever can be gleaned from informal visits by parent executives."

The use of different performance/success measures is not a problem per se. The problem is that previous researchers have paid little attention to articulating the relationship between the different measures. Therefore, previous research findings are hardly comparable. The use of the traditional financial performance measures at the practical level is fully understandable because it represents a standard, legitimate, and familiar business practice. However, this approach may suffer from losing sight of the significant differences between a joint venture and a wholly owned subsidiary, leading to an oversimplification of the additional challenges of managing joint ventures. In addition, a practical problem with this approach is that financial and objective measures are frequently unavailable for many joint ventures as quasi-subsidiaries (Beamish and Delios 1997).

The situation becomes more complicated when the different perspectives on performance and the diversity of performance measures are examined simultaneously. While in many cases the partners may share some common objectives and use similar performance measures, in many other cases each party's idiosyncratic perspective is combined with a quite distinct set of performance criteria. In the majority of international alliances, the partners and the venture's management consent on some, but differ on other performance dimensions. This is particularly true for partnerships created between developed country and developing country participants. Osland and Cavusgil (1996) interviewed both the foreign and the local partners and the venture's management for eight international joint ventures in China and convincingly documented the significant differences among these parties' goal sets. As a result, they caution that performance for joint ventures should consider multiple parties' interests. In his study of U.S. manufacturing joint ventures in China, Yan (1993) generated a comprehensive list of strategic objectives of joint venture sponsors. While some objectives (e.g., profit and business growth) are shared between the partners, others (e.g., market penetration by the U.S. partner and acquisition/learning of advanced technology by the Chinese partner) are different yet possibly complementary, and still others are potentially conflicting (e.g., the U.S. firm's interest in the local market and the Chinese firm's desire to export). The multiple perspectives and the lack of clarity in measures can create serious problems in performance assessment. As Anderson (1990) explains,

> a venture may enjoy excellent market acceptance and provide high return on investment, which is good performance from one parent's viewpoint. Yet another of the parents may be unhappy because the venture refuses to use one of its divisions as a supplier. From one parent's perspective, then, the joint venture is performing poorly. Indeed, the same venture may be rated very differently depending on the viewpoint adopted. Parents that evaluate performance strictly in accord with their own interests, as they do with subsidiaries, risk alienating their partners. Performance evaluation requires incorporating multiple viewpoints, if only to forecast the partners' reactions and future behavior. (p. 20)

Appropriateness of Different Measures at Different Times

The third and final controversy in performance assessment concerns the effect of timing. For example, traditional financial indicators can serve as appropriate measures of performance for mature ventures. However, it is often unrealistic to expect joint ventures to be profitable or to bring substantial financial gains early in their operations. Therefore, it may be misleading to use financial indicators to assess the performance of joint ventures without specifying their stages of maturation with respect to long-term goals. Anderson (1990) proposed a conceptual framework in which joint venture performance is assessed on an "input-output continuum." While "output" measures such as profitability, cash flows, and market share are ultimate indicators of performance, "input" measures such as harmony and trust among partners are determinants of performance. For relatively mature ventures that operate more like independent businesses, "output" measures may be appropriate; whereas for young ventures that are not yet ready to generate positive cash flows, input measures of performance are necessary. Particularly during the early stages of development, it is often necessary to rely on subjective assessments to judge progress.

To summarize, the above three major issues concerning performance assessment have had significant implications for joint venture research as well as practice. For scholarly research, the controversies involved have made previous empirical results suspect and comparisons across studies futile. For practitioners, the coexistence of multiple perspectives and performance measures has created tremendous problems and conflict among joint venture partners and venture management. As a matter of fact, the lack of congruity of performance measures among the different parties involved has been argued as a major determinant of joint venture success (Beamish and Delios 1997). Next, we draw research on organization effectiveness to reconcile the controversies and to construct an integrative framework of joint venture performance.

Organizational Effectiveness

Organizational performance, a concept that has been extensively studied by strategic management researchers, refers to the economic and social outcomes associated with organizational actions (Hrebiniak, Joyce, and Snow 1989). In the organization theory literature, however, a broader notion of performance is organizational effectiveness. Since joint ventures have important similarities to stand-alone, independent organizations, the extensive research on organizational effectiveness may prove useful for an understanding of joint venture performance. Given the trademark features of joint ventures, such as diverging partner strategic goals and objectives, involvement of multiple organizational entities, and high rates of change and instability, an analysis of performance in comparison with independent organizations will also help to highlight the critical complexities and challenges.

The Concept of Effectiveness

To the novice, it seems to be a straightforward affair to define and measure the effectiveness of an organization: to analyze effectiveness is to assess how well an organization is doing against a set of performance standards. However, the pursuit of the seemingly simple endeavor will lead us into some complexities and controversies. Although every organization wants to be effective, reaching agreement among different conceptualizations of effectiveness has not been easy. Georgopoulos and Tannenbaum's (1957) early work views effectiveness as the extent to which the organization, with given resources and means, fulfills its objectives without incapacitating its resources and placing undue strain on its members. Taking the organization as the appropriate level of analysis for assessing effectiveness and considering effectiveness in the context of the organization's interaction with its external environment, Yuchtman and Seashore (1967) suggest that a relevant view of effectiveness answers the question "How well is the organization doing for itself?" They argue that the effectiveness of an organization depends on its bargaining position, as reflected in its ability to acquire scarce resources from the external environment. Similarly, from a resource-dependent perspective, Pfeffer (1977) defines effective organizations as those that (1) accurately detect the patterns of resource interdependence in organizational and interorganizational interactions; (2) accurately perceive and understand internal and external demands; and (3) carefully and timely respond to those demands, particularly to those made by the groups that control the most critical interdependencies. Considering that possible constraints and multiple goals may exist in organizations, however, Pennings and Goodman (1977) argue that an effective organization should satisfy relevant constraints and produce organizational outcomes that meet the multiple expectations of its stakeholder groups. Arguing for a social psychological criterion for assessing organizational effectiveness, Cummings (1977, 60) proposes that "An effective organization is one in which the greatest percentage of participants perceive themselves as free to use the organization and its subsystems as instruments for their own ends." This perspective is consistent with Cyert and March's (1963) theory of the firm in which organizations are viewed as composed of various coalitions—groups of individuals with political agendas pursuing their own interests.

Two Models of Effectiveness

Regardless of the controversial conceptualizations, two prominent models of organizational effectiveness emerge to be most relevant to international joint ventures: the Goal Model and the Strategic Constituencies Model. As we illustrate later in the chapter, while each model has distinctive strengths as well as identifiable weaknesses, an integration of the models provides the best insights into our understanding of performance and performance assessment in joint venture.

The Goals Model

Originating in traditional measures of performance used in accounting, the Goals Model is unquestionably the most popular and dominant approach for assessing organizational effectiveness (Bedeian 1984). Viewing organizations as rational, goal-driven systems, this model focuses on the organizational ends, and is concerned with the extent to which an organization achieves it goals. This position is best presented by Reddin (1970, 3) who argues that "there is only one realistic and unambiguous definition of managerial effectiveness. Effectiveness is the extent to which a manager achieves the output requirements of his job." The criteria of effectiveness emphasized in this model usually include the ultimate outcomes of the organization, such as the number/amount and quality of products, benchmarks on profit for a for-profit company, bed occupancy for a hospital, number of championship titles for a sports team, or a nationally favorable ranking for an MBA program. The appeal of these criteria is that they are quantifiable, unambiguous, and easy-to-compare performance levels among different organizations or between different periods of time for the same organization.

The Goals Model primarily rests on two implicit but critical assumptions: First, organizations are rational systems in which the necessary human and material resources can be dutifully manipulated for achieving certain given or agreed-upon goals. The second assumption, derived from the first, is that in order to measure effectiveness, these organizational goals must be valid, identifiable, well defined, widely shared, and measurable. This is an assumption that can be challenged, however, and has called the validity of the entire model into question. First, it is unrealistic to use goals as the single standard of organizational effectiveness (Etzioni 1960). Goals, as norms or targets, specify ideal states. Organizations, as social systems, tend to be less consistent and less perfect than anticipated. As a result, discrepancies between goals (an ideal state) and performance (a real state) are inevitable. Second, organizations generally seek to accomplish multiple different goals simultaneously. Scholars have assembled lengthy lists of valid goals for organizations to pursue (Scott 1992). For example, Campbell (1977) lists thirty different criteria for measuring organizational effectiveness, ranging from productivity and profit to growth, turnover, stability, and cohesion. Unsurprisingly, many of these goals may be inconsistent or conflicting with each other such that the achievement of one of them may inhibit the attainment of others. For instance, a high rate of return on investment may well be achieved at the expense of long-term growth or long-term research and development. Given the scarcity of organizational resources, it is impossible to achieve all goals. A recent example is the state of Oregon's attempt, phrased as "a goal to end all goals." Among the countless benchmarks, it was an official state policy that by the year 2010, 90 percent of Oregonians would exercise aerobically for twenty minutes three times a week. It is also enshrined in state law that 70 percent of children would be free of tooth decay by then, and that 50 percent of adults would have entertained a foreign visitor. While some of the Oregon benchmarks were clearly effective when put to work, things got out of control when everyone wanted a benchmark, including one for earthquake prepared-ness by the state geologist and one for animal control by dogcatchers.

A third shortcoming of the Goals Model rests on the difficulty in establishing unambiguous criteria for measuring effectiveness. While profitability, sales, market share, and the like are easily measurable, other goals are not. For example, employee morale, organizational adaptabil-ity, and improvement in leadership are important indicators of perfor-mance, but they are less likely to be measured objectively. More importantly, a potential danger of using the Goals Model is that it can mislead the organization to paying attention only to those measurable goals while ignoring the ones that are more difficult to quantify.

The Strategic Constituencies Model

Intended to address the shortcomings of the Goals Model, a relatively recent perspective argues that organizational effectiveness should be measured by the extent to which it satisfies the demands placed by its "strategic constituencies"—various internal and external groups on which the organization depends for survival and growth (Pfeffer and Salancik 1978). A constituency is said to be strategic when it can create signifi-cant uncertainty for the focal organization, its influence on the organi-zation is critical yet nonreplaceable, or it is able to take direct action to disrupt the operations of the organization (Miles 1980). This approach is consistent with the political perspective on organization, which ar-gues that within and around organizations there are multiple coalitions, each with different interests and agendas (Cyert and March 1963; Mintzberg 1983).

According to this perspective, an effective organization must meet the multiple expectations of its stakeholder groups (Pennings and Goodman 1977) and serve as an arena in which the different interest groups perceive themselves as free to use the organization and its sub-systems as instruments for their own ends (Cummings 1977). Unlike the Goals Model, which regards organizations as rational, goal-seeking devices, the Strategic Constituencies Model views organizations as political entities where vested interests compete for control over critical resources. This model argues that the "official" goals of an organization, frequently articulated solely by the "dominant coalitions" (Cyert and March 1963), are seldom widely shared or supported by other interest groups.

An implication of the Strategic Constituencies Model is that organizational effectiveness is in the eye and value of the evaluator, and, therefore, there is no one best set of criteria for measuring effectiveness. The criteria used to assess effectiveness depend on who the assessor is. Pickle and Friedlander (1967) provided empirical evidence consistent with the argument that organizations confront incompatible demands. Using a sample of small businesses in Texas, these researchers identified several internal and external interest groups (including the owners, the employees, the customers, the suppliers, the creditors, the local community, and the federal government), and developed a measure of effectiveness for each group on the group's own criteria. For example, the owners were postulated to be interested in profit, while employees were postulated to be interested in their satisfaction with work. The central interest of the study was to examine how the satisfaction of one group's demands is related to the satisfaction of other groups. The results of statistical analysis suggest that the correlation between the satisfactions of different groups varies (i.e., is higher between some groups than between others), is generally positive, but is overall fairly low. Out of the twenty-one pairs of relationships examined, only seven were statistically significant.

The Strategic Constituencies Model has its own problems. First, it is unable to capture changes in strategic constituencies over time. As the environment turbulence occurs rapidly and frequently, some interest groups that are strategic today might not be tomorrow. In addition, the demands of the same group are also subject to change over time. Second, although it is able to address some of the shortcomings of the Goals Model, the Strategic Constituencies Model suffers from a lack of clarity. In many cases, it may be a challenging task even to identify who the relevant strategic constituencies are. Once they are identified, however, it may still be very difficult to detect what each constituency's demands are, because in a political context, interest groups often feel it is to their advantage to conceal their real interests. Third and finally, this model may create incentive problems for the management of the organization.

Unlike the Goals Model, in which the higher the level of achievement of goals, the more effective the organization, the Strategic Constituencies Model does not necessarily propose a close and positive relationship between maximization of the satisfaction of all its constituencies and organizational effectiveness. In fact, an effective organization must be able to differentiate its various strategic constituencies and make commitment only to those demands that are placed by the most critical interest groups. It has been argued that, ironically but understandably, organizational effectiveness becomes "the ability of the organization to *minimally* satisfy the demands of various constituencies central to its survival and development . . . because each of an organization's constituencies has different goals and value orientations that are unlikely to be satisfied completely" (Banner and Gagne 1995, 118).

An Integrative Framework of Performance Assessment

The Complexities in Joint Ventures

If it is a challenging task to assess performance in single, freestanding organizations, performance assessment in joint ventures is even more complex and controversial. First, from the Goals Model perspective, joint ventures deal with not only multiple goals and objectives, but also mutually noncongruent or conflicting expectations of the sponsors (Anderson 1990; Yan and Gray 1994). Second, a strategic constituency analysis suggests that international joint ventures involve a far more complex set of organizational entities as stakeholders than independent firms do. In addition to the "regular" constituency groups such as suppliers, customers, creditors, government agencies, and employees, an international joint venture involves at least two different sponsoring organizations, the venture's own management, and the national and local government agencies in different countries, each holding distinct stakes in and placing different demands on the partnership. For example, many international joint ventures in developing countries are equipped with two parallel accounting systems to accommodate different constituencies: one to conform to the multinational firm's worldwide corporate rules and standards, the other to satisfy the local government's unique requirements.

To incorporate the strengths of both the Goals Model and the Strategic Constituencies Model approaches, we now propose an integrative framework of joint venture performance measurement. While we agree that the extent to which organizational goals and objectives are achieved is a valid measure of performance, we consider the interests of the multiple constituencies involved in the partnership to be also critical. Therefore, the key idea on which this framework is based is that the perspectives of all critical players in the venture as strategic constituencies have to be considered, and the specific measures used to gauge the venture's performance have to be matched with the achievement of the individual goals/objectives of the parties. Our underlying assumption is that a high-performing joint venture should be able to fulfil the strategic expectations of all the parties. Because joint ventures consist of several actors whose assessments of performance may differ substantially, we believe it is essential that performance be measured in reference to the specific goals of each party involved. As previous researchers proposed, joint venture performance should be assessed according to the participants' expectations and objectives at the formation of the venture (Hebert 1994, 28).

Multiple Sets of Goals/Objectives

Consider the simplest scenario: a joint venture is created between two partner firms, one from overseas and the other local, and operated by a separate management team (either formed by the partners' nominees or hired from a third party). If we do not consider other important strategic constituency groups such as local government agencies for the sake of simplicity of presentation, there are three immediate organizational entities involved: the two parent firms and the venture management. The achievement of the goals and objectives of all these parties is critical.

First, the objectives of the parent firms provide the fundamental benchmark for performance measurement, because as a sponsor of the venture, each parent commits critical resources to the venture and, in return, expects the satisfaction of particular goals. By all means, joint ventures are formed to pursue the sponsors' strategic interests. Therefore, assessment of the degree to which the parents' interests are met should serve as an essential basis for measuring venture performance. If a joint venture is unable to meet the key expectations of both or either of its parents over a considerably long period of time, it is not a high performer. In fact, its survivability may become questionable.

Meanwhile, however, the joint venture management's objectives are also important to performance assessment. Dymsza (1988) noted that a key factor that leads to success or failure of a joint venture is achievement of the major goals set for the venture management. Although theoretically it is ideal that these goals integrate and operationalize the goals of both parents in a congruent manner, in many cases the venture management's goals stand as a separate system existing in parallel with the parents' goal sets. The achievement of these goals usually determines the extent to which the joint venture strategies and plans are effectively executed and the parents' interests are effectively and efficiently pursued. In fact, previous scholars have argued that "joint ventures should be evaluated primarily as stand-alone entities seeking to maximize their own performance" (Anderson 1990, 23). Achievement of venture management's goals is particularly important for highly autonomous joint ventures in which neither partner firm is actively involved in the venture's strategic and daily operational decisions.

In fact, the three sets of goals coexisting in a joint venture, one for each parent and one for the venture itself, may be mutually related. Some goals may be shared, but others may be significantly different. Let us consider a real example, NUMMI, the GM-Toyota joint venture in Fremont, California, to illustrate the coexistence of different sets of goals. Toyota's overall goal was to penetrate the automobile market in the United States. Toyota also had several other objectives for joining NUMMI: placation of the U.S. and Japanese governments in the hope of avoiding U.S. import constraints, testing the feasibility of producing Toyotas in a U.S. plant, reducing financial costs and risks associated with oceanic shipments, locating a good labor pool, and locating supplies for high-quality, inexpensive parts (Weiss 1987). GM's objectives, on the other hand, included building a replacement for its aging and not-profitable Chevette model, strengthening both domestic and international competition in subcompact markets, responding to union complaints about layoffs at its closed Fremont plant, meeting fuel standards to protect profitable large cars, learning Japanese manufacturing techniques in order to lower the $1,500 to $2,000 per car Japanese cost advantage, and attracting customers back to GM products in the U.S. markets (Weiss 1987). Finally, the goals jointly defined by the partners for the venture management included the installation and operation of Japanese-style production and management systems (e.g., the just-in-time delivery of components, the total-quality principles, and the practice of continuous improvement), a team-based, flat organizational structure, a collaborative, trust-based corporate culture, and reaching nominal annual capacity of 200,000 cars.

As this example shows, parents' goals for participating in joint ventures can be numerous. Among the most frequently observed are market penetration, gaining access to local markets and learning local marketing expertise, diversification by starting new lines of business, transfer of technology, learning manufacturing or management techniques, absorbing extra capacity, striving for economies of scale, and risk sharing. For example, the major goal of a transnational partner may be to gain market access to a developing country that has considerable market potential. In contrast, the local partner may have the goals of entering into a profitable business operation, getting access to advanced technology, business know-how, and trademarks (Dymsza 1988).

Similarly, the goals for joint ventures resulting from the founding negotiations vary from one venture to another, ranging from specific, unambiguously defined (e.g., annual production of 200,000 Nova cars for NUMMI, the New United Motor-Manufacturing Inc., a joint venture between GM and Toyota) to relatively vague targets (e.g., conducting six-to-ten-year "medium-term" research on artificial intelligence/ knowledge-based systems, database management systems, expert systems software, etc. for Microelectronics and Computer Technology Corporation (MCC), an R&D collaborative formed among twenty-one American firms) (Ouchi and Bolton 1988). These objectives, including the expected benefits occurring to each partner and goals for major stages of the venture development, are usually deliberately negotiated and written in the venturing agreement (Harrigan 1986). Often, these objectives can be found in specific "purpose clauses" in which the expectations of the parents and the goals set for the venture are provided (Hall 1984).

With the three sets of objectives identified, the next step is to decide the appropriate measures against which the level of achievement of these objectives can be evaluated. Table 7.1 provides an illustration of what objective measures of each party's goals might look like. For simplicity of presentation, we assume that while the partners have a shared goal of financial prosperity, each partner has a distinctive objective: Parent A (the local partner) intends to acquire a new technology to be transferred from parent B (the foreign partner), whereas parent B's target is to penetrate the local market in the country where parent A is located. Operationally, both objective and subjective measures can be developed for measuring the achievement of each of these goals. For example, successful technology transfers can be indicated by such measures as the number of patents adopted in local operations that are associated with a particular product/production process, advanced machines and equipment installed for manufacturing the product, and the number of local employees trained in the technology. These relatively objective measures can also be supplemented by some subjective satisfaction measures such as the overall degree of learning and the estimated amount of tacit knowledge or know-how acquired. Similarly, parent B's goal of market penetration can be measured by the number of linkages developed with local institutions through the venture, accessibility to local dealership networks, brand recognition, market share, and market share growth. Subjective measures may include satisfaction with the overall learning gained through the joint venture about the local market and the increase in this partner's competence in marketing in the country.

Regarding the shared goal for business growth, some traditional growth measures are relevant, such as growth rates of sales, assets, and number of employees and the relative growth rates against industry average. Among subjective measures, the venture's perceived potential sustainability, well-developed strategic plans for growth, and the venture's ability to have access to local or international financial institutions or private investors may be important. Performance gauged in these relatively "soft" measures may be indicative of the venture's longer-term potential for growth.

We also considered a general goal for the joint venture management in Table 7.1, that is, an effective and efficient operation of the venture in order to achieve the parents' objectives. The achievement of this goal can be measured in the following objective measures: quantity and quality of outputs, productivity/efficiency of the operation, introduction of new products, pricing with respect to the competition, market share, various financial indicators, and employee turnover rates. Additionally, some subjective measures are necessary, such as perceived partner commitment, harmony and trust between the partners' appointees, venture partner and interpartner working relationship, relationship with local government, venture management competence, and employee morale and satisfaction.

Different Patterns of Performance Assessment

When performance measures are calibrated with respect to the goals and objectives of each partner and of the venture management, we be-

Table 7.1

Multidimensional Measures of Joint Venture Performance

Goals	Objective Indicators	Subjective Judgments
Specific to parent A: Technology transfer	Number of patented technologies transferred Advanced equipment installed Number of people technically trained	Degree of learning about advanced technology Perceived increase in technological competence Amount of tacit knowledge learned
Specific to parent B: Market penetration	Number of linkages developed with local customers Accessibility to local dealership networks Brand recognition Market share/market share growth Sales volume/sales growth	Degree of learning about the local market Perceived increase in marketing competence
Shared by both parents: Business growth	Growth rate of sales, assets, number of employees Relative growth against industry average Converting/repatriating profit in hard currencies	Potential sustainability of the venture Well developed strategic plan for growth Competence of the venture management in terms of long-term development
The joint venture: Effective and efficient operation	Product quality and quantity Productivity The venture's market share, ROI, ROA, ROE Employee turnover rates/satisfaction	Partner commitment Harmony and trust between expatriates and locals Venture partner and interpartner working relationship Relationship with local government Venture management competence Employee morale and satisfaction

lieve that patterns of performance as gauged by the achievement of these parties' objectives can offer useful management implications and are predictive of the future development of the joint venture. These patterns may prompt different organizational and managerial actions (e.g., structural reconfiguration or termination of the joint venture). Assuming that each party's level of goal satisfaction can be aggregated into a single indicator (e.g., overall percentage of satisfaction) according to the formula below, the result will be three performance evaluations, one for each parent and one for the joint venture.

$$P_i \;=\; \sum_{j=1}^{n} S\;(A_j{*}W_j) \quad j = 1, 2, \ldots, n.$$

where P_i = the aggregated indicator of performance evaluation for the ith party; $i = 1, 2, 3$ (representing parent A, parent B, and the joint venture management, respectively).

W_j = the weight assigned to the jth goal according to the party's perceived importance, the highest for the most important goal, subject to $\sum W_j = 1$.

A_j = the degree to which the jth goal is achieved, subject to $0 < A_j < 100$ percent.

For simplicity of presentation, let us classify each of the performance assessments into two categories, high and low. A comparison among the three parties' evaluations (i.e., whether their evaluations agree in terms of "high" or "low") will result in six combined patterns of performance assessment. For example, if performance evaluations for all three parties are in agreement (either all "high" or all "low"), a consensus pattern (pattern 1 or 5) will be observed. However, if the parties disagree in their evaluations of performance (e.g., one rates it as "high" while the other two rate it as "low"), patterns of disagreement (patterns 2, 3, 4, and 6) occur. These six patterns are depicted in Table 7.2.

Each of the six different patterns represents a distinct profile of the venture's current performance. Again, using our earlier scenario that the local partner wants technology transfer whereas the foreign partner is interested in market penetration, the different performance patterns can be described as follows:

Table 7.2

Patterns of Performance and Associated Structural Changes

		Performance to Parents		
		Both high	One high and one low	Both low
Performance to joint venture	High	1 No change necessary	3 Reconfiguration or redirection	5 Tuning or adjustment
	Low	2 Tuning or adjustment	4 Reconfiguration or redirection	6 Overhaul or termination

Pattern 1: Performance assessments for all actors (both parents and the venture management) are high. Parent A successfully acquired the new technology, while parent B gained access to the desired market. At the same time, the venture successfully produced and marketed its products. In this case, the joint venture's success is evident. The venture should continue its current practice and no changes are necessary.

Pattern 2: Performance is assessed as high for both parents, but low for the joint venture. This occurs when parent A has successfully acquired new technology while parent B effectively penetrated the market (probably with parent B's own products). However, the joint venture failed to produce or market its locally manufactured products (possibly because of its lack of autonomy to run its own business). In this situation, adjustments of the objectives set for the venture management are necessary in order for the cooperation to be sustained. Or, the venture's function may be reduced to a common arena in which each partner independently pursues its own individual interests.

Pattern 3: Performance is high as assessed by only one parent (say, parent A was successful in transferring new technologies while parent B failed to penetrate the desired market). In addition, the joint venture management rates performance as high, because the venture has successfully manufactured and marketed its product. This type of venture is unstable if parent B's needs for market access remain unsatisfied. This situation creates a high likelihood of major structural reconfiguration or termination. Acquisition of the venture by parent A, the satisfied partner, is highly possible. Or, the venture will spin off to a third party, if parent A was interested only in technology transfer but not long-term benefits from operating the venture.

Pattern 4: Performance is assessed as high for one parent but low for the other parent and the venture management. This occurs when either parent A acquired the technology or parent B gained access to the market, but not both. In addition, the venture management objectives are not achieved. For example, the venture acted primarily in the service of one of its parents and did not focus on achieving its own goals. This type of joint venture results in an unsatisfied partner as well as ineffective venture management. Therefore, it needs substantial reconfiguration. Otherwise, the likelihood of termination is fairly high.

Pattern 5: Both parents rate the venture's performance as low, despite a high-performance rating by the venture management. This scenario occurs when the joint venture successfully produces and markets its product while neither of the parents achieves its strategic goals. Although this seems less likely, it is possible when the joint venture is highly independent of its parents, and the venture management runs the venture opportunistically to pursue its own interests. In this case, a significant change is expected to bring the parent firms' interests back to the venture's agenda. For example, the parents may increase their level of involvement in the venture's decision and management, or the venture may be spun off as a freestanding company completely separated from its parents.

Pattern 6: This is the most straightforward case of joint venture failure, because none of the actors in the joint venture has satisfactorily achieved its goals. The most probable destination for ventures of this type is overhaul or termination.

Conclusions

The framework proposed in this chapter helps resolve several major problems. First, it incorporates, instead of assuming away, the different perspectives on performance measurement by taking all the key players' perspectives into consideration. In this way, we promote a balanced view of performance assessment in which the interests of all the key players in the collaboration are represented. This view contrasts with the dominant approach in previous work in which performance is assessed only from the multinational partner's perspective while the legitimate interests of the local partner are ignored and the role of the venture's management is downplayed. Second, our framework promotes a more meaningful and accurate use of traditional performance measures. We do not simply turn away from these measures by claiming that they are useless or irrelevant. Instead, we reduce the level of application from the generic level of the entire partnership to the level of each party involved in terms of the achievement of this party's particular objectives. We argue that these measures are still highly applicable and effective if the critical individual parties are identified (the foreign or the local partner, the venture management, or a local government agency), and if a fine connection is built between the measures and each specific party's strategic objectives. In addition, the use of measures can follow a contingent approach by choosing different measures for different stages of the venture's development. Third, this framework improves upon the subjective measure of satisfaction. An overall generic judgment of satisfaction (no matter from whose perspective it is assessed) is less reliable because it depends solely on the assessment by executives whose self-interest in the outcomes may make their assessment highly subjective. Subjective measures can suffer from evaluation errors caused by interpersonal and emotional factors. For example, superior or poor working relationships between the boundary spanners within each parent firm may color the overall satisfaction measure. Even when such a judgment is made from an organizational instead of individual perspective, the results can still be questionable because the expectations, intentions, and objectives of each partner can change over time. With the parties' objectives clearly identified and understood, the satisfaction can be assessed at a more objective or at least intersubjective level, and the accuracy and usefulness of such an assessment can significantly increase.

However, it seems that there is an important condition for the new framework to work properly. That is, the partners to a joint venture have to be open about each other's strategic expectations right from the outset. During the negotiation and formation stages, the strategic goals and expectations of the partners should be made explicit and a congruent set of performance measures matching the goals jointly developed. Both theoretical and empirical evidence is available, suggesting that hidden agendas held by any partner tend to hurt the partnership's long-term performance, although they may bring some immediate benefits to the opportunistic player. For a relatively long-term cooperative arrangement like joint ventures, it is pivotal that partners raise the level of discussability of each other's strategic intentions, make each other's goals known and clearly understood, and update each other as any changes in strategic interests occur.

A Mini-Case Example

Du Pont: Joint Venture Pioneer

Du Pont first engaged in joint ventures near the turn of the century and has pursued more than forty joint ventures since 1950, in a broad array of businesses. Widely regarded as a company with a cohesive culture, Du Pont is supported by a program of internal management development, promotion from within, and rewards for being a "team player" (versus "turf protector"). Today, Du Pont profits from that cohesion in the thorough yet flexible way it evaluates joint ventures. However, this was not always the case.

Before 1970, Du Pont joint-ventured primarily in response to government pressures in such countries as Mexico and Japan, exercising 100 percent ownership wherever possible. Ventures were evaluated in a formal, stylized manner, using financial criteria for the most part. Although it still preferred 100 percent ownership, after 1970 Du Pont began to undertake joint ventures for a variety of reasons. And as Du Pont's motivations for venturing became broader, more complex, and more strategic, so too did its criteria for evaluating venture performance.

Today Du Pont is organized into worldwide business centers, which may be centered on either a product or a market. Annually, the venture head and a representative from the most closely related worldwide business center set profit goals and evaluate performance. In addition to financial measures, mostly relating to return per resource committed, other criteria are used. These include:

- how safely and ethically the venture operates;
- environmental impact of the venture;

- the venture's innovativeness;
- degree to which the venture satisfied the other partner (this is to forestall discontent);
- degree to which the venture fills the need of its host country (this is to forestall government interference);
- degree of learning about industries, technologies, management techniques, the partner's skills, or countries;
- how smoothly the venture runs (personnel and coordination issues);
- ability to repatriate profits; and
- how well the venture meets goals based on the reasons it was created. Some of the reasons are utilizing capacity, affecting competition, gaining market share, generating other opportunities, and helping spur the scale of other Du Pont products.

Performance criteria vary by venture and strongly reflect the reasons the venture was created. Du Pont considers that flexibility is necessary because each venture is unique; the performance criteria must also be unique. One constant exists: Safety, health, and environmental dimensions (what Du Pont personnel call "the SHE issues") are always a must. The company refuses to venture with partners who do not meet its SHE standards. Should a venture violate these standards, Du Pont will buy out the partner, fix the problem at its own expense, or, if all else fails, leave the venture.

As ventures mature and markets change, criteria change. In particular, once a project is authorized, it has a "proof period." After year three (proof year for established products) or year five (proof year for ventures involving new product categories), much greater emphasis is placed on financial measures, reflecting the maturing of the venture and the parent's correspondingly appropriate shift from input to output measures.

Potential conflicts with partners are explicitly focused upon when the venture is created. At that time, Du Pont presses for agreement about goals. Afterward, the venture is evaluated as to how well it meets the partner's goals as well as Du Pont's. This is based on Du Pont's experience-based belief that the venture must be a win-win situation if it is to be healthy and survive. Hence, ventures are not forced to suboptimize their own performance to benefit Du Pont.

A striking feature of Du Pont's procedure is its relatively low level of procedural formality. This appears to be a conscious strategy whose purpose is to reduce bureaucracy, focus on action, encourage initiative, retain flexibility, and stimulate broad-ranging evaluation. As mentioned earlier, while performance criteria are well defined, neither weights nor scores are formalized, although they are used. Subjective information is widely used by Du Pont to judge whether the broad objectives of the venture are being met.

In short, Du Pont appears to focus on subjective strategic performance as well as formal performance criteria—and to recognize that a strong emphasis on outputs is inappropriate for young ventures, though appropriate for mature ones.

(Adapted with permission from Erin Anderson. 1990. "Two Firms, One Frontier: On Assessing Joint Venture Performance." *Sloan Management Review* [winter]: 19–30.)

—— 8 ——

An Empirical Study
of Interpartner Fit
and Performance

It is a strong belief of joint venture researchers and practitioners alike that "fit" or "compatibility" between joint venture partners is key to venture success. However, in previous research the phenomenon of interpartner fit has been inconsistently conceptualized and operationalized. As a result, empirical studies of the phenomenon have either failed to confirm theoretical predictions or produced inconsistent findings that are difficult to reconcile. In this chapter, we report a comparative case study of four joint ventures in an attempt to develop a grounded theory model. The research results suggest that interpartner fit consists of four fundamental dimensions: (1) compatibility of strategic objectives, (2) complementarity and joint management of critical resources, (3) consensus on the venture's operating culture and strategy, and (4) consistency between the partner's perceptions of interpartner relative bargaining power and control. These dimensions of fit tend to evolve over time and may exert a significant effect on joint venture performance.

Introduction

In chapter 2, we conceptually discussed the issue of fit between joint venture partners in the context of partner selection. In this chapter, we reexamine this issue by reporting an empirical study of interpartner fit and its performance implications. Particularly, interpartner fit achieved at the venture's founding may change over time as a result of changes in the partners or the venture's external environment. Therefore, fit or misfit stands as an ongoing concern of joint venture partners beyond the initial partner selection stage.

This chapter was adapted in part from a working paper with Xiansheng Duan.

The cross-cultural and interfirm nature of international joint ventures is a key source of the additional complexities and challenges in the management of this cross-border, hybrid form of organization. Unlike independent firms in which organizational activities and processes are syndicated under a single governance structure and a shared cultural scheme, international joint ventures are formed between firms with different organizational and cultural characteristics. While acting as economically and legally independent entities (Pfeffer and Nowak 1976), the trademark feature of joint ventures is the interdependence and interaction between the parent firms.

Prior research has articulated a linkage between interpartner "fit" and venture performance. Fit, however, has been postulated by using different notions such as strategic symmetry (Harrigan 1986, 1988a), interfirm diversity (Parkhe 1991), match of partner characteristics (Geringer 1988), or interpartner compatibility/complementarity (Beamish 1988; Chi 1994; Hill and Hellriegel 1994; Inkpen 1995; Inkpen and Currall 1998). The conceptual laxity of fit has created problems for operationalization (Inkpen and Currall 1998). As a result, prior empirical work has either failed to confirm theoretical predictions or produced inconsistent findings that are difficult to reconcile.

In this chapter, we use a comparative case study method to examine interpartner fit and its effect on venture performance. We report a study of four U.S.-China manufacturing joint ventures and build a multidimensional model of fit that takes into consideration interpartner compatibility in strategic objectives, contribution and joint management of critical resources, operating cultures, strategies and policies, and structure of partner bargaining power and control.

Below we first present the conceptual background on which the case studies were conducted. Next, we describe the research method, which is followed by our case-study results. In light of the findings, we offer several propositions for future research. The chapter concludes with the theoretical and practical implications of the study.

Theoretical Background

Fit in Strategic Management

The concept of fit is not entirely new. It has been widely used in the strategic management literature to denote a congruent relationship between the firm and its environment or between its strategy and its structure and processes. The classic contingency theory (Lawrence and Lorsch 1967) argues that a firm whose internal features best match the external environmental demands will achieve superior performance. Chandler's milestone work (1962) demonstrated that a diversification strategy requires a firm to install a multidivisional organizational structure. Based on rich field data collected from several industries, Miles and Snow (1978) developed a typology of business strategies—Prospector, Defender, Analyzer, and Reactor—and proposed a co-alignment between a specific business strategy and the firm's organizational structure, technology, and organizational processes. For instance, firms pursuing a Defender type of strategy would enact a highly stable environment, adopt a functional structure, use highly efficient technologies, and install centralized control processes. According to these authors, the absence of such a match would lead to administrative inefficiency and undesirable performance.

Applying the same thesis to joint ventures, some scholars argue that venture performance depends on the congruence between the global strategy and structure of the multinational corporation (MNC) parents (Gomes-Casseres 1990; Harrigan 1984; Herbert 1984). Based on Franko's (1971) empirical work, Geringer and Hebert (1989) propose that international ventures having a fit between the MNC's strategy and its control over the venture are expected to perform better. Although examining fit in the context of joint ventures, this stream of research focuses solely on the MNC parent's perspective and treats the joint venture as no different from the wholly owned subsidiaries of the MNC firm.

Fit in Mergers and Acquisitions

Research reviewed above has treated fit as a congruent or co-aligning relationship among *intra*organizational variables. However, the central concern of fit in joint ventures is the matching relationship between the sponsoring firms, which is *cross*-cultural and *inter*organizational in nature. To this extent, research on mergers and acquisitions (a branch of strategic management research) offers useful insights. Although there are substantive differences between mergers/acquisitions and joint ventures (i.e., the former calls for a consolidation of *all* assets of the two firms while the later represents only a *partial* combination of the sponsors' assets), the idea of fit between two separate firms working together is common in both types of arrangement. In essence, both are designed to pursue strategic interests through collective strategies (Astley and Fombrun 1983).

Previous studies have shown that superior postmerger performance occurred when some level of relatedness (e.g., product, market, etc.) existed between the target and the bidder firms (Kusewitt 1985; Lubatkin 1987; Singh and Montgomery 1987). The notion of interfirm relatedness has been extended to other variables (e.g., production technologies, organizational cultures, product functions, customer groups, etc.). For example, fit or misfit between the corporate cultures on dimensions such as risk-taking attitude, reward orientation, innovation orientation, and autonomy orientation was found to have performance implications (Chatterjee, Lubatkin, Schweiger, and Weber 1992). Jemison and Sitkin (1986) argue that mergers between organizations similar in culture, human resource policies, and administrative processes will demonstrate better fit and thereby better performance. Similarly, Datta, Grant, and Rajagopalan (1991) found that incompatibility in the management styles between the merging firms was negatively related to performance. With respect to interfirm similarities in resource allocation patterns and strategic skills and competencies, however, findings have been inconsistent. For example, *dissimilarities* between targets and bidders on R&D intensity, administrative intensity, debt intensity, and capital intensity were found positively related to performance (Harrison, Hitt, Hoskisson, and Ireland 1991). Ramaswamy (1997), however, found that mergers between strategically *similar* firms resulted in better performance than those between dissimilar firms.

Fit in International Joint Ventures

Previous research on joint ventures has deemed the formation motives, relational and structural characteristics of the partners, and their interactive contingencies critical factors in venture performance (Hill and Hellriegel 1994; Parkhe 1993b; Park and Ungson 1997; Zeira and Shenkar 1990). Significant attention has been paid to the static comparative/configurational features of the sponsors, particularly in the stage of partner selection. Geringer (1988) argues that selection of a joint venture partner needs to consider a fit in both task-related characteristics (e.g., resources and skills) and partner-related characteristics (e.g., size, objectives, and operating policies).

Harrigan (1986, 1988a, b) proposes that venture performance depends on strategic symmetry between the partners, which occurs when they "possess complementary strategic missions, resource capabilities, managerial capabilities, and other attributes that have a strategic fit such that the relative bargaining power of the partners is evenly matched" (1986, 11). Using variables of interpartner relatedness, parent-venture relatedness, and the relative size, nationality, and joint venture experiences of the parent firms, she reported significant relationships between strategic symmetry and performance. More recently, Park and Ungson (1997) tested the effect of a similar set of independent variables on joint venture dissolution but found no support for most of the hypothesized relationships. However, they found a significant effect of interpartner nationality on partnership termination, but in a direction opposing to previous findings: the greater the cultural distance, the less likely the venture is to dissolve.

A number of fit studies have focused on the partners' contribution of critical resources to the joint venture (i.e., who brings what to the party) and the interdependence between the partners in terms of competencies and skills (Pfeffer and Nowak 1976). The long-term mutual need between the partners for each other's resource commitment was argued to be critical to venture performance (Beamish and Lane 1983; Beamish 1984). Chi (1994) characterizes joint ventures and strategic alliances in general as an arena in which strategic resources are traded across firms. When these resources are complementary, desirable performance is expected because of the synergistic effect. Among the very few empirical studies, Hill and Hellriegel (1994) tested the performance implications of partner complementarity, measured as the distinctiveness between the two partners' resource contributions, but failed to confirm the proposed positive effect.

Summary

As the review above, as well as our discussion in chapter 2, suggests, the notion of fit has been explored from a wide variety of perspectives. However, important deficiencies exist in prior research. First, although prior scholars have postulated different statements and concepts, there is a lack of consistency in the definitions of fit. As Galbraith and Nathanson (1979, 266) noted, "Although the concept of fit is a useful one, it lacks the precise definition needed to test and recognize whether an organization has it or not." Second, prior research has not established an appropriate correspondence between general statements of fit and concrete, operationalizable analytical schemes (Venkatraman 1989). Geringer (1988, 163) notes that previous studies of international joint ventures have failed to provide "an underlying conceptual model which could specify traits that would be 'complementary' for a particular firm or joint venture. They provide little guidance as to whether complementarity entails similarity or dissimilarity between organizations on one or more dimensions." Without specifying the critical features of the phenomenon or suggesting appropriate measures of these features, studies of interpartner fit can provide only very limited insights for bridging the current disconnection between theory building and theory testing.

Third, previous research on fit tends to compare the characteristics of the parents in separation from the focal joint venture (with Geringer [1988] and Hill and Hellriegel [1994] as exceptions). We argue that interpartner fit or misfit assessed by comparing the static and indirect parental predispositions (e.g., the parents' size, age, or nationalities) may be long-shot and unreliable, because this approach ignores the specific context of the venture in terms of the sponsoring firms' strategic expectations, the mission/goal set for the joint venture to accomplish, as well as the venture's external environment (e.g., industrial characteristics, market competition, and the technological features of its products).

Fourth, prior research on interpartner fit has either focused on initial partner selection or taken a snapshot view after the venture's inception, but paid little attention to how fit or misfit changes over time as it evolves. This static approach is insufficient at best, because fit is a process of "shooting at a moving target of co-alignment" (Thompson 1967, 148). Finally, previous research has fallen short of offering joint venture practitioners any guidelines as to whether there is a fit or how to correct misfit when it occurs. The relevance of research will significantly increase if some specific facets of fit are identified and action-oriented recommendations are provided.

A Four-Dimensional Model of Interpartner Fit

Interpartner fit is a rich and complex concept evolving from a variety of factors (Inkpen and Currall 1998; Osborn and Hagedoorn 1997). Therefore, a dimensionalized approach is justified (Geringer 1988; Hill and Hellriegel 1994). Based upon the multiple dimensions of interpartner fit that we presented in chapter 2 (i.e., compatibility of partner goals, complementary resources, commitment of the partners, and partner capability), we developed a refined model to take into consideration interpartner fit both at the time of the joint venture's founding and during the post-formation dynamics. We define *interpartner fit as the extent to which compatibility is achieved between the joint venture partners with respect to (1) their strategic objectives; (2) contribution of critical resources; (3) agreement upon the venture's operating culture, strategy, and policies; and (4) the structure of the partners' relative bargaining power and control over the venture's operation.* This framework guided our case studies.

Congruence of Strategic Objectives

Interpartner fit depends on the congruence between the two sets of strategic objectives of the partners in respect to the particular joint venture. Compatible partner interests are a primary factor in venture success (Inkpen and Currall 1998; Tomlinson and Thompson 1977; Tung 1984) because congruent objectives minimize transaction or agency costs associated with partner opportunism and with the installation of surveillance mechanisms (Alchian and Demsetz 1972; Williamson 1975). Tomlinson and Willie (1978) argue that partners' goal congruence defines the underlying basis of their perception of mutuality of interests.

Congruence does not necessarily require commonality, however, although perfect congruence occurs when both partners share a common set of strategic objectives. In this case, when one partner's goals are achieved, the goals of the other partner are achieved automatically. A high level of congruence also can be reached when the partners hold different but complementary goals. As a most frequently observed scenario, goal complementarity occurs when the multinational partner is interested in penetrating an underdeveloped country market for a specific product, while the local partner is currently importing the product but desires to manufacture it locally. Conflict in interests and incongruent strategic objectives between joint venture partners are not uncommon, however, in which case it is difficult for the venture to satisfy both partners.

Complementarity of Resources

Resource dependence theory (Pfeffer and Salancik 1978) argues that firms cooperate to manage their interdependence and reciprocal needs for critical resources. The interdependence between joint venture partners in terms of skills and competencies entails the notion of complementarity (Harrigan 1986). Chi (1994) states that "complementarity exists between two sets of resources when a joint use of them can potentially yield a higher total return than the sum of returns that can be earned if each set of resources are used independently of the other" (p. 275). In more specific terms, Hill and Hellriegel (1994, 595) argue that complementarity occurs "only when the partners bring distinctive competencies that are different and nonoverlapping," thereby stressing the "nonredundant" nature of partner resources.

Consensus on Operating Culture, Strategy, and Policies

Addressing interfirm relationships, Ring and Van de Ven (1994) note that it is pivotal for the participating firms to create consensus on the key cultural expectations, purposes, and values that govern the interfirm arrangement. Such consensus, according to these authors, serves as a "psychological contract among parties" (p. 101) and increases the partners' formal commitment to the cooperation. Hill and Hellriegel (1994, 603) argue that superior performance is associated with the sharing of "similar operating philosophies" or "the same business style" between the partners. When joint ventures are governed by an integrated management system that is either developed independently or adopted from one of the parents, performance can be enhanced (Killing 1983). Similarly, Yan (1993) found that consensus among the partners on the venture's mission, strategy, and operating principles significantly contributed to performance. Partner consensus minimizes destructive conflicts, political behaviors, and confusion of authority among the joint venture's employees.

Co-alignment Between Bargaining Power and Management Control

As we have discussed in chapter 6, a partner's bargaining power is its ability to favorably change the bargaining relationship, to win accommodations from the other party, and to influence the outcomes of a negotiation. Management control is the process by which an organization influences its subunits and members to behave in ways that lead to the attainment of its objectives (Flamholtz, Das, and Tsui 1985). A positive link between bargaining power and control has been documented in previous research (Blodgett 1991; Child, Yan, and Lu 1997; Killing 1983; Lecraw 1984). Using a partner's resource contributions as the key base of bargaining power and its involvement in the venture's strategic decision making as a measure of managerial control, respectively, Yan and Gray (1994) found that joint ventures with an equally matched bargaining power between the partners were equipped with a shared control structure. However, the venture in which bargaining power was unequally divided adopted an unbalanced control structure in which the more powerful partner dominated.

A logical extension of the correspondence between bargaining power and control is that when co-alignment exists between the two variables (i.e., the control structure is consistent with the structure of bargaining power), each partner achieves the level of control it deserves so that its position in relation to the other in the partnership is justified. As a result, the venture's stability increases. When such a co-aligning balance is tilted, however, it produces unhappy players who will feel that the control exercised by their partner is undeserved. The perceived inequality and injustice will give rise to interpartner politics and juggling-for-control activities, which will hurt performance.

Methodology

Intended to enhance a multidimensional approach to interpartner fit and to address the limitations of previous research, the study reported here used an inductive method, arguably the most appropriate for theory building when existing theories are inconsistent (Eisenhardt 1989; Yin 1989). Parkhe (1993a) noted that rigorous comparative case studies are particularly needed in international joint venture research.

The Cases and Data Collection

This study involved four U.S.-China manufacturing joint ventures (see Table 8.1). We considered several factors in case selection. First, international joint ventures have rapidly proliferated in China since the early 1980s, and U.S. companies have been active participants in creating these ventures. Research on Chinese joint ventures, however, has been quite limited until recently (Luo 1998; Peng, Lu, and Shenkar 1998). Second, we focused on manufacturing ventures to minimize extraneous

Table 8.1

A Summary of the Major Characteristics of the Joint Ventures

Characteristics	IndusCon	OfficeAid	FeedProc	R-Seals
Product	Industrial process control	Electronic office equipment	Hog and chicken feed	Rubber seals
Length of negotiation in years	3	4	1	2
Formation	1982	1987	1986	1983
Total invest-ment in millions of dollars	10	30	9	1
U.S.-China equity shares:				
At founding	49/51	51/49	50/50	49/51
In 1997	51/49	65/35	50/50	49/51
Contracted duration in years	20	30	20	20
Product market	Local for import substitution	Mainly local but small percent-age for export	Mainly local but small percentage for export	Local

variation (Eisenhardt 1989) that might result from the differences be-tween service and manufacturing partnerships. Third, the sample was representative of U.S.-China ventures, of which about 70 percent are in manufacturing (U.S.-China Business Council 1990). The ventures in-cluded in the study represent industrial sectors in which about half of all U.S.-China joint ventures were found. A fourth factor considered was that the ventures had to be in operation for a period of time so that data on performance and changes over time were available. Finally, accessibility to informants was important, because, by design, we needed multiple infor-mants from each venture to agree to be interviewed longitudinally.

Following a structured protocol, interviews were conducted with ex-ecutives at both the parent firms and the joint venture. Each executive was interviewed at least twice over the five years between 1991 and

1996. Most interviewees were top-level executives who personally participated in the venture's founding negotiations (see Appendix 8.1). Each interview lasted about two hours and was tape-recorded unless informants objected. To ensure accuracy, we performed member checks (Lincoln and Guba 1985), in which transcripts/interview notes were verified by the original interviewees.

We also collected archival data for each venture, including its contracts/agreements, the venture's as well as the parents' organizational charts, the joint venture's corporate brochures, progress reports, and newspaper/magazine reports about these ventures.

Data Analysis

The study adopted a content analysis procedure (Lincoln and Guba 1985; Strauss 1987) in which the researchers jointly developed the coding scheme and coded the case studies independently. The outcomes (maps and tables recorded on flipcharts) were compared, and differences were reconciled upon consensus.

Data analysis was first conducted at the within-case level, in which we assessed the coded data to identify different dimensions of interpartner fit. Interpartner fit at each joint venture was assessed based on data collected up to 1993 when the first round of interviews was finished. The dynamics and changes in fit were examined based on data collected in 1996 when the last round of interviews was conducted. Venture performance was assessed at an aggregate level considering the venture's history up to 1996. Finally, cross-case comparisons were undertaken to identify similarities and differences, on which the linkage between the different dimensions of fit emerged in the earlier analysis, and performance was established. The analysis also traced the dynamics and changes in each joint venture over time to assess the impact of these changes on interpartner fit.

Case Study Results

Interpartner Fit

Congruence of Strategic Objectives

Interpartner fit in terms of founding objectives is summarized in Table 8.2. IndusCon showed the highest level of fit among the four ventures,

Table 8.2

The Founding Strategic Objectives of the Partners

	IndusCon	OfficeAid	FeedProc	R-Seals
U.S. partner strategic objectives	Business growth Local market penetration Profit	Profit Local market penetration/ market share Low-cost sourcing	Local market penetration Profit	Local market penetration Gaining business experience Profit
Chinese partner strategic objectives	Import sub-stitution Manufacturing technology Upgrade suppliers' technology	Manufacturing technology Management know-how Export for foreign exchange	Feed recipes and manufac-turing technology Import substitution Export	Trademark and manu-facturing technology Domestic market growth Export for foreign exchange
Level of congruence	High	Moderate	Low–moderate	Moderate

in which the U.S. partner was seeking "international business growth" and "penetrating the Chinese market," while the Chinese partner's most important objective was "import substitution." By jointly establishing a local manufacturing facility, both partners' objectives could be achieved simultaneously. As we stated earlier in the chapter, this is a typical case of complementary goals. Among the partners' other objectives, the lo-cal partner's expectation of acquiring and upgrading its manufacturing technology and the foreign partner's to profitably grow its business in China through the partnership could possibly be achieved at the same time.

Congruence in strategic objectives was the most problematic at FeedProc, in which the U.S. partner intended to penetrate the local mar-ket and to make a profit in China, while the Chinese partner desired to acquire advanced manufacturing technology and feed recipes, to substitute imports, and to export to other Asian countries. While penetration of the local market by the Americans and import substitution for the Chinese were congruent goals, the Chinese partner's objective of exporting a large portion of the venture's products was directly in conflict with the U.S. partner's key interest in the local market. Since the U.S. firm had already been manufacturing similar products in other Asian countries surrounding China, it did not want to create possible internal competition between its Chinese joint venture and its other operations in Asia.

Interpartner goal congruence was moderate at OfficeAid and R-Seals. In both ventures, the U.S. partner was interested in the local market while the Chinese partner was interested in advanced technology, representing possibly complementary goals. However, there was a potential conflict between the partners: While the fundamental interest of the U.S. partner was to penetrate the local Chinese market, the local partner was under the strong governmental pressure of earning hard currency to pay back their loans made in foreign exchange. Therefore, it was a strong Chinese motivation to export at least a portion of the venture's product.

Complementarity of Critical Resources

Following Hill and Hellriegel (1994), resource complementarity was assessed by gauging the distinctiveness between the partner's contributions. Resources were examined along the joint venture's critical functional lines, such as product design, manufacturing technology, material/components procurement (both locally sourced and imported), marketing and distribution (both local and international), product service and support, human resources, and local knowledge, networks, and political connections and influence (Yan and Gray 1994).

As summarized in Table 8.3, the four ventures showed highly similar configurations in partner contributions, in which a complementary, symbiotic relationship (Astley and Fombrun 1983) was apparent. The U.S. partners contributed product and manufacturing technologies and channels for procuring imported material/components, while the Chinese partner contributed expertise in local marketing and distribution, procurement of locally sourced raw material/components, and the general local contacts and political connections. When a venture was involved in export (as OfficeAid and FeedProc), the U.S. partner was in charge of gaining access to the international market.

Table 8.3

Partner Resource Contributions

	IndusCon	OfficeAid	FeedProc	R-Seals
U.S. partner resource contributions	Product and manufacturing technologies	Product and manufacturing technologies	Manufacturing technology	Well-known trademark and manufacturing technology
	Procurement channels for imported material	Procurement channels for imported material	Management know-how	Procurement channels for imported key ingredients
	Management know-how	Management know-how	International marketing experience	
		Channels to international market	Procurement channels for imported key ingredients	
Chinese partner resource contributions	Expertise in local marketing and distribution	Expertise in local marketing and distribution	Cheap land and labor	Cheap skilled workers
	Procurement of locally sourced raw material	Procurement of locally sourced raw material	Local government support	Management know-how
	Management know-how	General local contacts and political connection	Local distribution	Local marketing experience
	General local contacts and political connection		Procurement of local materials	General local contacts and relationships
Degree of complementarity	High–moderate	High	High	High

The ventures differed, however, in the partners' contribution of managerial know-how and participation in managing the venture's resources. Both partners at IndusCon contributed managerial expertise and jointly managed the use of the resources by mutual consultation (in this respect, the venture possessed some redundant resources). In OfficeAid and FeedProc, the U.S. partner contributed most management know-how to the venture while the local partner's input was limited only to the areas of personnel, administration, and government relations. In both cases, the venture's management system was duplicated from the U.S. parent. Partner contribution of managerial expertise at R-Seals was the opposite: The local partner designed the venture's management system and installed an all-Chinese management team. Both partners agreed that the venture was managed very much like "a Chinese enterprise."

Consensus on Operating Culture, Strategy, and Policies

Interpartner consensus on the joint venture's operating culture and strategy was assessed based on the evaluation by the venture's executives. Interpartner fit on this dimension was the highest at IndusCon, in which a consensus-based culture was created. As an ex-general manager noted, "Mutual consulting between us continued throughout my term . . . . All important decisions were consensus-based." This culture featured the venture's initial technology transfer agreement in which the U.S. partner transfered new technologies to the venture on a continuing basis upon the approval of the venture's board of directors. This was done because both parents believed that a continuing flow of new technology to the venture was vital in this highly competitive and technology-intensive industry. Furthermore, both partners shared a long-term vision: They agreed at the outset that every penny earned in the venture's first five years would be reinvested to enhance the venture's financial strength. In addition, an operational principle shared by the partners was to have "no hidden agenda" from each other.

Interpartner consensus on operations was low at both OfficeAid and FeedProc, in which the joint venture's culture and management were copied from the U.S. parent but not sincerely shared by the venture's Chinese-partner nominated managers. As the following quotes suggest:

> The Americans always consider the joint venture as one of their own children and use their own "standard model" to format it. . . . Here is China, not U.S.A. (OfficeAid's Chinese deputy general manager)

> They (the U.S. partner) have adopted a complete American management system here without considering the peculiarities of the Chinese situation. . . . Although it was written in the joint venture agreement that major decisions have to be made by consensus at the board of directors' meet-

ings, in practice the American manager unilaterally makes all the decisions without even consulting with us. (aFeedProc's Chinese deputy general manager)

At OfficeAid, there was a lack of cross-partner consensus on decision authority exercised by the general manager and the deputy general manager. The U.S. manager insisted "I was the general manager, he was the deputy. If we didn't agree on anything, I made the decision." His Chinese counterpart, however, indicated, "I am representing one of the two equal parties. From a long-term point of view, joint ventures have to localize." As a result, OfficeAid experienced a struggle for power and control between the partners.

At FeedProc, there was a conflict between the partners on the issue of internal transfer pricing in the joint venture's trading relationship with its U.S. parent, in both procuring raw materials and disposing of the venture's products. The Chinese side saw the trading with the U.S. firm as "unfair" in that the U.S. partner was playing a "dirty game"—making a unilateral profit at the cost of the partnership. The internal transfer arrangement was especially annoying to the Chinese because the venture had been losing money since its inception.

Partner consensus on operations was moderate at R-Seals, which was managed by an all-Chinese team. Because of the venture's small size and high maturity of technology, the U.S. partner elected not to be involved in the venture's daily operation. Interpartner conflicts, as they occurred, were resolved at the annual meetings of the board of directors.

Co-alignment of Bargaining Power and Management Control

We assessed the partners' relative bargaining power and management control based on their contribution of critical resources to the venture and the perceived level of involvement in making strategic decisions for the venture, respectively. Our assessment, as summarized in Table 8.4, suggests that a high level of alignment between the two variables existed in all joint ventures except R-Seals. Partner bargaining power at IndusCon was equally matched because the venture had a 49–51 ownership structure and the partners' contribution in other resources was comparable. It was also apparent that the venture was jointly managed, and that both partners were actively involved in decision making (Killing 1983).

Table 8.4

The Co-alignment Between Bargaining Power and Management Control

	IndusCon	OfficeAid	FeedProc	R-Seals
Non-equity-based bargaining power	Approximately equal	U.S. higher	U.S. higher	Approximately equal
Equity-based bargaining power (U.S.-China)	49–51 Approximately equal	51–49 Approximately equal	50–50 Equal	49–51 Approximately equal
Overall bargaining power	Approximately equal	U.S. higher	U.S. higher	Approximately equal
Management control	Shared and consensus-based	U.S. dominant	U.S. dominant	Chinese dominant
Bargaining power–control co-alignment	High	High	High	Low

At OfficeAid and FeedProc, unbalanced bargaining power was aligned with a dominant control structure. In both cases, the U.S. partner, as a world leader in each of their businesses, contributed advanced product and manufacturing technologies, arguably the most critical input to the venture, and accordingly exercised a higher level of management control. Although both partners were equally represented on the board of directors in both cases, each venture installed a dominant general manager and a management system adopted from the U.S. parent.

Unlike the other three cases, there was a lack of alignment between bargaining power and control at R-Seals. In this symbolic Chinese majority (51 percent) joint venture, resource contributions were approximately balanced between the partners, in which the American advanced technology and strong trademark met the Chinese local knowledge and market/distribution expertise. However, control at both the strategic and the operational levels was dominated by the Chinese partner, which nominated the majority of board members (three out of five) and an all-Chinese management team. Consider the following example: Soon after the venture's opening, the Chinese parent decided to fire the first general manager (who had served as a key negotiator on the Chinese team) without the U.S. partner's consent. Upset, the Americans protested and demanded "a due process" through the board of directors. A board meeting was soon called, at which all three Chinese members voted in favor of the firing. A majority vote of three to two ousted the manager legitimately. It is important to note, however, that in this case the U.S. firm very much accepted the current control structure by choice, because as a large multinational company, it regarded the joint venture as too small to exercise hands-on control from cost-efficiency considerations.

Dynamics and Changes in Interpartner Fit

Taking advantage of our longitudinal interview data, we were able to track the dynamics and changes in interpartner fit that occurred in the joint ventures after their formation. As a result, we were able to identify several major sources of change across the case studies: unforeseen environmental contingencies, changes in parent firm strategies, the growing independence of the venture itself, and interpartner learning. Each of these factors prompted dynamic currents and changes in the interactions between the venture partners and exerted a significant effect on interpartner fit.

Environmental Contingencies

Unanticipated events in a joint venture's environment can trigger significant changes in interpartner fit. These events included adjustment of governmental policies with respect to foreign direct investment, unforeseen development in the venture's market, and changes to the parents beyond their control. Relaxation of the Chinese government's restrictions resulted in IndusCon's acquisition of the sales and services company formerly wholly owned by the local parent to consolidate local marketing with manufacturing. This significantly changed the fit between the partners on two dimensions. First, the overall structure of resource complementarity shifted from the original match of the U.S. partner's technology and the Chinese partner's local knowledge to a match of the U.S. partner's technology, the joint venture's marketing knowledge, and the Chinese partner's political connections. Second, the acquisition significantly reduced the local partner's relative bargaining power because local marketing and services had been a major function performed by the Chinese partner. Similarly, as the economic reforms proceeded, the Chinese government became more tolerant about foreign-majority joint ventures and wholly owned foreign holding companies. OfficeAid's U.S. partner was able to establish two new partnerships in China, with both a majority ownership and a wholly owned holding company. As our last round of interviews was being conducted, the parent firms were about to close their renegotiations in which OfficeAid's ownership structure was proposed to change from a symbolic U.S. majority (51 percent) to a substantive U.S. majority (65 percent). Finally, as a result of the Chinese government decentralization, each individual state-owned hog farm was able to make its own purchasing decisions. Therefore, the local partner of FeedProc, a government agency, lost its monopolized distribution channels. This change reduced the U.S. firm's reliance on the local partner, and consequently it set up a wholly owned subsidiary to sell the joint venture's output. The new arrangement significantly changed the original alignment of interpartner interests and the partners' consensus on the venture's operating strategy and policies.

R-Seals was created upon the predicted exponential increase in demand for high-quality seals in China as the government designated automobile manufacturing as one of the "pillar" industries of the national economy. The market development, however, surprised R-Seals: Most foreign automakers brought their own seals-making facilities to China, while the local state-run auto companies, experiencing increasingly severe financial difficulties, could not afford the high prices of the joint venture's products. As a result, not only did interpartner fit, as perceived at the venture's founding, not result after its formation, but misfit between the partners emerged over time.

Uncontrollable changes to joint venture parent firms also played a role in shifting interpartner fit from its original configurations. IndusCon lost its original local parent (a government agency) as a consequence of governmental reforms, but was subsequently "assigned" to another agency as a "foster" parent. Similarly, FeedProc's partner from the central government gradually de-coupled itself from the venture by withdrawing its involvement in the venture's operations and calling back the deputy general manager it had nominated. Similar events also took place on the foreign partner's side, as evidenced by the British acquisition of IndusCon's U.S. parent. Although beyond the partner firms' control, these events had considerable impact on interpartner fit.

Changes in Parent Firm Strategies

Strategic redirections of joint ventures by their parent firms or changes in a parent's strategic interest in the venture were also found to reshape interpartner fit. A primary founding objective of FeedProc's U.S. partner was to make a profit, which was not in conflict with the Chinese partner's interests. However, over time, the U.S. firm found that it could make more profit out of selling the joint venture's outputs to its wholly owned operations in China under internal transfer prices. Therefore, it shifted its strategic interest from the joint venture to its entire operation network in China. While the major objective of the U.S. partner was being unilaterally served, the overall interpartner compatibility in the partnership was adversely affected. Similarly, OfficeAid's U.S. parent bought back a portion of the venture's products under internal transfer prices and made a unilateral profit by exporting them to the South American markets.

Effect of changes in partner strategic interests on interpartner fit is more dramatic at IndusCon following its U.S. parent's acquisition by a British conglomerate in 1995. While business growth remained as a strategically important objective for the foreign parent, the means to achieve growth was changed from depending on advanced technology to relying on operation scale/volume. This change led to a major decrease in the number of new products transferred to the joint venture, thereby prompting considerable concerns by the local partner, because the Chinese firm believed that the key competitive advantage of the venture was its technological superiority. This major shift in the U.S. partner's strategy triggered a series of events: Complaints increased from the local partner, which disturbed the partners' consensus on the operating strategy and policies at the venture. The formerly sincere cooperation was gradually replaced by frequent bargaining between the local and the expatriate managers. Attempting to control the situation, the U.S. partner proposed a change to the venture's equity structure. After several rounds of painful negotiations, a symbolic 2 percent change in ownership was agreed, in which the U.S. partner shifted from a minority (49 percent) to a majority owner (51 percent). Both parties found, however, that the trusting relationship between them had been significantly undermined.

Growing Independence of the Venture

As international joint ventures mature over time, they build their own knowledge bases, becoming independent of their parent firms (Prahalad and Doz 1981). While this tendency can increase the venture management's autonomy, thereby creating a positive effect on performance (Killing 1983), it can disturb fit or create misfit between the partners. For example, as IndusCon acquired the sales company from its local parent and as its local parent was replaced, it became more independent of its Chinese sponsor. On the other hand, the increased reluctance of the foreign partner to transfer new technology increased the venture's technical independence. The net effect of these changes called for a redefinition of interpartner fit on all dimensions.

Increased independence was also observed at R-Seals. The mediocre performance of the joint venture over the years minimized the level of interest by its U.S. parent. Meanwhile, the Chinese governmental reform significantly decreased the local partner's direct involvement in the venture's decision making. As a result, the partners' strategic interests became less binding and the venture's own managers' aspirations became more relevant and influential. With its U.S. parent company's support, R-Seals recently shifted its attention to international market opportunities.

Interpartner Competitive Learning

Joint ventures and strategic alliances in general have been characterized as a strategic game in which firms form alliances to extract and internalize the skills of their partners and thus either improve their own competitive position or reduce their partner's capability for autonomous action within and outside the partnership. Therefore, joint ventures become an arena in which the partners are engaged in a "race to learn" (Hamel 1991). Luo (1997) recently reported that because of the effect of learning, first movers significantly outperformed late entrants into the Chinese market. We observed interpartner learning across all joint ventures in this study. For example, the U.S. partner of OfficeAid preferred a joint venture to a wholly owned option when it first went to China, as the head negotiator of the U.S. firm and the venture's founding general manager suggested during an interview in 1991:

As a foreign company, who will you see for water? For electricity? Who will you talk to for the right employees you need? In a country full of uncertainty, you need a local partner at least to start with. I was against the wholly owned scenario from the outset even though we might have had that option then.

Four years later, however, the same executive, now the U.S. firm's general manager for China operations, created two more U.S.-majority ventures and was involved in the establishment of a wholly owned holding company in China. In an interview in 1996, he stated:

I believe [the U.S. partner] now, as an American company, knows how to do business in China. Over the years, we have learned a great deal in doing business in that country. We have piggybacked on our partner's initial dealers network and built our own. We have developed very good relationships with Chinese government officials.

Learning-oriented motives, however, can complicate the cooperation and develop misfit between the partners. The achievement of learning-driven objectives can directly upset the compatibility of partner goals. Since learning changes the pattern of partner resource contributions and partner interdependency (Inkpen and Beamish 1997), partner complementarity and the congruence between bargaining power and control will be altered. In addition, a competitive learning motive promotes the mentality of opportunism prevention and interpartner politics, making consensus building on the venture's operational strategies and policies difficult.

Finally, our longitudinal data suggest that venture performance may have a feedback effect on interpartner fit. As noted by previous studies, successful performance of a joint venture can serve as a confirmation of the current organizational arrangements and the patterns of partner interaction, while in less than successful ventures, the current structure and processes are the target to criticize and to initiate a change (Killing 1983; Yan and Gray 1994).

Venture Performance

We assessed performance by using three generic indicators: objective measures (profit or loss and market share), achievement of partner strategic objectives, and the quality of interpartner relationship. Since detailed financial data are confidential, we assessed financial performance based on our interviewees' estimates. The achievement of partner objectives and the interpartner working relationship were assessed in a similar manner.

IndusCon stands as the highest performer among the four joint ventures. This venture had been profitable since the second year in operation (average profitability above 20 percent). By 1996 it had gained a market share of 25 percent in the increasingly competitive Chinese market and earned a good reputation on its superior product quality. By and large, both the foreign and the local partner achieved their initial strategic objectives; therefore, the venture was viewed as successful by both parents. The working relationship between the partners had been exemplary over many years. In fact, it was elected one of the best-run international joint ventures in China several times in its operational history.

We assess FeedProc as the least successful venture in the study. First of all, it has been operated at a loss since its inception. Its growth rate and market share were both far short of meeting expectations. Both partners had only partially achieved their founding strategic objectives, mainly short-term ones (e.g., market entry, import substitution, and high-tech equipment). The interpartner working relationship had been poor throughout the venture's history. There was constant tension between the U.S. partner and one of the two local partners.

As shown in Table 8.5, we assess the overall performance of OfficeAid as "moderate" and that of R-Seals "low–moderate." OfficeAid had gained a high market share in China (about 40 percent) and it was "very profitable" compared with its competitors, although it lost money on exporting. The U.S. partner had achieved two out of the three strategic objectives (market share and profit). However, the Chinese partner had achieved only one of its four founding objectives (profit). The working relationship between the partners was far from desirable. At R-Seals, it took the venture five years to break even, and it has remained only slightly profitable since then. Its profitability was "far lower than the industry average," according to an informant. The venture was stagnant in growth and about average in meeting its parent firms' expectations because both parents had only partially achieved their founding objectives. The working relationship between the partners had been "neither good nor bad," according to the Chinese general manager.

The Relationship Between Fit and Performance

Table 8.5 integrates the case study results for cross-case comparison. At the overall level, interpartner fit at IndusCon was ranked the highest, FeedProc the lowest, while OfficeAid and R-Seals are in between. This pattern is consistent with our ranking of performance, in which the ventures range (from the highest to the lowest) from IndusCon to OfficeAid, R-Seals, and FeedProc, suggesting a close relationship between interpartner fit and performance at a generic level.

The relationship between each of the dimensions of fit and performance is more complex. First, the congruence between the partners' strategic objectives was found to be an important contributor to performance. IndusCon, in which the partners' strategic expectations are highly compatible, is highly successful on all three measures, while the other three ventures that were featured with moderate levels of goal congruence performed either moderately or poorly. A particularly tight relationship was found between the congruence of the partners' strategic objectives and the perceived achievement of these objectives. This is not surprising because we considered a venture as "High" in achieving its parent objectives only when it had met the strategic expectations for both parents. Therefore, high performance occurs only when the two sets of objectives of the parents are congruent so that they can be achieved simultaneously. With respect to other performance measures, the fit-performance linkage is also evident.

A cross-case comparison reveals consistent patterns between interpartner consensus on the venture's operating culture, strategy and policies, and venture performance, suggesting a close relationship between the two variables. The relationship of fit on this dimension to two performance variables, namely financial performance and interpartner relationship, is particularly strong. For example, the consensus dimension of interpartner fit is high at IndusCon and low at FeedProc with OfficeAid and R-Seals in between. The same pattern is observed in financial performance and the quality of the interpartner working relationship.

The effect of the other two dimensions of fit on performance is less than straightforward. First, since resource complementarity was rated high for all four joint ventures, the sample lacked necessary variance to indicate its effect on performance. However, a detailed examination of the cases suggests that the partners' contribution in management exper-

Table 8.5

Relationship Between Interpartner Fit and Performance

	IndusCon	OfficeAid	FeedProc	R-Seals
Goal congruence	High	Moderate	Low–moderate	Moderate
Resource complementarity	High–moderate	High	High	High
Joint management	High	Low–moderate	Low	Low*
Consensus on operations	High	Low–moderate	Moderate	Moderate
Power-control co-alignment	High	High	High	Low*
Partner agreement on bargaining power–control	High	Low–moderate	Low	Moderate–high*
Overall fit	High	Moderate	Low	Moderate*
Financial performance	High	Moderate–high	Low–moderate	Low–moderate
Achievement of objectives	High	Moderate	Moderate	Low–moderate
Working relationship	High	Low	Low	Moderate
Overall success	High	Moderate	Low	Low–moderate

* This arrangement was made upon the consent of the foreign partner, which elected not to be involved in the venture's daily management for cost-saving considerations.

tise and their participation in managing the venture may have a significant effect on performance. At InducCon, the most successful venture in the sample, both partners contributed management know-how and more importantly, jointly managed the venture's operations.

Management at FeedProc, the least successful venture, reveals a different pattern, in which the foreign partner contributed significantly to management know-how and dominated the venture's operation, while the local partners' managerial contribution was minimal and involvement in management control was limited. In this joint venture, the larger local partner (a government agency owing 40 percent equity) was a silent partner (Killing 1983), which neither contributed to nor was involved in the venture's management. Although the smaller local partner (with 10 percent equity) nominated a deputy general manager to the venture, no significant sharing of decision making occurred at the top management level, because the U.S. general manager single-handedly made most of the important decisions. Consistent with previous reports that shared management positively affects venture performance (Beamish 1984; Hill and Hellriegel 1994), our results suggest that interpartner fit in managerial know-how and joint management of resources contributes to performance.

No evidence was found for the effect of the co-alignment between bargaining power and control on performance because no consistent patterns were observed between this dimension of fit and any performance indicators. However, we found that agreement or disagreement between the partners' perceptions of each other's bargaining power and control has an important effect on venture performance. At IndusCon, both partners were in strong agreement that the partners' bargaining power was evenly matched and their involvement in co-managing the venture is about equal. In the cases of OfficeAid and FeedProc, such an agreement was absent. In fact, the partners at both ventures had been in dispute about the value and importance of each other's contributions. The American general manager of OfficeAid described the local partner's expertise in local marketing and government relationships as "looking good on the surface but absolutely rotten beneath it." Similarly, the American parent of FeedProc viewed its local partners as less important to the venture's success. As the U.S. expatriate manager commented, "The [Chinese partner] was very helpful in gaining access to the Chinese market. They were instrumental in opening the door to gain the business from various operations in the early days. Today, however, most of their control over these local operations has vanished. The local farms are more independent of Beijing." FeedProc's Chinese partners, however, resented the American's dominance in management. They claimed that "the Americans do not deserve the right to impose on the venture a complete American management system." In fact, there was a long-lasting tension between the expatriate general manager and his Chinese deputies.

At R-Seals, there is an apparent misalignment between bargaining power and control (both partners' resource contributions are about equal, but the venture is under the Chinese partner's dominant control). However, in this partnership, the control structure in favor of the local partner was voluntarily accepted by the U.S. firm. In other words, there are no disputes between the partners about the current structure of management control.

Discussion and Conclusions

In light of our case study findings, in Figure 8.1 we offer a grounded theory model of interpartner fit. Consistent evidence generated across the case studies suggests that there is a strong and close relationship between interpartner fit and joint venture success. Generally, when all four dimensions are considered, ventures with a higher level of fit between the partners demonstrated a higher level of performance, whereas ventures with a lower level of fit were found less successful.

While our case studies provided general support for our initial conceptual framework, there are several issues that deserve further discussion. First, in all the joint ventures in our study, partner resource contributions were complementary, but not all ventures were equally successful. We found that the degree of joint contribution of managerial expertise and joint management of these resources were related to performance. Second, we found that an "objective" assessment of the coalignment between partner bargaining power and control was less predictive of performance than the agreement/disputes between the partners' "subjective" perceptions of each other's bargaining power and control. In particular, when Party A perceives that Party B has "inflated" its own resource contributions but "devalued" the resources committed by Party A, disputes about whether a fair control structure is in place will occur. This suggests that the consistency of perceptions between the partners about each other's bargaining power and the level of control they exercise has an effect on performance. Third, out of our analysis of the dynamic aspects of the joint ventures, several key environmental and organizational contingents emerged to prompt changes in interpartner fit over time. Specifically, unexpected events in the venture's external environment, redirections of the partners' strategic interests in the venture, increase in the venture's independence, and interpartner competitive learning were found to change the patterns of interpartner

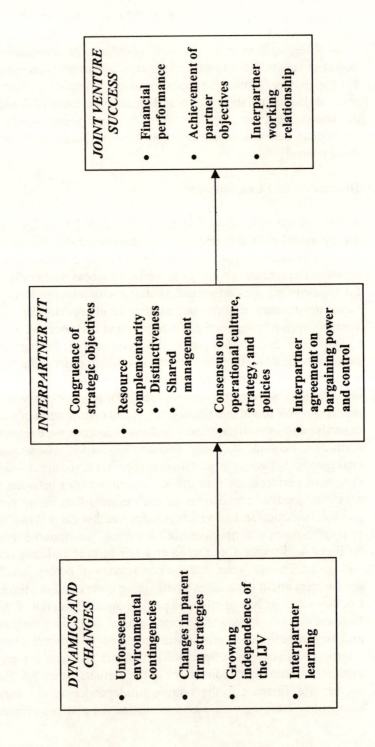

Figure 8.1 A Grounded Theory Model of Interpartner Fit in International Joint Ventures

compatibility and to create misfits between the partners. Finally, the venture's ongoing performance and successful experience may exert a feedback effect on interpartner fit.

Theoretical and Practical Implications

This study contributes in several ways. First, although interpartner fit in international alliances has been a familiar notion to both scholars and practitioners, few systematic efforts have been made to rigorously examine the phenomenon. There has been a considerable lack of clarity about how "fit" is conceptualized and how it can be appropriately measured (Geringer 1988; Venkatraman 1989). This chapter represents a systematic attempt to investigate the phenomenon. Second, this study proposes a migration of focus in fit studies from the comparison of the static features of the parents to the examination of parent configurations within the venture's specific context. Without focusing on the particular venture, parent potentials will not guarantee to generate synergy. Therefore, the weak/inconsistent prior empirical results should not be surprising. Our case studies provided evidence that the generic features of the parent firms, such as nationality and vertical or horizontal relationship, are poor predictors of performance: All the joint ventures in this study were created between the U.S. and the Chinese firms and all were horizontal ventures as the parent firms for each venture operated in the same industry. However, radical differences in performance were observed among these ventures. Theoretically, the features of the venture parents may depict only a rough and incomplete contour of potential fit between them. The actual compatibility can be developed only when the parents' potentials for fit (e.g., strategic expectations and resource availability) are effectively realized and implemented in jointly managing the partnership's operations.

A third contribution of this study concerns whether interpartner fit entails similarity or dissimilarity in the partners' resource contributions, a long-time unsolved mystery in the joint venture literature (Geringer 1988). Our results confirm Hill and Hellriegel's finding (1994) that dissimilarities in partner resources do not exert an effect on venture performance. The lack of support for this widely held thesis may be attributed to the fact that partner contribution in distinctive skills and competencies is a necessary but not sufficient condition for joint venture success. That is, without mutually distinctive resources, a partnership is unlikely to succeed (or there is no need to form joint ventures in the first place). However, contribution of nonredundant resources per se will not guarantee venture success.

In contrast, we found that a shared base of resources, particularly managerial know-how, and the joint management of these resources by all partners may be critical factors in performance. Partners possessing similar expertise are able to understand each other better, reduce unnecessary conflict, and cultivate mutual appreciation of each other's commitment, while the partners with distinctive competencies in different functional areas may experience difficulties in integration (Hill and Hellriegel 1994). A conceptual extension of our findings is that, for synergy to occur, interpartner resource complementarity may entail several aspects: (1) distinctiveness to take the advantage of symbiotic cooperation (Astley and Fombrun 1983); (2) similarity for the partners to understand and appreciate each other's contributions and expertise; (3) sufficiency of the jointly created resource pool (i.e., whether the partners' resource contributions are collectively sufficient to enable the venture to pursue its stated mission in the face of competition); and (4) effective deployment of the resources. Future research should further investigate each of these aspects.

Our case data supported the premise that interpartner fit in joint ventures is a dynamic phenomenon evolving over time upon changes in the venture's external environment as well as in its internal strategic and structural changes. Since fit represents a task of "shooting at a moving target of co-alignment" (Thompson 1967, 148), attention to the dynamic aspect of fit is particularly important. Our results illustrate that interpartner fit is far from an issue exclusively relevant to joint venture partner selection such that once a compatible partner is chosen, the partners would fit forever. Since "changes will occur in every venture's design because managers rarely can anticipate exactly how their agreement to cooperate will evolve" (Harrigan 1986, 34), the achievement of a dynamic fit between the partners is a paramount challenge and a long-term task.

Finally, this study has important practical implications. Our multidimensional framework can help joint venture practitioners assess interpartner fit and to diagnose misfit. The specific dimensions identify the key areas in which partner compatibility is pivotal. These managers may find our results on partner similarities or dissimilarities and their impact on venture performance particularly helpful, because the debates and controversies in the academic literature to date have provided them with few clear and actionable directions. Our identification of the dynamic factors and changes prompting interpartner misfit can also prove helpful for managers in detecting these changes and undertaking actions to reinstall fit.

This study has some limitations that warrant attention. First, all our case studies were drawn from U.S.-Chinese manufacturing joint ventures. Characteristics idiosyncratic to the two countries, particularly China, such as the short history of foreign direct investment, the quasi-political goals of the local partners, and the highly uncertain and dynamic environment during the reforms, might have affected our results. Therefore, generalization of our results to other international alliance populations should be done with caution. Second, as in most case studies, the analyses conducted in this study were partially based on retrospective data, which might have introduced a source of bias as a result of faulty memory or retrospective sense-making on the part of our informants. However, this problem has been attenuated as we collected data from multiple sources, and interviews were conducted with the same informant more than once. Finally, our measures of the dimensions of interpartner fit may be still too simple, given the complexity of the phenomenon. More data are needed to capture the richness of the concept and to validate our measurement. Future research should refine the measures of the variables and examine the relationships proposed in the grounded theory model with larger samples.

Appendix 8.1

Sources of the Interview Data

Joint Venture	Interviewees*
IndusCon	Managing director for international joint ventures of the U.S. parent, member of the joint venture's board of directors, and former deputy general manager of the venture
	General manager and former deputy general manager of the joint venture, member of the joint venture's board of directors, former member of the Chinese negotiation team
	Manager of marketing of the joint venture
OfficeAid	Former general manager for China operations of the U.S. parent, member of the IJV's board of directors, former head negotiator of the U.S. team, and the first general manager of the joint venture
	General manager of the joint venture and vice president for China operations
	Former chairman and general manager of the Chinese parent firm
	Deputy general manager of the joint venture, member of the venture's board of directors, and former executive general manager and head negotiator of the Chinese partner
	Manager of marketing of the joint venture
FeedProc	Senior corporate vice president and president of the feed milling group of the U.S. parent, former head negotiator of the U.S. team, member of the joint venture's board of directors
	Deputy general manager of the venture, a key member of the Chinese team of founding negotiations, member of the venture's board of directors
R-Seals	President of the U.S. parent's Sales Division and a former key member of the U.S. negotiation team
	General manager of the joint venture, member of the venture's board of directors

*Each paragraph represents one individual. The firms and individuals are disguised to ensure confidentiality.

——— 9 ———

Two Empirical Studies of Bargaining Power, Parent Control, and Performance

This chapter reports two empirical studies of the bargaining power-control-performance relationships. The first study, using a multiple case method, is an inductive examination of four manufacturing joint ventures between U.S. and Chinese firms. The hypotheses developed as a result of the case studies were subsequently tested in the second study using firsthand survey data collected from a sample of ninety American-Chinese joint ventures in China. The results of both studies indicate a positive linkage between partner bargaining power and control and a significant effect of the venture's control structure on performance. In addition, a strong link was found between the interpartner working relationship and the venture performance.

Introduction and Methods

In this chapter, we continue our discussion of parent management control in international joint ventures. Based on the conceptual discussion presented in chapter 5, we now report two specific empirical studies of parent control. These two studies adopted a perspective of interpartner negotiations, and incorporated bargaining power, control, and performance into an integrative framework, as depicted in Figure 9.1. This preliminary framework guided our case analysis in the first, qualitative study; and a revision of it was subsequently tested in the second, quantitative study.

This chapter was adapted in part, with permission, from Aimin Yan and Barbara Gray. 1994. "Bargaining Power, Management Control, and Performance in U.S.-China Joint Ventures: A Comparative Case Study." *Academy of Management Journal* 37 (6): 1478–1517; and a working paper by the same authors.

Figure 9.1 **A Preliminary Model of Bargaining Power, Management Control, and Performance**

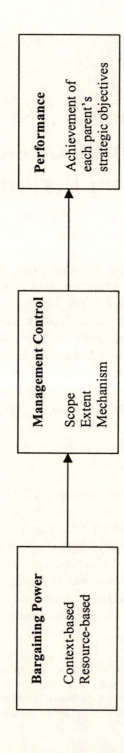

Both studies focused on U.S.-Chinese manufacturing joint ventures in China. We limited the studies to manufacturing partnerships because (1) about 70 percent of U.S. joint ventures in China are involved in manufacturing (U.S.-China Business Council 1990); and (2) we wanted to avoid problems of combining alliances in manufacturing sectors and those in service industries (Chowdhury 1988). Both qualitative and quantitative approaches were undertaken to enhance the rigor and richness of the research.

The Comparative Case Study

This comparative case study was intended to accomplish several objectives. First, by adopting an in-depth, qualitative approach, we wanted to critically examine and enrich our understanding of the relationships between bargaining power, control, and performance and to sort out the confusion and inconsistencies with respect to these relationships. Inductive inquiries are important because they can inform theory building by providing detailed understanding and explanations for the phenomenon under investigation and help verify possible stereotypes in previous theories (Glaser and Strauss 1967; Yin 1989). Eisenhardt (1989) argues that case studies are particularly appropriate for theory building when there is no theory, or existing theories are in conflict. Second, previous researchers have used highly idiosyncratic measures for such theoretical variables as bargaining power and control, and performance of joint ventures has been measured in multiple ways. Without a thorough understanding of how these variables are manifested in practice, their operationalization in theory testing could suffer from serious problems with construct and/or measurement validity. Inductive studies are appropriate to operationalize theoretical models by suggesting appropriate and reliable measures of the variables. Finally, in-depth case studies can help reveal the details of the rationales and causalities among the variables, thus providing reliable and convincing explanations and interpretations for the results of quantitative studies.

The case studies included four joint ventures in industries ranging from electronic equipment and peripherals to industrial control equipment, personal hygiene products, and pharmaceuticals. Two out of these four cases were also used in the study of interpartner fit reported in the previous chapter. For each case study, data were collected, following the same procedures as described in the previous chapter, through in-depth personal interviews with multiple executives of both the U.S. and the Chinese partners as well as the managers of the joint ventures. Our informants at the parent companies were senior executives who either were personally involved in the initial negotiations for the venture or were directly responsible for overseeing the joint venture's operation. Interviewees from the joint ventures include the general manager or president, the deputy general manager or executive vice president, and some key functional managers. Except for one joint venture, three or more informants were interviewed for each partnership. The key characteristics of the four joint ventures are summarized in Table 9.1.

In data analysis, we followed strictly the logic of analytic induction (Cressey 1953; Glaser and Strauss 1967), an incremental case study method in which multiple cases are analyzed sequentially and the findings from each case are compared and contrasted with the "theories" generated from previous case results. In this way the previously formulated theoretical components are challenged, revised, and enriched; and theories are built incrementally until a certain level of saturation is achieved.

The Survey Study

Based on the findings in the comparative case studies, a survey study was conducted among U.S.-Chinese manufacturing joint ventures in China. The questionnaire was prepared in both English and Chinese versions, which were mailed to the American and the Chinese general managers of a joint venture, respectively. In addition, a separate questionnaire was sent to the U.S. parent company. We administered the questionnaires in China as a collaborative effort with the business school of a Chinese university. We secured support from the municipal governments of several Chinese cities in which a large number of the targeted joint ventures were located.

Respondents at ninety joint ventures completed and returned the questionnaire (response rate of 32.3 percent). For sixty-eight ventures (75.6 percent of the sample) the respondents were top executives (the venture's chairman, president, general manager, or deputy general manager). For thirteen ventures (14.4 percent), the respondents were assistant general managers or chief staff members. For the remaining nine ventures (10.0 percent), a lower-level manager responded to the questionnaire. From twenty-seven joint ventures in the sample, two responses to the ques-

Table 9.1

A Summary of the Major Characteristics of the Joint Ventures

	Office Aid	IndusCon	Daily Product	Bio Tech Ltd.
Product	Electronic office equipment	Industrial process control	Personal hygiene products	Pharmaceuticals
Years of negotiation	4	3	2	3
Formation	1987	1982	1981	1982
Total investment	$30 million	$10 million	2.85	10
Equity share (US/PRC)	51–49	49–51	50–50	50–50
Contracted years	30	20	20	15
Product market	Mainly local; small % export	Local, for import substitution	50% for export	Mainly local; small % export
U.S. partner objectives	Profit Market share Low-cost sourcing	Business growth Market penetration Profit	Learn business practices Establish credibility Profit Business expansion	Market Profit
PRC partner objectives	Technology & management Export for foreign exchange	Import substitution Manufacturing technology Upgrade suppliers' technology	Profit Export for foreign exchange Technology Growth	Technology Learning management Business expansion

tionnaire were generated, typically one from the Chinese general manager and the other from the expatriate general manager. Respondents from fifty-five joint ventures (61.1 percent) had personally participated in the initial negotiations that led to the formation of the partnership.

The ninety joint ventures in the quantitative sample were formed be-

Table 9.2

Industrial Sectors and Provinces/Municipalities Represented in the Sample

Industry sector*	No. of ventures	%	Province/city	No. of ventures	%
Chemicals	16	17.8	Shanghai	31	34.4
Electronics	14	15.6	Beijing	10	11.1
Miscellaneous light industry	13	14.4	Hebei	9	10.0
Food and agriculture	10	11.1	Guangdong	7	7.8
Miscellaneous industrial equipment	10	11.1	Jiangsu	5	5.6
Metals	6	6.7	Tianjin	5	5.6
Medical	5	5.6	Shandong	4	4.4
Building materials	5	5.6	Hubei	3	3.3
Telecommunications	4	4.4	Liaoning	3	3.3
Engineering services	3	3.3	Shaanxi	3	3.3
Resources	3	3.3	Fujian	2	2.2
Transportation equipment	1	1.1	Heilongjiang	2	2.2
			Anhui	1	1.1
			Henan	1	1.1
			Hunan	1	1.1
			Ningxia	1	1.1
			Shanxi	1	1.1
			Zhejiang	1	1.1
Total	90	100.0		90	98.8**

*The categories are those suggested by the U.S.-China Business Council (1990).
**Total is not equal to 100.0 because of rounding.

tween 1982 and 1992. All joint ventures in the sample are manufacturing partnerships in twelve industrial sectors (see Table 9.2). The majority of the joint ventures (71 percent) operated within five industrial sectors: chemical materials or products, electronic components or equipment, light industry manufacturing, food processing and agricultural products, and miscellaneous industrial equipment. The ventures were located in eighteen Chinese provinces and municipalities.

Sample representativeness and triangulation of data collected from different sources were performed to ensure the study's validity. Multiple statistical methods were used in analyzing the quantitative data, including correlation analysis, multivariate analysis, path analysis, and multivariate regression.

Case Study Results

Bargaining Power

Across the four cases, two components of negotiation context-based and seven of resource-based bargaining power were identified respectively (Table 9.3). For each case, only those components that both partners acknowledged are listed.

Negotiation Context–Based

Evidence supporting the two components of context-based bargaining power (the venture's strategic importance and availability of alternatives) was present in all four cases. The perceived strategic importance of the joint venture to the overall business of each parent reflects each partner's strategic stakes in, and thus dependence on, the partnership. For example, Bio Tech was critically important to its U.S. parent because this parent regarded China as one of its worldwide strategic markets. For the U.S. parent in Daily Product, on the other hand, because the joint venture was nothing more than an experiment to test the Chinese market, the stakes were only marginally important.

Context-based bargaining power can also be derived from having alternatives (e.g., alternative partners with whom to negotiate and/or availability of existing channels through which to accomplish the same mission as the joint venture). For example, the Chinese partner in IndusCon was simultaneously engaged in negotiations with a Japanese

Table 9.3

Relative Bargaining Power Between the Partners

Components of Bargaining Power	Office Aid		IndusCon		Daily Product		Bio Tech, Ltd.	
	U.S.	China	U.S.	China	U.S.	China	U.S.	China
Context-based:								
Alternatives available	Higher		Moderately lower		Equal		Equal	
Strategic importance	Moderately higher		Moderately lower		Moderately higher		Equal	
Resource-based:								
Technology	Higher		Higher		Moderately higher		Moderately higher	
Management expertise	Moderately higher		Equal		Higher		Equal	
Global support	Higher							
Local knowledge	Moderately lower		Lower		Moderately lower		Moderately lower	
Marketing and distribution	Moderately lower		Moderately lower		Higher		Lower	
Material procurement	Moderately higher		Moderately higher		Equal		Equal	
Capital investment	Approximately equal		Approximately equal		Equal		Equal	
Overall bargaining power	Higher		Approximately equal		Higher		Approximately equal	

firm and the U.S. partner. This enabled the Chinese to choose between two rival foreign firms, thereby increasing their bargaining power in negotiating with the U.S. company. In Daily Product, because the local partner was "assigned" to the U.S. parent by the Chinese government, the U.S. firm had no alternatives. As another example, additional bargaining power accrued to the U.S. parent of Office Aid because the U.S. company had existing business channels in China that could serve as alternative outlets. The U.S. firm's regional division in Hong Kong had previously exported to China, which remained a viable alternative to the joint venture.

Resource-Based

The components of resource-based bargaining power signify the resources and capabilities committed by the partners to the joint venture. These resource contributions are either explicitly specified in the joint venture agreements (contracts, memorandums or licenses) or verbally recognized by both partners during the negotiations. A consistent, complementary pattern is observed across all four cases with regard to the types of resource committed by the partners. Predictably, the foreign firms contributed more heavily than their local partners in technology (product design, manufacturing know-how, and special equipment) and global support (technical, marketing, and maintenance services) while the Chinese firms contributed more in knowledge about, and skills to deal with, the local government and other institutional infrastructures. IndusCon's U.S. parent's comments were illustrative:

> We have the technology and certain know-how. The Chinese partner knows how to make things happen in China. You put the two together right, it works.

In other areas, while both partners made contributions, apparent complementarity also existed. The U.S. partner tended to provide imported materials, channels for exporting the joint venture's products, and expertise in production management; while the Chinese partner contributed in areas of local sourcing, domestic distribution, and personnel management. In equity investment, both partners injected roughly the same amount of capital in all four joint ventures.

While both partners possessed bargaining power during the initial negotiations, the patterns of the relative bargaining power between the partners varied from one partnership to another. Since data with which to assess the relative importance of each component to bargaining power were not available, we assessed the relative bargaining power of the partners in each joint venture by assuming that all components contributed equally. In two of the four joint ventures (IndusCon and Bio Tech), bargaining power was balanced, or approximately equally shared between the partners. On the other hand, a significant imbalance in the partners' bargaining power existed in the other two ventures (Office Aid and Daily Product), with much more bargaining power accruing to the U.S. partner. The bottom of Table 9.3 summarizes the overall patterns of relative bargaining power in the ventures studied.

Management Control

Our data analysis revealed several unambiguous indicators of management control, which is congruent with the notion that control is multidimensional (Geringer and Hebert 1989). Like Schaan (1983, 1988), we found that nominations of a venture's board of directors and general manager were important control mechanisms. Both interview and archival data supported the importance of the role played by the boards of directors in making strategic decisions for the joint venture and solving critical problems regarding the partnership in general. The following quotes provide some evidence:

> We [the board] approve the annual budgets submitted by Daily Product's management and decide everything important for its operation. When anything unexpected happens in China, I have to be there to talk to the Chinese chairman (Vice-chairman of Daily Product).

> The board of directors is empowered to discuss and take actions on all fundamental issues concerning the venture, namely, expansion projects, production and business programs, the budget, distribution of profits, plans concerning manpower and pay scales, the termination of business, the appointment or hiring of the president, the vice-president(s), the chief engineer, the treasurer and the auditors as well as their functions and powers and their remuneration, etc. (The Law of The People's Republic of China on Joint Ventures Using Chinese and Foreign Investment)

The board of directors of each joint venture in this study met at least twice a year to set biannual goals, review performance, and approve operational plans for the venture.

Our data also suggest that substantial power is associated with the position of general manager in joint ventures. In each of the four ventures in this study, the general manager had always been a board member and served as the executive officer of the joint venture. The general manager made important operational decisions for the ventures and represented each parent in negotiations with the other partner on issues that arose unexpectedly. However, difference in decision power attached to the general manager and deputy general manager of a venture, each of whom is nominated by a different parent, varied significantly across our cases. In two joint ventures, Office Aid and Daily Product, the general manager exercised more control than the deputy general manager, but in the other two, the positions were roughly equal in terms of control. For example, the former U.S. general manager of Office Aid, who was from the U.S. parent, stated:

> Eighty percent of the time he [the Chinese deputy general manager] would say "yes" when I made a decision . . . because I was the general manager, he was the deputy. If we didn't agree on anything, I made the decision.

This pattern was confirmed by a Chinese manager at Office Aid, who observed that "in the offices where there is an American manager, he will be in control though we have a deputy manager there." However, the IndusCon and Bio Tech data suggest different stories, as the following quotes reveal:

> The Chinese general manager and I were equals, co-managers. Mutual consulting between us continued throughout my term. This relationship was passed on to me from my predecessor. And it's true even today. (IndusCon's former deputy general manager from the U.S. parent)

> In organization design, our president [of the joint venture] should report to the Chinese chairman. However, in managing the joint venture, they are equally involved in making important decisions. (A representative of the U.S. parent of Bio Tech)

Joint venture parents also exercise control through structuring the partnership. We found that when the management system, decision process, and corporate policies of a joint venture were similar in structure to those of one parent, that parent exercised a higher level of control than its partner did. In fact, the ability of this partner to replicate its way of managing in the joint venture reflects its level of control over the partnership, as the following quotes suggest:

> Three weeks after we hired the senior staff, we started training them in our corporate principles. . . . We wanted to go through a process which is

part of our management process, our management styles. . . . I created a culture at the joint venture. (Office Aid's first U.S. general manager)

We structure the joint venture in China exactly the same way as we structure our organizations in other countries. In comparing with the Chinese state-run enterprises, we don't have the [communist] party event and the union plays a very small role. (Daily Product's U.S. vice chairman)

Our data also provide information about the overall control by each parent, as perceived by the interviewees. This indicator reflects both the scope and the extent of control (Geringer and Hebert 1989). The following comments suggest that this indicator of control is also important:

[The U.S. company] always considers the joint venture as one of their own children and uses their own "standard model" to format it. They try to control it in great detail. (Office Aid's Chinese deputy general manager)

In making important decisions for Bio Tech, both sides make compromises. "Compromise" is the most appropriate word here. (Bio Tech's U.S. parent)

Table 9.4 summarizes the degree of control exercised by the partners in each case. Overall, an imbalance in control favoring the U.S. parent occurred in Office Aid and Daily Product. In contrast, control in IndusCon and Bio Tech was approximately balanced between the parents.

Venture Performance

There were considerable differences in the strategic objectives of the partners (see Table 9.5). The Chinese partners focused on upgrading technology and management and earning foreign exchange through export, and the U.S. partners aimed at penetrating the local market and earning a profit in China. These divergent, though potentially complementary, objectives implied that significant bias would occur if performance were assessed from only one partner's perspective or by simply using available standard financial indicators. Moreover, we found that the joint venture management did not provide performance assessments independent of those of the parents because all the joint ventures operated under a close parent control. A joint venture's managers did not represent the partnership itself; rather, each acted as the representative of the parent firm of his or her nation. Therefore, it was inappropriate in

Table 9.4

Partner Management Control

Components of Management Control	Office Aid		IndusCon		Daily Product		Bio Tech, Ltd.	
	U.S.	China	U.S.	China	U.S.	China	U.S.	China
Percent of board membership	Equal		Slightly lower		Equal		Equal	
Nomination of key personnel	Higher		Approximately equal		Higher		Slightly lower	
Similarity of management systems to parents'	Higher		Approximately equal		Higher		Approximately equal	
Perceived overall control	Higher		Approximately equal		Higher		Approximately equal	
Overall pattern of management control	Higher		Approximately equal		Higher		Approximately equal	

this study to count the joint venture managers' assessment of performance as independent of their parents,' as previous researchers have suggested doing (Anderson 1990; Killing 1983).

The performance measure we used was the extent to which a venture's partners had achieved their strategic objectives in initiating the joint venture. If an objective represented a long-term goal of a partner, we measured the extent to which satisfactory progress had been made. Using this measure fits well with the ways that partners actually evaluated performance. The following comments by a U.S. firm are representative:

> The only appropriate criterion for performance evaluation is whether or not the partners and their stakeholders are happy with the joint venture's operation. The happiness for us is measured by its profitability and market share—the two most important goals we had. . . . Our stakeholders are happy with what we have done in China.

Table 9.5 presents information about performance assessment for the joint ventures.

Table 9.5

Achievement of Strategic Objectives by the Partners

Strategic objectives	Degree of Achievement			
	Office Aid	IndusCon	Daily Product	Bio Tech Ltd.
U.S. Partner				
Profit	Yes	Yes	Yes	Yes
Market share	Yes	Yes		Yes
Growth		Yes	Partially	
Local sourcing	No			
Learning			Yes	
Credibility with Chinese government			Yes	
Overall	Largely achieved	All achieved	Largely achieved	All achieved
Chinese partner				
Technology	Partially	Mostly	Yes	Yes
Export	No		Yes	
Growth			Partially	Partially
Learning management			Yes	
Import substitution		Yes		
Upstream technology	Yes			
Profit			Yes	
Overall	Largely not achieved	Mostly achieved	Largely achieved	Largely achieved

Relationship Between Bargaining Power and Management Control

The theoretical framework in Figure 9.1 shows a positive relationship between the relative bargaining power of a venture partner and the management control it exercises. Data from all four of our cases support this relationship. The relative bargaining power between the partners in two joint ventures (Office Aid and Daily Product) was uneven: The U.S. parent had higher bargaining power than the local parent. Accordingly, in these two joint ventures, the U.S. partner exercised a higher level of management control than its Chinese partner for all indicators except the representation on the board, which was equal. For these two ventures, unevenly distributed bargaining power is associated with imbalanced management control. The partner who gained more bargaining power during the negotiations exercised more management control

Table 9.6

Patterns of Bargaining Power, Management Control, and Performance

Variables	Office Aid		IndusCon		Daily Product		Bio Tech, Ltd.	
	U.S.	China	U.S.	China	U.S.	China	U.S.	China
Relative bargaining power	Higher		Approximately equal		Higher		Approximately equal	
Management control	Higher		Approximately equal		Higher		Approximately equal	
Venture performance	High	Low	Very high	Very high	High	High	Very high	High

in the venture. In the other two joint ventures, IndusCon and Bio Tech, each partner possessed roughly even bargaining power and exercised equal management control over the venture. Overall, the pattern of partners' relative bargaining power is consistent with, and positively related to, the pattern in which management control is shared between the partners (Table 9.6).

Relationship Between Management Control and Performance

In the theoretical model, we predict a direct, positive relationship between management control and performance. The bottom two rows in Table 9.6 depict the general patterns of management control and performance for each joint venture. Our findings suggest that the relationship between management control and performance was not as straightforward as was predicted. To better understand how the cases deviate from the prediction, we focus on each case in the "step-wise" manner the analytical induction method suggests (Cressey 1953).

Office Aid

As discussed above, Office Aid's U.S. parent exhibited more control than the Chinese parent. With regard to performance, the U.S. parent had achieved its two most important objectives, profit and market share, though its objective of building a low-cost sourcing base in China had not yet been achieved (see Table 9.5). In contrast, the Chinese partner had only partially achieved one of its two equally important objectives, updating technology. Because the joint venture exported at a loss, the second Chinese objective, generating foreign exchange through export, had not been achieved. The significant imbalance at Office Aid in achieving its parents' strategic expectations hindered the overall performance of the venture, which is the lowest among the four joint ventures.

The Office Aid data seem to support the positive relationship between control and performance reported by previous studies (Killing 1983; Lecraw 1984). In other words, the partner who exercises more management control achieves a higher level of performance from its own point of view.

IndusCon

In IndusCon, the strategic objectives of both partners were realized (see Table 9.5). The U.S. partner had achieved its objectives of profitability and business expansion. IndusCon had been very profitable since its second year of operation. Because both partners reinvested all profit the joint venture earned in the first five years, the venture grew rapidly. Regarding market penetration, a representative of the U.S. parent made the following assessment:

> Probably a couple of companies are bigger than we are in terms of volume per year. Nevertheless, I think, the market sees us as a quality company. . . . We are definitely the leader in quality. On an overall basis, if you ask the most potential customers in China who they consider as the quality leader company, they would probably say "IndusCon."

Nonetheless, the U.S. parent perceived IndusCon as still having room to grow because its market share was still below 10 percent and the Chinese market was far from saturated.

The Chinese partner had also achieved its three objectives. First, by manufacturing locally, the joint venture enabled the Chinese to reduce its imports of industrial control equipment, its principal objective. In the past ten years of operation, IndusCon had produced a variety of control systems installed in many key Chinese industries. Second, regarding the objective of updating technology, the Chinese were satisfied to the extent that IndusCon had become an important source of high-technology products in China. Third, IndusCon's efforts to upgrade the technical capacity of the local suppliers had increased localization of material sourcing, creating a ripple effect on the Chinese economy. As a result, the Chinese government had twice selected IndusCon as one of the "best run China-foreign joint ventures" in China in recent years. The Chinese partner was satisfied with the progress of technology transfer to date, though the U.S. partner still held the key technology. Overall, IndusCon stood as the best performer among the four ventures in this study because it had achieved the objectives of both of its parents.

In IndusCon, the partners exercised equal management control, and both had achieved their strategic objectives. This finding contrasts previous studies' prediction of inferior performance in joint ventures with shared management (Killing 1983) but is consistent with Beamish's (1984, 1985, 1993) findings that shared or split control is superior for international joint ventures in developing countries. The inconsistencies between the Office Aid and IndusCon data suggest that the previously proposed relationship between control and performance (as being proportional for each parent) underspecified the relationship. The inconsistencies can be reconciled, however, if we raise the level of analysis from the individual-parent level to the between-parents level. In Office Aid, a relatively *unbalanced* level of management control (control was unequally shared) between the parents was associated with *unbalanced* levels of performance (high for the U.S. parent while low for the Chinese parent). Similarly, in IndusCon, the *balanced* management control of the partners resulted in *balanced* levels of performance (both "high" in this case). To sum up, then, balance or imbalance in partners' management control is associated with a similar pattern of performance assessed in terms of the achievement of both partners' strategic objectives.

Daily Product

Three out of the four strategic objectives of the U.S. partner—namely, learning how to do business in China, establishing credibility with the Chinese government, and earning a profit in operating the joint venture —have been completely achieved. The U.S. partner indicated that the joint venture achieved a 49 percent profit margin. With regard to the U.S. partner's fourth objective, expanding the Chinese market for personal hygiene products, some progress had been made—the venture's production had exceeded the planned capacity by 50 percent. However, their hope for market expansion had been achieved to only a limited extent.

The Chinese partner had achieved its three most important objectives: earning a profit, exporting for foreign exchange, and updating the manufacturing technology at the joint venture. The Chinese objective of growth had been achieved only to the extent that the volume of the existing products had been increased beyond the original expectation. However, since the U.S. partner had some reservations about transferring other products to the joint venture, the Chinese partner had not yet fulfilled the objective of expanding to its partner's other businesses. Nevertheless, Daily Product had been successful in meeting most of its parents' expectations. Its overall performance was much higher than Office Aid's, though slightly lower than IndusCon's.

The relationship between control and performance at Daily Product somewhat differed from what we found in the two ventures we previously described. Management control was unequally shared between the parents, but performance had been balanced, with both partners achieving their most important strategic objectives. In other words, at Daily Product unbalanced control was associated with balanced and moderately high performance. This pattern forced us to reconsider the proposed direct relationship between balanced (unbalanced) control and high (low) performance.

Further examination suggests that the superior interpartner working relationship might have accounted for the exceptional pattern between control and performance revealed by Daily Product. First, unlike the previous two ventures, in which the partners had radically different strategic goals, the Daily Product partners were able to work out some common objectives, such as profitability in hard currency. Because the partners shared a common destiny, the issue of conflict over how to operate the business was less likely to occur. Common goals may serve as an informal control mechanism that renders the pattern of formal management control less critical than it is when the partners' objectives radically diverge.

A second factor in the interpartner working relationship at Daily Product is that the partners built consensus on the specific operational goals for the joint venture. For example, both parties agreed that within the first eighteen months after start-up, the joint venture should (1) achieve annual capacity of 50 million units for product one and 4 million units for product two; (2) make a profit; (3) achieve surplus in foreign exchange; and (4) export 30 percent for product one and 70 percent for product two. These benchmarks, clearly specified in the joint venture contract and thus institutionalized, probably served as an alternative means of control for both partners to ensure that their interests were pursued. The interpartner working relationship was further strengthened in Daily Product after the first eighteen months of operation, when these specific plans had been realized. After that, "trust was no longer a problem. They trust us and leave the business to us," the U.S. partner's informant observed. Therefore, the superior working relationship between the partners may be an additional critical variable to impact performance when the management control of the partners is unequal. Another possibility is that the interpartner working relationship may have a moderating effect on the formal control-performance relationship.

Bio Tech

The U.S. parent of Bio Tech had achieved both of its strategic objectives, market share and profit. Bio Tech had been very profitable and acquired the highest market share of all international pharmaceutical joint ventures in China. The Chinese partner had achieved its first and second objectives: to update manufacturing technology and to learn the advanced Western management techniques for running a high-technology pharmaceutical enterprise. The Chinese were satisfied with the venture's business growth because it had continuously added new pharmaceutical products. However, this objective had been achieved to only a limited extent because the Chinese expectation of extending the business to the U.S. partner's other products (e.g., nutrition products) had not yet been met. Overall, like Daily Product, Bio Tech demonstrates strong performance in achieving most of its parents' objectives.

The Bio Tech data provided confirmatory evidence for the relationship between management control and performance revealed in the previous cases: equal management control was associated with balanced and relatively high performance for both partners. In fact, Bio Tech's control-performance relationships were very similar to IndusCon's.

Summary: An Enriched Model of Management Control

Our results regarding bargaining power, management control, and performance and their relationships are summarized in a grounded theory model in Figure 9.2. Among the major findings, the study identified several concrete and measurable components of each of the key variables. Two different components of bargaining power were identified: context-based and resource-based power. The sources of context-based power included the alternatives available to the joint venture partners during the partner selection and negotiation stages and the strategic importance of the joint venture to each partner. Resource-based bargaining power consisted of the partners' contribution to the venture of strategic resources and expertise in seven categories (technology and know-how, management expertise, global support, local knowledge, distribution channels, material and/or components procurement, and financial capital resources). Supporting the notion that parent control is multidimensional (Geringer and Hebert 1989), we found that parent control was exercised by each partner at the venture's board of directors level (strategic control), the venture's top management level (operational control), and organizational structural level (structural control) (i.e., the similarity of the venture's structure and organizational processes to each of the parents).

An important finding of the study concerned performance measurement, a topic of considerable debate in the literature (as discussed in chapter 7). Our interview data suggested that the achievement of the partners' founding objectives was an appropriate measure of performance. This measure reflects the nature of joint ventures as interfirm arrangements, captures both partners' perspectives on performance, and is able to assess the partner's idiosyncratic expectations.

Overall, the consistent evidence generated across all the case studies has corroborated and enriched the conceptual model: A direct, positive relationship exists between bargaining power and management control and between management control and venture performance. In addition, interpartner relationship in co-managing the joint venture may have a significant effect on venture performance.

The Survey Study

Hypotheses Tested

Building upon the results of the comparative case studies, we developed a set of hypotheses for testing in the subsequent quantitative study. These hypotheses included the following variables:

Figure 9.2 A Grounded Theory Model of Management Control in International Joint Ventures

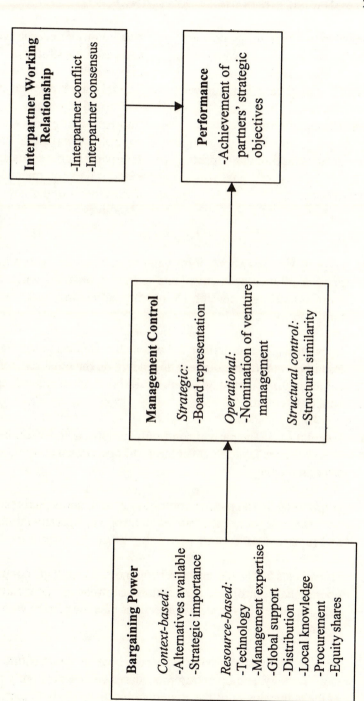

Context-based bargaining power: Availability of alternatives
                                     and venture's strategic
                                     importance
Resource-based bargaining power: Capital-based resource and
                                     noncapital resources
Management control: Strategic control, operational
                                     control, and structural control
Interpartner working relationship: Interpartner consensus and
                                     perceived interpartner conflict
Performance: achievement of partner
                                     objectives

Hypothesis 1: Within a joint venture, the partner with a greater number of alternatives available in the negotiations will achieve more (a) strategic control, (b) operational control, and (c) structural control.

Hypothesis 2: The partner for whom the venture is strategically less important (therefore less dependent on the other partner) will achieve more (a) strategic control, (b) operational control, and (c) structural control.

Hypothesis 3: The partner contributing more capital resources will exercise more (a) strategic control, (b) operational control, and (c) structural control.

Hypothesis 4: The partner contributing more noncapital resources will exercise more (a) strategic control, (b) operational control, and (c) structural control.

Hypothesis 5: The parent exercising more (a) strategic control, (b) operational control, and (c) structural control over the venture will achieve more of its strategic objectives than the partner with lesser control.

Hypothesis 6: Interpartner consensus about the joint venture's mission, strategy, and operating procedures will be positively related to the achievement of the strategic objectives for both partners.

Hypothesis 7: The perceived interpartner conflict in co-managing the joint venture will be negatively related to the achievement of the strategic objectives for both partners.

Operationalization of Variables

Most joint ventures in the sample (seventy-nine out of ninety) involved only two partners, one American, the other Chinese. For the ventures that had more than one local partners, we consolidated their response because they tend to take "party lines" in important decisions (Pearson 1991).

Achievement of Partner Objectives

We used the extent to which the partner's strategic objectives at the formation of the venture have been achieved as a performance indicator, an "approach proposed by Killing (1982) and later used by a variety of researchers" (Hebert 1994, 28). In the survey, sixteen potential objectives drawn on prior research, particularly our own inductive study, were listed. We asked the respondent to choose four most important objectives for each partner and rank them (1 to 4) according to their strategic importance. Then they rated the extent to which, at the survey's administration, each strategic objective identified had been achieved on a 7-point Likert scale ranging from "not achieved at all" to "achieved." If an objective was a long-term goal, the informant was asked to assess the extent to which the venture was on the "right track toward the achievement of this objective." We weighted the ratings by using a multiplier of $(1/n)$, where n is the nth most important objective. Specifically, Objectives 1, 2, 3, and 4 were weighted by one, a half, a third, and a quarter, respectively. In case there was a tie between two rankings, the respective weights were averaged. (While this specific weighting scheme was arbitrarily selected, we also conducted analysis without weighting under the assumption that all objectives for a partner are equally important. Both methods produced highly consistent results). An achievement score for each parent was calculated by taking the weighted average of the ratings for that parent's objectives. For example, if a partner had three strategic objectives, ranked 1, 2, and 3, with achievement rankings of 3, 5, and 1, respectively, the score of achievement for this partner would be

$$\frac{3 \times (1/1) + 5 \times (1/2) + 1 \times (1/3)}{(1/1 + 1/2 + 1/3) \times 7} = 0.46$$

where the denominator is the sum of the highest weighted ratings possible. A relative measure of achievement of partner objectives was represented by the ratio of the U.S. partner's score to the Chinese partner's.

We used the achievement of both partners' strategic objectives as a measure of overall performance, based on the assumption that a high-performing joint venture should be able to satisfy the strategic interests of all sponsors (Killing 1983). For illustration, assume that in a hypothetical joint venture, the U.S. partner had four strategic objectives (ranked as 1, 2, 3, and 4) while the Chinese partner had three (ranked as 1, 2, and 3). Further assume that the ratings for the extent to which the strategic objective had been achieved were 7, 4, 6, and 5 for the U.S. partner, and 3, 5, and 1 for the Chinese partner. The overall performance score for this venture will be:

$$\frac{7 \times (1/1) + 4 \times (1/2) + 6 \times (1/3) + 5 \times (1/4)] + [3 \times (1/1) + 5 \times (1/2) + 1 \times (1/3)}{(1/1 + 1/2 + 1/3 + 1/4) \times 7 + (1/1 + 1/2 + 1/3) \times 7} = 0.66$$

Management Control

All three dimensions of control were assessed as per the time of the joint venture's founding. Strategic control was measured by the ratio of the number of U.S. to Chinese directors on the joint venture's board. Although it would be ideal to collect both quantitative and qualitative data for this variable, it is practically very difficult and costly to do so for a large sample because of the limited access to richer, process-oriented data. Operational control was measured by nomination, as well as the decision power, of the venture's top managers. Respondents were asked to indicate which parent nominated the joint venture's general and deputy general managers (1 for nomination while 0 for non-nomination) as well as the amount of decision power exercised by each manager on a 7–point Likert scale. The operational control score is the ratio of the ratings for the U.S. and the Chinese parent, respectively. Overall, the operational control scores could vary between 0 and 7. Finally, structural control was measured on

7–point scales in terms of the similarity of the venture's organizational structure and operational processes to those of each of its parents. A measure of structural control is the ratio of the U.S. parent's aggregated score to the Chinese parent's.

Bargaining Power

The alternatives available were indicated by the number of alternative partners each party contacted or with whom it negotiated during the joint venture's founding negotiation on a scale ranging from 0 to 6 or more. The perceived importance of the venture was assessed as the perceived strategic importance of the partnership to each parent's overall business portfolio at the venture's founding. The responses were reversely coded because of the proposed negative relationship between strategic importance and control. For each variable, the ratio of the U.S. partner's score to the Chinese partner's indicates the relative contextual power between them.

Capital-based bargaining power was measured by the ratio of the U.S. partner's equity share to the Chinese partner's at the venture's founding. Measurement of noncapital-based power considered partner resource inputs in the following categories: technology, management expertise, marketing skills, material procurement channels, political clout and relational networks, and customer service. Under the assumption that bargaining power gained by contributing different types of noncapital resources is cumulative, an overall score was derived for each partner by summing this partner's contributions across the six dimensions. The ratio of the U.S. partner's score to the Chinese partner's indicated the structure of noncapital resource-based bargaining power.

Interpartner Working Relationship

The interpartner working relationship was composed of two variables: interpartner consensus and perceived interpartner conflict. Four Likert-scale items measured interpartner consensus regarding the venture's (1) overall mission and strategy, (2) structure and processes, (3) operating routines, and (4) mutual consideration of the partners. Two items were used to assess perceived interpartner conflict, including the frequency of serious interpartner conflict in the joint venture and the perception of the difficulties in co-management.

Results

Assessment of the Overall Model

The descriptive statistics and Pearson's product moment correlations for the variables are shown in Table 9.7.

Multivariate analyses (MANOVA) were performed on bargaining power, management control, the interpartner working relationship, and achievement of partner objectives to assess the overall appropriateness of the model. Results (Table 9.8) indicate that the bargaining power variables (alternatives available, partner stakes, capital resources, and noncapital resources), as a set, were significantly related to the set of management control variables (strategic, operational, and structural control), which in turn was significantly related to the achievement of the partner's strategic objectives. As predicted, the bargaining power variables as a set were not directly related to the achievement of partner objectives. A strong linkage was found between the interpartner working-relationship variables (interpartner consensus and perceived conflict), as a set, and the achievement of the strategic objectives for both partners. These results provide strong support for the theoretical soundness of the overall model presented in Figure 9.2.

Test of Hypotheses

Hypotheses 1 to 5 were tested by using path analysis, an analytical technique to identify the relative magnitudes of the direct and indirect effects of multiple sets of variables (Duncan 1971). The path analysis consisted of four regression equations:

Achievement of:

Partner objectives $= a + b1$ strategic control $+ b2$ operational control $+ b3$ structural control $+ b4$ alternatives $+ b5$ strategic importance $+ b6$ capital resource $+ b7$ noncapital resources $+ e$ (1)

Strategic control $= a + b1$ alternatives $+ b2$ strategic importance $+ b3$ capital resource $+ b4$ noncapital resources $+ e$ (2)

Operational control $= a + b1$ alternatives $+ b2$ strategic importance $+ b3$ capital resource $+ b4$ noncapital resources $+ e$ (3)

Structural control $= a + b1$ alternatives $+ b2$ strategic importance $+ b3$ capital resource $+ b4$ noncapital resources $+ e$ (4)

Table 9.7

Descriptive Statistics and Pearson Product-Moment Correlation ($n = 90$)

	Mean[a]	S.D.	1	2	3	4	5	6	7	8	9	10
1 Alternatives	1.38	1.09										
2 Strategic importance	1.30	.89	.0658									
3 Capital resource	1.07	1.17	.4307**	.0598								
4 Noncapital resources	1.22	1.37	.0753	.0782	.0703							
5 Strategic control	.82	.39	.4965**	−.0178	.6043**	.1673						
6 Operational control	1.43	1.23	.2715*	.2405*	.2747**	.3154**	.4546**					
7 Structural control	1.45	1.14	−.0243	.0473	−.0278	.2113*	.2512*	.4679**				
8 Perceived conflict	3.27	1.45	.2973**	.2576*	.2760**	.2069	.2616*	.4470**	.2182*			
9 Perception of consensus	4.42	1.18	.2200*	.0343	.3546**	.0827	.2285*	−.0187	−.2687*	−.1145		
10 Achievement of partner strategic objectives	1.11	.47	−.0112	−.1023	−.0229	.1901	.0284	.3068**	.1536	.1679	−.1421	
11 Achievement of strategic objectives for both partners	.68	.18	.0597	.1199	−.0274	.1284	.1284	−.0062	.0072	−.0628	.5374**	−.1785

* $p < .05$, ** $p < .01$

[a] The mean values of all but three variables (variables 8, 9, and 11) represent ratios measured based on a comparison between the U.S. and the Chinese partners.

Table 9.8

Multivariate Analysis Results

	Wilk's Lambda	F-statistic	df	p<	Theory confirmation
Relationship between:					
Relative bargaining power and management control structure	.4224	7.0551	12, 22	.000	Yes
Management control structure and achievement of partner strategic objectives	.8699	4.2873	3, 86	.007	Yes
Relative bargaining power and the achievement of partner strategic objectives	.9491	1.1391	4, 85	.344	Yes
Interpartner working relationship and achievement of strategic objectives for both partners	.7112	17.6649	2, 87	.000	Yes

The beta coefficients in these equations represent the path coefficients of the model and the direct effects of the antecedents (bargaining power) and the independent (management control) variables on the dependent variable (achievement of partner objectives). Table 9.9 reports the results of this analysis.

The hypothesized relationship between negotiation context-based bargaining power and management control is partially supported: Significant relationships were found between availability of alternatives and strategic control ($t = 3.22$, $p = .002$) and between strategic importance and operational control ($t = 2.06$, $p = .04$). These results confirm Hypotheses 1(a) and 2(b), respectively. The more alternatives a partner has for a joint venture, the more strategic control over it this partner will exercise; and the less important a joint venture to a partner and therefore less dependent on the partnership, the more operational control this partner is able to gain. Other relationships predicted in Hypotheses 1 and 2, however, were not supported. Significant effect was found for the rela-

Table 9.9

Results of Path Analysis

Variables	Beta[a]	t–value	R²	F–value	df
Achievement of partner strategic objectives			.1857	2.6717*	7,82
Alternatives	−.0031	−.026	.0000		
Strategic importance	−.2223	−2.128*	.0450		
Capital resource	.0400	.170	.0003		
Noncapital resources	.1114	1.057	.0111		
Strategic control	−.2627	−1.786	.0317		
Operational control	.4384	3.317***	.1093		
Structural control	−.0823	−.676	.0000		
Strategic control			.4517	17.5053***	4,85
Alternatives	.2871	3.220**	.0669		
Strategic importance	−.0744	−.922	.0055		
Capital resource	.4768	5.350***	.1846		
Noncapital resources	.1180	1.460	.0138		
Operational control			.2264	6.2191***	4,85
Alternatives	.1631	1.540	.0216		
Strategic importance	.1979	2.063*	.0387		
Capital resource	.1733	1.637	.0244		
Noncapital resources	.2755	2.870**	.0750		
Structural control			.0482	1.0768	4,8
Alternatives	−.0286	−.243	.0007		
Strategic importance	.0344	.324	.0012		
Capital resource	−.0325	−.227	.0009		
Noncapital resources	.2130	2.000*	.0448		

* $p < .05$, ** $p < .01$, *** $p < .001$.
[a] All beta coefficients are standardized.

tionship between capital-based bargaining power and strategic control ($t = 5.35$, $p = .000$), which supports Hypothesis 3(a). Thus, the party who commits more capital resources than its partner gains more strategic control. Hypotheses 3(b) and 3(c), regarding the relationships of capital resource contribution with operational or structural control, were not supported at $p < .05$. Noncapital-based bargaining power was not related to strategic control (Hypothesis 4[a)]), but its hypothesized relationships with operational control ($t = 2.87$, $p = .005$) and structural control ($t = 2.00$, $p = .05$) were significant. Therefore, Hypotheses 4(b) and 4(c) are both supported. These results suggest that the parent who gains more bargaining power by contributing more noncapital resources is able to exercise more operational and structural control, but not strategic control, over the joint venture.

Table 9.10

Achievement of Strategic Objectives for Both Partners

Variables	Beta	t–value	R^2	F-value	df
Achievement of strategic objectives for both partners			.3280	8.1987***	5,84
Perception of consensus	.5242	5.706***	.2605		
Interpartner conflict	−.0195	−.212	.0004		

*** $p < .0001$.

Regarding the effect of management control on the achievement of partner strategic objectives, support was found for operational control (Hypothesis [b]) ($t = 3.32$, $p = .001$), suggesting that the greater the control a parent exercises in the venture's operations, the greater the extent to which this parent achieves its strategic objectives. The hypothesized relationships of strategic and structural control with achievement of partner goals (Hypotheses 5[a] and 5[c]) were not supported.

The effect of the interpartner working relationship on the achievement of both partners' strategic objectives (Hypotheses 6 and 7) was tested by regression analysis (see Table 9.10). The overall regression model (with the achievement of both partners' goals as the dependent variable and the perceived interpartner consensus and level of conflict as independent variables) was significant ($p = .0000$). The relationship between interpartner consensus and the achievement of both partners' objectives (Hypothesis 6) was strongly supported ($p = .0000$). However, Hypothesis 7, regarding the predicted negative effect of interpartner conflict on the achievement of partner strategic objectives, was not supported, although the regression coefficient was correctly signed.

Implications of the Results and Explanations for the Unsupported Hypotheses

While the negotiations perspective on management control proposed in this chapter received significant support, confirmation was not generated for all hypotheses. The lack of support for the proposed effect of the availability of alternatives on operational and structural control (Hypotheses 1[b] and 1[c]) may be related to timing. Simultaneous negotiations with multiple partners-to-be are likely to occur only in the early, exploratory stage of negotiations (e.g., in partner selection). At this stage, the potential partners are likely to reach general agreement on the overall mission and the long-term strategic goals for the proposed joint venture, but details pertaining to its structure and operation may remain unclear. Thus, early negotiations may focus primarily on strategic control over the proposed partnership (Newman 1992). As our case studies indicated, potential joint venture partners in China see agreement on strategic control (reflected in ownership split) as a threshold to cross before the start of formal negotiations. "You either accept it, at least in principle, to start the negotiation; or you reject it. Then, negotiations will never happen." In this stage, the partners are most likely to manipulate their contextual-based power (e.g., alternatives available) to gain strategic control. As negotiations proceed to the later stages in which operational and structural control become central issues for bargaining, sunk costs have accumulated (e.g., extensive time that executives spend on international travel and negotiations [Mann 1989]) and partner-specific commitments have been made, thereby rendering alternative partners irrelevant and other forms of bargaining power more salient.

The effect of the venture's strategic importance was found significant on operational control, suggesting that when a partner has greater stakes in a joint venture, it will be more dependent on its partner and thereby gain lesser operational control over the venture. The predicted effects of strategic importance on strategic and structural control were not significant. A plausible explanation is that when the venture is highly important to a partner, this partner may increase its commitment toward the venture, thereby instilling confidence in its participation and enhancing this partner's bargaining position in the negotiations. Or, as Harrigan (1984) suggested, partner stakes may be paradoxical in determining bargaining power. Positive and negative perceptions of partner stakes in a venture may offset each other, producing nonsignificant net effect.

The relationship between resource-based bargaining power and parent control received strong support. First, consistent with many previous studies (e.g., Blodgett 1991; Lecraw 1984), we found that the firm that commits the greater amount of capital resources gains more strategic control. However, no effect was found for capital-based power on operational or structural control, which seemed to be more heavily affected by contribution of noncapital, tacit resources. It is clear in our results that ownership is not the only vehicle through which partners gain control. Noncapital resources, including a variety of expertise, skills, and capabilities, can serve as important leverage for shaping the control structure. This result corroborates previous findings that joint venture sponsors can gain control disproportionate to their equity holdings (Killing 1983). Given Harrigan's (1986) observation that many firms strive for at least a symbolic majority of ownership in order to win control over the joint venture's operation, our results are important to practitioners.

The effect of control structure on the achievement of partner objectives received partial support. Hypothesis 5(b) regarding the effect of operational control is supported, suggesting that control exercised by a partner over the routine operations of the joint venture, has a direct impact on the achievement of this partner's strategic objectives. This result confirms the transaction costs and agency theory arguments that the partners controlling the venture's operations employ the common pool of resources opportunistically to pursue their own interests. This relationship between operational control and performance was also evident in Hebert and Beamish's (1994) recent study of Canadian joint ventures.

The lack of effect of strategic control on the achievement of partner objectives was surprising. A factor that may account for this is the process by which strategic decisions are made. If decisions are made by the board of directors by the simple majority rule, then interpartner competitive motives will likely drive decisions that mirror the pattern of power distribution between the partners. Therefore, a closer relationship between strategic control and the achievement of partner objectives would be expected. However, if strategic decision are consensus-based, as is consistent with Japanese and Chinese cultures (Triandis 1986), strategic control would not likely have a direct effect on achievement of objectives. To this extent, our results may have reflected a unique feature of international joint ventures in China.

The unsupported effect of structural control on performance may be explained by Kilduff's (1992) argument that it is difficult for parent firms to implement their own operating routines in their international subsidiaries, because each parent's systems may be deeply rooted in certain cultural assumptions and values not necessarily shared by the joint venture. Therefore, chances for successful replication of a parent's corporate culture in the joint venture may be limited.

The strong positive association between interpartner consensus and the achievement of objectives for both parents is not surprising. Because joint ventures are high-stake, longer-term alliances, agreement between the sponsors with respect to the venture's strategic and operational goals helps to develop shared understanding between the partners and to achieve smooth coordination among the venture's operations (Hebert 1994; Hill and Hellriegel 1994). The unsupported relationship between perceived conflict and performance however, was surprising. One possible explanation is that conflict is not always counterproductive. A certain amount of conflict between the partners may stimulate creativity and improve the quality of decisions, thus positively contributing to venture success. Therefore, the unsupported effect of interpartner conflict may be a result of the inability of the two questionnaire items to distinguish subtleties in the informants' attitudes toward conflict.

Conclusions

The two empirical studies reported in this chapter strongly support the notion that joint ventures represent mixed-motive games in which competitive and cooperative dynamics occur simultaneously (Hamel, Doz, and Prahalad 1989). The significant association of the structure of operational control with a similar pattern in which the partners achieve their strategic objectives confirms the interpartner competition over how resources are allocated and what goals to pursue. Cooperative dynamics, however, were also found to be critical. The working relationship between the partners exerts a strong positive effect on the venture's overall success. To this extent, the joint venture's formal control structure and the interpartner working relationship may serve as alternative control mechanisms. Both types of control, like the clan form of organizational culture (Ouchi 1980), coexist in joint ventures and both affect performance.

Part IV

International Joint Venture Evolutions

—— 10 ——

Joint Venture Instability

This chapter offers an in-depth critique of previous research on the issues of instability of international joint ventures. We identify several major limitations of the previous literature: lack of clear conceptualizations and consistent operationalizations, lack of clarity in the relationship with performance, static focus on the eventual destination rather than developmental processes, and lack of managerial relevance. To overcome these deficiencies, we propose a significant reconceptualization in which instability is defined as a neutral, dynamic, process-based, and multifaceted phenomenon. We also propose directions for future research.

Introduction

It is a widely accepted premise that international joint ventures represent an inherently unstable and problematic organizational form (Das and Teng 1999; Franko 1971; Porter 1990). Reported instability rates of international joint ventures have ranged from 25 to 75 percent (Chowdhury 1988; Geringer and Hebert 1991). For ventures formed in developing or transforming economies, the turbulent political and economic environments together with the intercultural and interorganizational dynamics have made managing international joint ventures particularly challenging (Beamish 1993; Child and Markoczy 1991; Peng and Heath 1996; Reynolds 1979).

We intend to achieve three objectives in this chapter. First, we provide a theoretical synthesis and a critical review of previous research on

This chapter was adapted in part, with permission, from Aimin Yan and Ming Zeng. 1999. "International Joint Venture Instability: A Critique of Previous Research, a Reconceptualization, and Directions for Future Research," *Journal of International Business Studies* 30 (2): pp. 397–414.

joint venture instability. Over the past three decades, joint venture instability has been studied from different perspectives and, as a result, inconsistent empirical findings have been generated. Integration and consolidation of previous work can offer insights for further theoretical and empirical advancement. Second, we identify the major limitations in previous research. Among other deficiencies, the current literature is dominated by a static approach that treats instability as the end status of the joint venture (e.g., termination or liquidation), whereas the process aspect of the phenomenon is largely ignored. The third and the most important objective of the chapter is to provide a foundation for future research to overcome the identified deficiencies in previous research. Toward this end, we offer a comprehensive reconceptualization, in which instability is defined as a neutral, dynamic, process-based, and multifaceted phenomenon. We argue that instability is not necessarily a liability. Rather, the long-term success of international joint ventures is dependent upon effective adaptations and reconfigurations.

Below we first review prior research following three major threads: conceptualizations and operationalizations, major contributing factors, and the instability-performance relationship. Second, we critique the literature by pointing out the major limitations and deficiencies. We argue that these limitations have hampered this domain of research from making theoretical advances and contributing to joint venture practices. Third, we offer our reconceptualization of instability. Finally, we conclude with directions for future research.

Previous Research on Instability

With the rapid growth of research, it is a challenging task to review the instability literature both in breadth and in depth. In our review we primarily focus on those studies that directly and empirically examined joint venture instability. However, we analyze the issue of instability in the broader context of venture development whenever possible. While trying to be inclusive, our critique is organized around three fundamental questions: What is international joint venture instability and how has it been operationalized? What are the key contributing factors to instability? And what are the performance implications of instability? A brief sketch of the studies included in this review is listed in Table 10.1.

Table 10.1

A Summary of Previous Empirical Research on Joint Venture Instability

Study	Sample and Method	Operationalization	Key Findings
Franko (1971)	1,100 American-foreign joint ventures formed 1961–1968. Correlation and regression.	(1) Transformed to U.S. WOSs; (2) the U.S. firm increased equity to become a majority; and (3) selloff/liquidation.	28.5% instability rate. Policy changes of the partners, rather than interpartner conflicts, were responsible for international joint venture instability.
Berg and Friedman (1978)	123 domestic joint ventures in chemical industry formed 1924–1969. Tabulation.	Termination through either sell off or liquidation.	40.7% termination rate. Joint ventures are short-lived; but successful joint ventures were also found terminated.
Killing (1983)	35 international joint ventures in North America and Europe. Tabulation.	Major reorganization and termination.	35% instability rate. Joint ventures with dominant control or independent structure are more stable. Longevity is consistent with managers' perception of success.
Beamish (1984)	66 joint ventures in 27 less developed countries. Nonparametric statistics.	Major reorganization, equity changes.	Overall instability, 45%, with government partner, 58%; with foreign private partner, 23%. IJVs in developed countries more stable than those in developing countries.
Gomes-Casseres (1987)	5,933 foreign manufacturing subsidiaries of American firms 1900–1975. Tabulation.	(1) Transformed to U.S. WOSs; (2) sold to a local partner or a third party; and (3) liquidation.	33% instability rate. The rate of liquidation was lower in joint ventures than in WOSs. The rate of termination by selling off was twice as high for joint ventures as for WOSs. Instability is not equal to failure; it is often adaptive actions to changes in external environment.

(Table 10.1 continued)

Study	Sample and Method	Operationalization	Key Findings
Harrigan (1988)	895 interfirm alliances formed 1974–1985. Regression.	Termination.	54.8% termination rate. Strategic asymmetry between partners (differences in nationality, size, joint venture experience, etc.) increases instability.
Kogut (1989)	92 manufacturing joint ventures. Event history analysis.	Termination through dissolution.	29% dissolution rate. Concurrent ties among the same partners enhance stability, while changes in industry concentration and growth rates increase instability.
Kogut (1991)	92 manufacturing joint ventures. Event history analysis.	Termination through acquisition.	40% acquisition rate. Unexpected growth in the market increases the option value of the joint venture and thus its instability.
Bleeke and Ernst (1991)	49 cross-border alliances. Tabulation.	Termination through either acquisition or liquidation.	40% termination rate. Flexibility and ability to evolve beyond initial expectations are critical to joint venture success. An even split of ownership is more successful.
Blodgett (1992)	1,339 joint venture contracts. Event history analysis.	Contractual renegotiations.	Joint ventures are unstable when partners start out with uneven shares of equity, the contracts have been negotiated before, and they are formed in open economies.
Lee and Beamish (1995)	31 Korean manufacturing joint ventures in developing countries formed 1973–1988. Descriptive statistics and regression.	Equity changes and major reorganization.	19% instability rate. Stability differs between international joint ventures formed with government partners and those formed with private partners.

Makino (1995)	Japanese joint ventures in Asia. Toyo Keizai database, 1992. Nonparametric statistics.	The ratio of joint ventures terminated to total number of joint ventures formed, 1986–1991.	12.9% termination rate. Local ownership policy has no effect on performance but has negative effect on survival.
Park and Russo (1996)	204 joint ventures in electronics industry formed, 1979–1988. Event history analysis.	Termination either through liquidation or sales to a third party.	27.5% termination rate. Product stream and technology, home-industry competition, and other alliances between the same partners influence duration.
Park and Ungson (1997)	186 ventures in electronics industry formed, 1979–1988. Event history analysis.	Termination either through liquidation or sales to a third party.	No effect of cultural distance on dissolution, but U.S.-Japan ventures lasted longer than U.S.-U.S. ventures. Partner pre-venture relationships enhance stability.
Hennart, Kim, and Zeng (1998)	284 Japanese affiliates in U.S. in 1980. Event history analysis.	Three types of termination: (1) selloff; (2) liquidation; and (3) exit.	26.4% termination rate. A higher rate of exit was attributable to selloff. Factors in termination by selloff were different from those in termination by liquidation.
Hennart, Roehl, and Zietlow (1999)	57 U.S.-Japanese manufacturing joint ventures operating in the U.S. in 1980. Tabulation.	Cross-category changes in ownership structure.	63% instability rate. "Trojan horse" argument is not supported. Financial problems of the partners and/or the venture, interpartner conflict, etc. increase instability.

Instability: Conceptualization and Operationalization

Previous research has conceptualized and operationalized instability in two ways. An outcome-oriented approach characterizes instability as termination of joint ventures through various avenues or as change in the sponsors' ownership structure. A process-oriented approach, however, defines instability as major reorganizations or contractual renegotiations.

Instability as Termination or Changes in Ownership Structure

The dominant approach in literature treats instability as termination of the joint venture or change in its ownership structure. This approach was originated in Franko's (1971) pioneering study of U.S. manufacturing joint ventures abroad and was later adopted by a variety of scholars (e.g., Gomes-Casseres 1987; Hennart and Zeng 1997; Lee and Beamish 1995; Makino 1995). Franko considered three categories of instability: (1) the U.S. firm increased its ownership to more than 95 percent, thus converting it to a wholly owned subsidiary; (2) the U.S. firm increased its equity holding from a minority or 50–50 split to a majority under 95 percent; and (3) the joint venture was sold out or liquidated by mutual consent. Franko reported an instability rate of 28.5 percent.

Adopting Franko's measures, Gomes-Casseres (1987) studied 5,933 U.S. manufacturing subsidiaries abroad and reported that about a third of the ventures went through some form of ownership changes. However, he found that liquidation and bankruptcy were not primary forms of instability, accounting for only 10 percent of the unstable cases. Outright sales occurred in 37 percent of the ventures, and changes in ownership structures accounted for the remaining 52 percent of the unstable ventures. More recently, using similar measures, Hennart and Zeng (1997) studied Japanese joint ventures in the United States and observed very high ownership instability (68 percent). In contrast, relatively low instability rates have been reported among Japanese ventures in Asia (Makino 1995), Korean ventures (Lee and Beamish 1995), and joint ventures in China (Beamish 1993).

Some scholars have defined the instability concept more narrowly, that is, instability as termination (Berg and Friedman 1978; Bleeke and Ernst 1991; Harrigan 1988a; Hennart, Kim, and Zeng 1998; Kogut 1989, 1991; Makino 1995; Park and Russo 1996). Berg and Friedman (1978) measured instability as termination through either sales or liquidation, and observed an instability rate of 41 percent. Harrigan (1988a) reported that about 55 percent of the 895 interfirm alliances in her study were terminated and thus unstable. More recently, Barkema and Vermeulen (1997) built a longitudinal database of foreign entries by twenty-five Dutch multinationals in seventy-two countries between 1966 and 1994. Of the 228 IJVs in the database, 49 percent were terminated before 1994.

Kogut (1989, 1991) examined IJV termination by focusing on either dissolution or acquisition. Whereas a dissolution represents a failed IJV as a result of "either a business failure or irresolvable conflict among the partners" (1989, 187), acquisition occurs when the venture is acquired by one of the sponsoring partners or a third party due to different valuations of the joint venture. Of the ninety-two joint ventures in his sample, twenty-seven were terminated through dissolution and thirty-seven through acquisitions. Dissolution was found to be driven by changes in competitive rivalry within the venture's industry, while acquisition was driven by changes in the option values embedded in the venture's contractual agreement. Park and Russo (1996) found that, in a sample of 204 joint ventures in the electronics industry, 56 were terminated through liquidation and 82 through acquisition, representing an overall instability rate of 68 percent.

Instability as Reorganizations or Contractual Renegotiations

Several studies have paid attention to the structural and operational aspects of joint ventures. In addition to termination, Killing (1983) classified a joint venture as unstable when it had experienced a drastic shift in the venture's parent control structure. During the two-year observation period, seven out of the thirty-five joint ventures were terminated and five others underwent a major reconfiguration of their control structure due to poor performance. Therefore, about 35 percent of the ventures in this relatively small sample were categorized as unstable. Use of major reorganization as a measure of instability was also found in several other studies (e.g., Beamish 1984; Lee and Beamish 1995).

In the same vein, using joint venture data published in *Mergers and Acquisitions* between 1971 and 1981, Blodgett (1992) investigated instability by focusing on interpartner renegotiations of a prior contract. The unit of analysis of this study was the partnership contract rather than the venture itself, and incidence of contract renegotiations was used to indicate instability. The more process-oriented perspective represented by Killing (1983) and Blodgett (1992) is important because the focus has migrated from documenting the ultimate destinations/death rates of international joint ventures to investigating factors triggering or contributing to instability in operating these ventures.

Factors Contributing to Instability

In the majority of prior studies, instability has been treated as a dependent variable to signify the venture's ultimate destination. Consequently, various factors contributing to instability have been identified, including conflicts in shared management, cross-cultural differences, ownership structures, characteristics of the sponsors, and external environmental forces.

Interpartner Conflict in Co-management

A key feature of joint ventures is shared management between partners from different countries. Partners could disagree on just about every aspect of a venture's management. Therefore, interpartner conflict in co-management is often a driving force for instability (Killing 1983; Kogut 1989). Harrigan (1988a) found that differences between the partners in founding goals, strategic resources, and corporate cultures were responsible for shorter joint venture duration. On the other hand, joint ventures between direct competitors were found more likely to fail because potential interpartner competition and conflict undermined the partnerships (Park and Russo 1996; Park and Ungson 1997). Most recently, Das and Teng (1999) argue that joint venture instability occurs as a result of internal tensions developed within the partnership. From this point of view, joint ventures become unstable under the effect of several pairs of competing forces influencing the venture partners: cooperation versus competition, rigidity versus flexibility, and short-term versus long-term orientation.

Cross-cultural Differences

Cultural differences often influence the way in which the partners in a joint venture make strategic decisions and solve problems. For example, Japanese and American managers tend to see interfirm alliances very differently: The former treat them as primarily interpersonal relationships whereas the latter see them as enduring by design, irrespective of the specific managers involved (Turner 1987). Jones and Shill (1993,

131) point out that in international partnerships in Japan, cross-cultural differences "lead to endless, energy-and-time consuming debates—futile talk that produces a lot of heat and prevents the company making the decisions it has to." The positive effect of cultural differences on joint venture instability has also been evidenced in empirical studies with larger samples (Hennart and Zeng 1997; Li and Guisinger 1991; Pennings, Barkema, and Douma 1994; Shenkar and Zeria 1992). However, the findings of several recent studies demonstrate that the relationship between partner cultural differences and venture stability may be more complex and inconclusive than previous research has suggested. For example, Barkema and Vermeulen (1997) argue that the different dimensions of cross-cultural differences between joint venture partners might have different effects on the venture's instability. Based on Hofstede's (1984) typology, they found that interpartner differences in uncertainty avoidance and long-term orientation have a significant negative impact on joint venture survival, while differences in power distance, individualism, and masculinity did not affect survival. Similarly, Park and Ungson (1997) tested the effect of interpartner cultural differences on dissolution of joint ventures but found no support for most of the hypothesized relationships. However, they found a significant effect of interpartner nationality on venture termination, but in an opposite direction to previous findings: The greater the cultural distance, the less likely the venture is to dissolve.

Control/Ownership Structures

The structure of parent control has been found to influence venture instability, although the direction of this effect remains ambiguous. Killing (1993) found that a dominant management structure can minimize coordination costs and hence outperform shared control joint ventures. However, an unequal division of ownership may give the majority holder greater power, which may be used to the detriment of the minority owner. Therefore, a balanced ownership structure in which partners' bargaining power is evenly matched is more likely to produce mutual accommodations (Harrigan 1988). Empirically, Bleeke and Ernst (1991) found that alliances with an even split ownership had a higher success rate (60 percent) than ventures dominated by one company (31 percent). Beamish (1984) found that performance was enhanced when control was shared between the foreign and the local partner. Performance suffered, however, when the foreign partner exercised dominant control. Several recent dissertation research studies (Hebert 1994; Yan 1993, 1998) found that control over the joint venture's daily operations exerted the strongest effect on venture performance. Nevertheless, at a more general level, the control-performance relationship is nonlinear and more complex than previous researchers expected, and is likely to be contingent upon other organizational and interorganizational variables.

Characteristics of Parents

Franko (1971) concluded that policy changes in the multinational enterprise (MNE) partner were responsible for joint venture instability. When an MNE decides to tighten control over its foreign subsidiaries, it is likely to turn some joint ventures into wholly owned subsidiaries. Other partner characteristics, such as a parent firm's financial problems (Hennart, Roehl, and Zietlow 1999) and the partners' prior experience in joint venturing (Harrigan 1988a; Makino and Delios 1996; Park and Russo 1996) were also found to influence instability.

External Environments

Changes in external environments, such as local government policies and industry structures, may also influence joint venture instability. It has been widely documented that unanticipated major changes in local political environments (e.g., changes in government policies regarding foreign direct investment in general and equity joint ventures in particular) affect international business operations and contribute to venture instability (Blodgett 1992; Boddewyn and Brewer 1994; Brewer 1992; Vernon 1977). The past several decades have witnessed such drastic changes in many countries (Contractor 1990; Vachani 1995; Yan and Gray 1994).

Industrial dynamics may also influence the evolution of joint ventures. For example, joint ventures are found to be less stable in industries that experience intensive consolidation or volatile growth (Hennart and Zeng 1997; Kogut 1989, 1991).

Relationship to Performance/Success

Most previous studies have not examined instability and performance simultaneously and are therefore unable to establish an unequivocal relationship between the two variables. As an exception, Harrigan's (1988a) study included duration and sponsor-perceived success as well as stability as indicators of performance. In her sample, 66.7 percent of the "unstable" ventures were judged as unsuccessful by one or more sponsors, echoing a high correlation between instability and partners' assessment of performance. Killing (1983) used both longevity and parent assessments of performance to indicate joint venture success. The two measures were found consistent in assessing the failure cases in his sample. Similarly, Geringer and Hebert (1991) argue that longevity provides a necessary condition and a good proxy for international joint venture success.

Other researchers, however, have questioned the linkage between instability and performance. For example, using termination as a measure of instability, Berg and Friedman (1978) documented several cases in which a joint venture was terminated, not because of failure but as an outcome of success. They argue that a successful venture can become critical to one of its parent's overall businesses, therefore prompting this parent to turn the venture into a wholly owned subsidiary. Gomes-Casseres (1989) also argued that joint ventures may be terminated because they have successfully accomplished their initial objectives. The intended purpose of joint ventures typically is temporary and short-term in scope (Davidson 1982; Fayerweather 1982; Porter 1990). Whenever the joint venture's strategic mission is successfully achieved (e.g., a successful transfer of technology or the accomplishment of a specific joint research project), the venture is no longer needed. In these cases, the dissolution of the joint venture should be recorded as a success instead of a failure.

In fact, many successful joint ventures were found to undertake structural changes, but they did so as adaptive actions to changed external environments or internal strategies of their parents (Gomes-Casseres 1989; Yan and Gray 1994). Hennart, Kim, and Zeng's (1998) study reported clear differences between different types of instability (measured as termination by sell-offs versus liquidation). They found that variables that have been predicted to affect venture instability only influence the possibility of sell-off, not that of liquidation. Therefore, it would be misleading to treat instability as synonymous with failure.

To summarize, while most researchers conceptually agree that the linkage of instability to performance is more than complex, many used the former as a proxy for the later. Little research has been done to investigate the relationship and possible interactions between the two variables.

Limitations and Deficiencies in Stability Research

The above review suggests that significant research has been conducted to explore the phenomenon of joint venture instability. These studies have not only appropriately identified instability as a critical issue for research, but also contributed to our understanding of the fragility of international partnerships. It is arguable that the investigation of instability has become one of the most active domains of scholarly work in international management (Parkhe 1993). However, the literature is deficient in some important aspects, as we discuss below.

Conceptualization and Operationalization

While instability of international joint ventures has long been a major subject of study (Parkhe 1993), until very recently the literature lacked a theoretical definition for the concept. Most studies do not provide a conceptualization but "define" it by operationalizing it. Given the lack of theoretical work, not surprisingly, the empirical literature features a variety of measures of instability, ranging from dissolution and reorganization to renegotiation of contracts. Multiple ways to terminate a venture are also documented.

The use of different measures is not a problem per se. The problem rests in the fact that prior researchers have paid little attention to articulating the relationship between the specific measures they elect to use and the operational schemes adopted by others. Therefore, we know little about the relationships between the various measures of instability. To make the situation worse, the choice of a particular measure is often data-driven—more for the researcher's convenience or data availability than for theoretical rigor. These problems clearly have contributed to the noncumulative nature of previous findings. Since each measure used may be aligned with a unique set of theoretical assumptions or rationales (unfortunately, in many cases these assumptions or rationales are not explicitly specified), it is likely to produce highly idiosyncratic results (Kogut 1989; 1991). In addition, much previous work has depended solely upon static, second-hand data sources. For example, it is common that a joint venture is operationally categorized as "terminated" when, for potentially numerous unknown reasons, it fails to appear in the next issue of the same report.

Scholars of international joint ventures today have learned to be, and probably have become accustomed to being, extremely cautious when reading and interpreting previous findings. To what degree are the various measures different or correlated? To what extent is a specific measure appropriate to joint ventures across different populations? While some good exploratory efforts have been made (e.g., Geringer and Hebert 1991; Gomes-Casseres 1987; Hennart, Kim, and Zeng 1998), the above fundamental questions largely remain unanswered.

Relationship to Performance/Success

In the current literature, the instability-performance relationship remains unclear. While most researchers agree that instability is not equivalent to failure, operationally, many insist that longevity is a key measure of success and that termination indicates failure. Even Inkpen and Beamish's (1997) definition, the most conceptual and comprehensive so far, treats instability as something undesirable as it stresses the "unplanned and premature" nature of instability. The lack of clarity in the relationship between instability and performance has created difficulty in understanding previous research results, hindered communication among scholars, and significantly undermined the theoretical and practical value of prior research findings.

End Destinations as Instability

Previous work on instability (and on international alliances in general) has been dominated by a static approach (Doz 1996; Parkhe 1993a; Westney 1988) in which the focus is placed on the venture's end consequence, such as sell-out, acquisition, liquidation, or bankruptcy. The dynamic process by which stability or instability develops has been largely ignored in previous research.

Using the end consequences of joint ventures to conceptualize and operationalize instability has value, if the focus is placed on tracing the contributing factors to instability rather than counting the death rates. However, this approach has significant limitations. First, it is conceptually problematic to assert that all terminated ventures are unstable, because termination may be anticipated or "planned" by the partners at founding (Inkpen and Beamish 1997; Kogut 1989). It is equally problematic, on the other hand, to assume that all ventures that have not yet been terminated are stable. Joint ventures do not change from stable to unstable the night before their termination. Second, most previous studies used ownership changes as a proxy for instability. This approach is limited because instability can be multidimensional, as reflected in changes in the joint venture's strategy, core business processes, key products and markets, and partner contributions of critical resources. Without considering the developmental process, it is impossible to gain a rich understanding of these multiple manifestations of instability. The nature of instability can only be ascertained with detailed knowledge of the actual evolution of joint ventures (Doz 1996).

Practical Relevance

The commonly asked "so what" question is appropriate to pinpoint the lack of practical relevance of previous research on instability. What are the key managerial implications of the research findings produced over the past several decades? It is a challenging question for joint venture scholars to answer; but a good one to reflect upon. For example, from a modal choice viewpoint, we have warned practitioners that international joint ventures are more unstable than wholly owned subsidiaries, and that many joint ventures eventually turn out to be corporate odd couples. Even such general caution has not been effective, because in the past two decades a radical proliferation, rather than a decrease, of cross-border partnerships has been witnessed in both the United States and worldwide (Anderson 1990; Geringer and Hebert 1991). The real practical value of joint venture instability research rests on providing practitioners with insights regarding how to manage the venture's evolution, particularly how to reconfigure its structures and take adaptive actions over time in order to strengthen performance and prevent premature death. To this end, we now propose a reconceptualization of instability.

Reconceptualization of Joint Venture Instability

Recent Theoretical Progress

Since the last decade, several significant attempts have been made to explore the process in which instability of joint ventures evolves. For example, the interpartner competitive learning perspective (Hamel 1991; Inkpen and Beamish 1997; Lyles 1994) has provided a powerful explanation for venture termination. This perspective argues that venture partners are engaged in a race for learning to acquire each other's skills, resources, and competencies. Once one of the partners has successfully accomplished its learning objectives, the race is over and the partnership is terminated. This view was originally advanced by Hamel (1991) and further developed in Inkpen and Beamish (1997). Building upon the bargaining power argument (Harrigan and Newman 1990; Yan and Gray 1994), they argue that changes in bargaining power balance resulting from interpartner learning represent a key source of instability. Conceptually, they define instability as "a major change in relationship status that was unplanned and premature from one or both partners' perspectives" (p. 182). This definition, arguably the first to be theory-based, has considered a wide range of changes in IJVs, going beyond shifts in ownership structures or termination.

Another notable contributor is Doz (1996), who provided a detailed account of the interactions between initial conditions and organizational learning and the subsequent impact on the evolution of cooperation within joint ventures. The evolution of a venture is characterized by cycles of learning, re-evaluation, and readjustment. Initial conditions may determine alliance outcomes when these conditions are highly inertial and prevent meaningful learning between partners. Most recently, Yan (1998) provides an analysis of both the driving and the restraining forces for joint venture instability from an organizational theory angle. Drawing upon the organization stability/change paradox (Poole and Van de Ven 1989), it is argued that unexpected environmental and organizational contingencies, undesirable venture performance, obsolescing bargain, and interpartner competitive learning are major sources of IJV instability. On the other hand, the initial conditions of the venture—for example, the political and legal environments at the venture's founding, its initial resource mix, the balance of partner bargaining power, and the pre-venture relationship between the partners—serve as stabilizing forces for joint ventures. It is argued that joint ventures evolve under the effect of both sets of forces (see next chapter for a detailed discussion).

Reconceptualization

While development of a full theory lies beyond the scope of this chapter, we want to reconceptualize instability and to pinpoint several key dimensions of the concept. We propose that instability research refocus on the process of joint venture development, reveal the dynamic evolution and changes over the venture's life, offer insights on the effect of these changes on venture performance, and provide useful, practitioner-friendly implications with respect to initiation and management of organizational changes in joint ventures. Toward this objective, we provide the following redefinition:

> Instability refers to the extent to which the joint venture alters its strategic directions, renegotiates its contract/agreements, reconfigures its ownership and/or management structures, or changes the relationship with its parents or the relationship between the parents that may have a significant effect on the venture's performance.

Neutralization

This redefinition consists of several characteristics. First, the concept is neutralized. Because instability and stability are each defined as the opposite of the other, a value-based judgement of either term is biased and incomplete. If stability were assumed to be the primary, fundamental organizational state, instability would be defined as aberrations from the stable state or upheavals disrupting stability. However, from an organizational change perspective, organizations are not stable—they continuously evolve and are being renewed and reproduced over time (Poole and Van de Ven 1989). From this perspective, stability would be strange and abnormal. Perrow (1987) argues that although stability may stand for steadfastness and predictability, it can also represent stagnancy and unadaptiveness. Similarly, instability may signify change, adaptation, and progress as well as turbulence and unpredictability. Changes in joint ventures should be no surprise, as the ability to adapt has often been cited as one of the most important factors in joint venture success (Doz 1996; Killing 1983). Rather, it would be surprising if a joint venture remained unchanged over a long period of time. Organizational restructuring/reengineering has become an overwhelmingly popular practice worldwide, but no one seems to be alarmed by the vast instability created by such practices. Then, why should we be impatient about similar changes in international joint ventures? The following quote is illustrative:

> Alliances are often criticized as unstable because many of them last only several years. But compared to what? Are partnerships less stable, in gen-

eral, than organizational arrangements inside firms? In the 1980s, General Electric created roughly 100 strategic alliances; some prospered, others failed, and many needed redesign during their lives. But in the same period, General Electric reorganized itself dramatically, reduced total employment by 100,000, and bought and sold scores of businesses. GM and IBM both overhauled their internal operations and organization in the 1980s, and then made a multitude of corrections and refinements. During this period of organizational earthquakes and aftershocks inside GE, GM, and IBM, were the core operations of the companies less turbulent than their alliances? (Badaracco 1991, 127–128)

From the Static Outcome to the Dynamic Process

Our reconceptualization of instability calls for a shift from a static, ultimate outcome–oriented approach to a dynamic, process-oriented approach. Stability, or lack thereof, describes a pattern of behavior (of a physical subject, an individual or, by extension, a social or organizational entity) or alterations of the pattern over a period of time. A key dimension embedded in the concept is that it is longitudinal. It is necessary to study instability (or stability) as a process if the way in which original behavior, status, or structure is altered over time and the causes behind the observed changes are to be revealed. While outcome-based studies contribute to an understanding of the consequences of instability, a process-based approach is essential to capture the causes and dynamic development of instability. For example, while trust between joint venture partners has been proposed as a key factor in venture success, little is known about the process and mechanisms through which interpartner trust is established and maintained over time. As Madhok (1995) argues, a shift in focus from "ownership to relational dynamics" between joint venture partners is essential to our understanding of the evolution of joint ventures.

Relationship to Performance

The shift in focus to the dynamic process of joint ventures changes instability from a dependent to an independent variable. This change is nontrivial because it opens a new ground for theoretical and empirical exploration of the relationship between instability and performance. The complex but rich dynamics in the venture's evolution will present numerous contingencies for researchers to explore. Consequently, it may be arbitrary to claim a restructuring effort as good or bad because instability may exert positive and/or negative effects on joint ventures, or, as Blodgett (1992, 481) speculated, have nothing to do with performance. Similarly, the feedback effect of performance on instability also warrants attention. As previous research has revealed, superior performance is able to stabilize structural changes and reduce interpartner conflict and power struggles, as well as change the relative bargaining power of the partners (Yan and Gray 1994). On the contrary, poor performance often creates conflict and suspicion between partners, which in turn bring quick demise of the joint venture (Doz 1996).

The Multiple Facets of Instability

Instability is a multifaceted concept. First, new contingencies may be created when the joint venture redirects its strategic foci, changes its key objectives, repositions in the markets, or undertakes major growth or downsizing. These changes may be necessitated or prompted by environmental and interorganizational, as well as intraorganizational, factors. Second, instability occurs when the partners renegotiate contracts. The joint venture contract and major agreements (e.g., on technology transfer or management licensing) define the legal and institutional frameworks in which the venture operates. Any significant changes or attempts to change will make the venture unstable. Third, as well documented in the literature, reconfiguration of the venture ownership/control structure represents a major source of instability, because such changes create new bargaining dynamics and/or alter strategic stakes of the partners.

A fourth facet of instability concerns the venture's relationship with each parent and the relationship between parents. The joint venture becomes unstable when changes occur in the amount of decisional autonomy rendered to the venture's management or in the venture's role in each parent's overall business (e.g., the parent-venture quasi-internal transactions). Changes in interpartner relationship may result from major shifts in their relative bargaining power (Yan and Gray 1994), competitive learning (Hamel 1991; Inkpen and Beamish 1997), emergence/resolution of disputes and conflict, or building/deconstruction of trust between them (Madhok 1995).

In summary, our reconceptualization of joint venture instability helps reconcile inconsistencies in the literature (e.g., on the instability-performance relationship), integrates research on the different facets/aspects of instability, and opens a wide range of new research opportunities. Next, we offer several directions for future research.

Conclusions and Future Research Directions

By providing a comprehensive review and critique of the literature on instability, a key purpose of this chapter is to consolidate and integrate previous research. We contend that, by identifying the various conceptual and operational approaches to instability and revealing their interrelations, such an integration effort is useful for advancing research on international joint ventures. In this regard, our proposed reconceptualization of instability may serve as a fundamental first step toward future theory building. Now we offer the directions for future research.

First, a consistent conceptualization and operationalization of instability is essential for cross-study comparisons and, thus, knowledge accumulation. The proposed reconceptualization provides a possible framework to integrate different dimensions of instability. While substantial progress in this direction might take a long time, at the very least, studies should be clear in defining and measuring instability, articulating relationships with prior definitions and measures, and considering the underlying theoretical and methodological problems associated with a particular choice. If research focus is placed on instability as an outcome—thus, a dependent variable—independent variables need to be clearly defined and the relationship theoretically explored. However, as we argued above, instability is better treated as a multifaceted process variable; hence, integrative studies that examine the interactions among the multiple dimensions of instability are especially needed to advance theory building. For example, future research needs to spell out the relationships between contract renegotiations and strategic changes, and between changes in ownership structure and reconfiguration of the venture's management control structure.

Second, the proposed shift to a dynamic, process-oriented approach to instability is crucial for future research. The current joint venture literature has paid considerable attention to either the very beginning of the venture (in the tradition of modal choices) or the ultimate end of the venture (as reflected in the current research on stability), while the midlife of joint ventures has been left understudied, at best (Doz 1996). The complexity and richness of international joint venture as a unique form of organization rests on its cross-cultural and cross-organizational interactions. While focusing on only the opening and the closing games, current research has missed the most exciting and arguably the most challenging part of the story. One of the most promising areas for future research is to reveal the process by which joint venture development unfolds and thus offer insightful implications on how to initiate and manage organizational changes on an ongoing basis. While both conceptual and empirical work on the dynamic aspects of joint ventures has started to accumulate (e.g., Doz 1996; Hamel 1991; Inkpen and Beamish 1997; Yan 1998; Yan and Gray 1994), the field is in serious need of more rigorously designed, process-oriented, data-rich studies.

Third, future research has to offer convincing evidence on the instability-performance linkage. Making the concept of instability free from value judgment represents only the first step. Consistent with our reconceptualization, recent attention has been paid to the performance effect of internal and external changes in joint ventures, such as contract renegotiations (Blodgett 1992), interpartner competitive learning and knowledge transfers (Hamel 1991; Inkpen and Beamish 1997; Lyles 1994), and changes in bargaining power and reconfiguration of control structures (Inkpen and Beamish 1997; Yan 1998; Yan and Gray 1994). Future research should also examine the feedback effect of venture performance on instability. Killing (1983) initially observed the phenomenon that superior performance stabilizes joint ventures. Yan and Gray provided additional evidence for the performance feedback effect on changes in interpartner relative bargaining power and parent control structure (1994), and offered a conceptual framework that specifies how the levels of partner and venture management satisfaction prompt structural modification, reconfiguration, and termination (1995).

Fourth, both conceptual and empirical research are needed to compare and contrast the unique as well as common challenges in managing wholly owned subsidiaries, joint ventures, and other types of alliance. On one hand, Gomes-Casseres (1987) argues that instability in joint ventures and other organizational forms might be driven by the same set of factors. On the other hand, Inkpen and Beamish (1997) insist that the factors associated with joint venture instability are not necessarily the same as those for all types of alliance; therefore, generalization of the findings should be made with caution. The issue of instability in joint ventures can only be understood when compared with instability of other types of organizational forms (Hennart, Kim, and Zeng 1998). Future work should spell out the unique dynamics in each form, and at the same time identify the features shared by all forms. Cross-population comparisons, however, should be theoretically and methodologically rigorous and go beyond superficial contrasts of death rates.

Finally, we want to stress the issue of methodology in future research on instability. Our reconceptualization calls for a methodological readjustment. Changes in the venture's ownership and control structures, parent strategic objectives, and interpartner relationships, as well as the multiple-way interactions among these factors, and in the venture's performance require in-depth, longitudinal data and repeated-measure designs (Doz 1996). Simply relying on second-hand data and sophisticated statistical packages, as many previous studies did, is no longer adequate. In order to build rigorous joint venture theories, more inductive, grounded theory-building efforts are also warranted.

A Mini-Case Example

The Dunlop-Pirelli Union

The joint venture between Dunlop and Pirelli that began in 1970 and failed in 1979 has been analyzed in detail. These two leading European rubber and tire companies intended to integrate completely. Since the venture was both extensive and well publicized, much is known about the conditions leading to its demise. Its original, stated goals were to share R&D costs and risks, to reduce production costs, and to expand marketing opportunities. Geographical diversification, greater pooled financial resources, and stronger purchasing power were also expected.

Despite initial enthusiasm for establishing common management, Dunlop and Pierlli held separate preliminary meetings prior to their common monthly Central Committee meeting. They were unable to stop these preliminary meetings, and eventually the joint monthly meetings served merely as a forum to inform the other side of unilateral decisions. At the lower functional and operational levels, an effort to maintain equality in exchanges paralyzed decision making. Specifically, both sides were reluctant to share or adopt the other's technology, while the distribution networks were in direct competition.

Fundamentally, the two companies emphasized different paths to success. Whereas Pirelli believed it was absolutely vital to invest for new product development, which reflected its underlying industrial culture, Dunlop cut investment in a short-term perspective to improve financial performance, reflecting a strong adherence to its financial culture.

Nevertheless, the partnership was severely damaged when Pirelli was unable to meet its new-product-development target for radial tires. After the company invested heavily to create this new product, Pirelli's radial tire was a commercial failure, its production decreased 20 percent, and its Italian market share fell 5.5 percent. Dunlop lost confidence in Pirelli, wrote off its investment, and declined to participate in a recapitalization plan to restructure Pirelli's tire operations.

In essence, both companies moved apart at this juncture. Pirelli persisted with new product development, which eventually paid off. Moreover, it applied many of Dunlop's superior financial controls, and better coordinated its own international subsidiaries, partly as a result of its experience with Dunlop. While Pirelli focused on improving its own internal operations, Dunlop was preoccupied with measures intended to tighten financial control and to shore up short-term profitability.

In the end, Dunlop found itself with no new competitive products and obsolete production capacity as its market share in the United Kingdom declined in the face of foreign competition. In March 1979, Dunlop requested a 25 million pound sterling contribution from Pirelli to its restructuring plan. This investment request ultimately precipitated soon thereafter the termination of their very large joint venture.

(Adapted from The Conference Board, Report Number 1028: *Strategic Alliances: Guidelines for Successful Management*, p. 22. This case summary was based on *The Dunlop-Pirelli Union* case prepared under the direction of Professor Sumantra Ghoshal, London Business School.)

—— 11 ——

Structural Stability and Reconfiguration

Although it is a dominant premise that international joint ventures represent an inherently unstable and fragile form of organization, previous literature has failed to explain why many international joint ventures have an extended longevity and stability. In the last chapter we examined instability at a rather broad level. In this chapter, we focus on a specific dimension of instability—stability in the venture's management control structure. We draw upon the organization theory literature to develop two contrasting perspectives: structural instability and structural inertia, to trace both the destabilizing and the stabilizing forces in joint venture development. We argue that the structural stability of international joint ventures depends on the balance and interactions between the two sets of forces. A complete understanding of joint venture dynamics and evolution requires consideration of both forces.

Introduction

Despite the challenges of managing international joint ventures, a rapid proliferation of cross-border partnerships has been witnessed over the past several decades. The number of international cooperative arrangements formed in the 1980s exceeded the total number of international alliances created in all prior years combined (Geringer and Hebert 1991). Alliance formation in the United States has been growing at an annual rate of more than 25 percent since 1985 (Beamish and Inkpen 1995). From a practical point of view, the high growth of cross-border joint ventures justifies them as an effective strategy for internationalization.

This chapter was adapted in part from Aimin Yan. 1998. "Structural Stability and Reconfiguration of International Joint Ventures." *Journal of International Business Studies* 29 (4): 773–796. Reprinted with permission.

Successful joint ventures have frequently been observed, and some of them survive and prosper for many years (Beamish and Inkpen 1995; Killing 1983). Even among terminated ventures, many represent an accomplishment of the partners' initial expectations, and thus signify a success (Gomes-Casseres 1987). In countries like China, where the political and business environments have been perceived by the West as particularly uncertain, high stability and success rates of Western joint ventures have been reported (Beamish 1993; Davidson 1987; Newman 1992; Yan 1993).

These inconsistent observations present a challenging paradox, which previous research has not adequately addressed. On the one hand, the stream of research that stresses the inherent instability of international joint ventures fails to explain why many such ventures can survive and succeed over a long period of time. On the other hand, the literature does not provide a convincing theoretical rationale for successful ventures. At the center of the challenge is the critical task of identifying both the stabilizing and destabilizing forces in joint ventures. Although various factors have been reported as contributing to venture instability, prior research results have been noncomparable and noncumulative (Parkhe 1993b). Particularly the factors that stabilize joint ventures have received little attention.

The inconsistency in observations of instability may be theoretically rooted in the long-standing controversy between organizational stability and change in organization sciences (Poole and Van de Ven 1989). Like independent organizations, joint ventures are expected to be under the influence of both stabilizing and destabilizing forces. Because of their intercultural and interorganizational hybrid nature, however, the tension between stability and change in joint ventures may be considerably more complex than in single, stand-alone organizations. In this chapter, we take a theoretical approach to identify and analyze both the driving and restraining forces for structural reorganization in international joint ventures. We focus particularly on instability of joint venture governance and control structure, arguably one of the most active areas of joint venture research (Parkhe 1993). Because of the competitive and opportunistic behaviors in which the partners are likely to engage (Hamel 1991; Kogut 1989) and the impact of control on venture performance (Hebert 1994; Killing 1983; Lecraw 1984; Yan and Gray 1994), parent control structures and their change over time are critical issues for both scholars and practitioners.

The purpose of this chapter is to theoretically contribute to a more comprehensive understanding of the dynamic evolution of international joint ventures. The chapter proceeds as follows: After a brief literature review, the driving and restraining forces for restructuring in joint ventures are identified from the structural instability and the structural inertia perspective. This analysis results in several proposed relationships about structural reconfiguration in joint ventures for future empirical examination. Finally, the two sets of forces are combined into an integrative framework, and the implications of the framework are highlighted.

Previous Literature on Joint Venture Development

Previous research has paid significant attention to the early stages of joint venture development, such as formation. Scholars have focused on comparing joint ventures with other entry modes and on the associated incentive schemes from the multinational firm's perspective (Anderson and Gatignon 1986; Beamish and Banks 1987; Chi and McGuire 1996; Gomes-Casseres 1990; Hennart 1988; Hill, Hwang, and Kim 1990; Kogut 1988; Li 1995; Nordberg, Campbell, and Verbeke 1996; Tallman and Shenkar 1994), selecting appropriate partners and/or parent control structures (Geringer 1988; Geringer and Hebert 1989; Harrigan 1986; Killing 1983; Tomlinson 1970), and formulating strategies for and managing joint venture negotiations (Tung 1984, 1988; Weiss 1987, 1990). These research streams have generated useful insights about conditions leading to the venture's formation, and have increased our understanding about a series of important static decisions regarding alternative organizational designs, partner selection, governance and control structures, and negotiation strategies. What is less well understood, however, is the dynamic development of joint ventures after their inception, and the process by which the relationship between the partners unfolds.

Among the studies that have examined joint ventures beyond the formation stage, theoretical and methodological problems have been widely noticed. As we discussed in the previous chapter, lack of clarity and consistency in conceptualizing and operationalizing instability has been a concern of researchers for quite a while. Also, previous studies, with few exceptions (e.g., Blodgett 1992; Killing 1983), have focused on the termination of joint ventures, such as acquisition, liquidation, or bankruptcy, to characterize instability. The current literature has failed to provide theoretical explanations for the environmental and organizational forces that trigger instability, and the mechanisms through which instability occurs. We argue that an understanding of the key driving and restraining forces for joint venture restructuring is pivotal. The usefulness and relevance of joint venture research rest on its ability to suggest managerial actions that address instability rather than simply document the frequency of already terminated, thus "unstable," ventures. While researchers have called for more "process-oriented research on how the deals are managed once they are made" (Westney 1988, 346), the process of joint venture development has received "the least amount of systematic attention in the existing literature," representing "a critical omission in the development of a more complete theory of international joint ventures" (Parkhe 1993b, 234).

A critical aspect of joint venture development concerns changes in parent control structure over time. Because of the potential effect of control structure on venture performance, it is particularly important to study the process of structural change. In chapter 6, we defined parent control in joint ventures as the extent to which the sponsors of a joint venture influence its strategic and important operational decisions, and structure of parent control as the relative pattern in which the partners divide power in managing and governing the joint venture. However, previous research on control structure has been dominated by a static approach in which control and its determinants and effects are examined without considering changes over time. While studies examining the dynamic development of joint ventures are increasing, with few notable exceptions (Doz 1996; Inkpen and Beamish 1997; Hamilton and Singh 1991; Yan and Gray 1994), the specific forces driving toward or against structural reconfiguration, and the mechanisms through which structural changes, or resistance to them, affect venture performance have largely remained unstudied.

Focusing on the developmental process of joint ventures, we refer to structural reconfiguration as the extent to which the venture changes its structure of governance over time, so that significant reallocations of management control occur between the partners and/or between the parents and the venture management. A joint venture is structurally unstable if control over its strategic and operational management shifts frequently between the parent firms. However, it is structurally stable if its control structure remains unchanged for extended periods of time.

Driving and Restraining Forces for Structural Reconfiguration

Poole and Van de Ven (1989) argue that incompatible or inconsistent theoretical perspectives, which create "paradoxes," are an important resource for building management and organization theories. They further indicate that the tension between stability and change in organizations exemplifies such a paradox. In this section, we conceptually specify the driving and restraining forces for structural configuration in international joint ventures by considering two mutually opposing perspectives: the structural instability perspective and the perspective of structural inertia.

Although the theories advanced in this chapter can be applicable to all joint ventures, for simplicity of presentation we follow previous researchers (Geringer and Hebert 1989; Killing 1983) by assuming that a joint venture is sponsored by two parents (one foreign and one local). To the extent that joint ventures in developing countries may differ from their counterparts in developed countries, this chapter may be especially relevant to international ventures in developing economies.

The Structural Instability Perspective

This perspective portrays joint ventures as a transitional organizational form, which is inherently unstable by design (Davidson 1982; Porter 1990). "Joint ventures are a transitional form of management—an intermediate step on the way to something else" (Harrigan 1986, 193). While the dynamic nature of joint ventures has been discussed from different angles, the literature reveals four distinct explanations for structural changes and instability: instability prompted by unexpected contingencies; undesirable venture performance; obsolescing bargain with the local parties; and interpartner competitive learning. Each is discussed in detail below.

Unexpected Contingencies

Theoretically rooted in the contingency theory perspective (Lawrence and Lorsch 1967), this explanation attributes structural changes to organizational adaptation in which organizations alter their internal configurations to fit the new, changing environment. In the joint venture setting, structural instability is caused by contingencies unforeseeable at the venture's founding. As Harrigan (1986, 34) notes, "changes will occur in every venture's design because managers rarely can anticipate exactly how their agreement to cooperate will evolve." She further identifies a range of change stimuli leading to interpartner renegotiations. These stimuli emerge as a result of changes in the sponsors' strategies and bargaining power, changes in the venture's strategic importance to the parents, shifts in the parent-venture balance with respect to coordination and control, and dynamics in the venture's industry structure. Lecraw (1984) indicates that renegotiations will lead to an adjustment of ownership share if the relative bargaining position between the partners changes. Similarly, changes in a partner's ownership preference may be warranted when changes occur in a specific asset contributed by this partner (e.g., maturity of a technology) (Kobrin 1988).

A major source of unanticipated changes is the local political environment (i.e., government policies regarding foreign direct investment in general, and equity joint ventures in particular). Over the past several decades, drastic changes in host governments' attitudes toward foreign direct investment have been documented as a result of ideological transformation, the dynamics of global or regional politics, or bilateral relationships between countries, and increased globalization of the world economy (Contractor 1990; Vachani 1995; Vernon 1977). Such changes have been witnessed in Canada, Mexico, Taiwan, Korea, India, and China. Contractor (1990) found that government-imposed limits accounted for differences in the equity contribution of foreign direct investment in developing countries between 1977 and 1982. Similarly, Blodgett (1992) provided evidence that ownership structure changes as the host government shifts its policies on foreign direct investment from "restrictive" to "nonrestrictive." In their study of U.S. joint ventures in China, Yan and Gray (1994) found that unexpected changes in local governments' policies over time served as a stimulus for shifts in the partners' relative bargaining positions and the parent control structure. To summarize, these studies suggest that unanticipated changes in the joint venture's environment, as well as in the interpartner and parent-venture relationship, prompt structural instability.

It is important to note, however, that the effect of environmental contingencies on structural change may vary in different types of joint ventures. Generally speaking, joint ventures in developing countries, as compared to their counterparts in developed countries, have to deal with a more uncertain and dynamic environment. Therefore, unexpected environmental changes as a driving force for structural reconfiguration may be particularly strong for ventures in developing countries.

Undesirable Venture Performance

A second explanation argues that structural changes are undertaken by the joint venture sponsors as a response to the venture's ongoing performance. This feedback effect on control structure, however, can result in two mutually opposing outcomes. Superior performance of a joint venture may serve as a stabilizing force, while undesirable performance triggers instability. When a venture performs well, the interests of both partners are being served, thus providing incentives for both to keep the existing structure unchanged. Poor performance, however, implies that the alliance has failed to achieve at least one of the parent's objectives. Unsatisfied partner needs create stimuli for restructuring or reallocation of control. Killing (1983) observed that parents increased their intervention, and thus reduced the level of autonomy of the venture management, when the joint venture had not performed well. The parents elect to exercise more control because they tend to attribute poor performance to a lack of competence by the venture's management team. Yan and Gray (1994) note that the performance of a joint venture can reshape the relative bargaining power between the parents such that superior performance creates an additional bargaining chip for the dominant partner, thus further enhancing its control. When the venture does not perform well, however, structural instability will occur because poor performance provides a stimulus, or sometimes a legitimized excuse, for the subordinate partner to propose a more active role in governing the venture's operations.

Additional complexity arises when the partners do not agree with each other in assessing performance, which, as we discussed in chapter 9, is not unusual in an intercultural setting, particularly in ventures between developed and developing country partners. For example, the lead strategic objective of U.S. firms in their joint ventures in China was to earn a profit, whereas the most important motive of the local partner was to acquire advanced Western technology (Yan 1993). Out of this divergence in the partners' expectations, interpartner disagreement about the venture's performance and, more fundamentally, about appropriate performance measures is likely to emerge. When this happens, there is a perception of inequality, which, in turn, can prompt the partner that feels unequally treated to try to renegotiate the control structure or benefit distribution. As Contractor and Lorange (1988) argue from a contribution-inducement-balance point of view, adjustments must be made as joint ventures evolve so that relative benefits are commensurate with the partners' ongoing contributions. Based upon the way the two parents and venture management evaluate performance, as we predicted in chapter 9, different types of action can be taken to reconfigure the parent control structure including no change, structural adjustment, reconfiguration, and termination. For example, no change is deemed necessary when all the three parties involved agree that the joint venture is performing well; termination is expected if all consider the venture a poor performer, while adjustments or reconfigurations are predicted in other scenarios. In sum, superior venture performance attenuates structural instability; whereas undesirable performance or interpartner disagreement about performance assessment prompts instability.

Obsolescing Bargain

A third explanation for structural change is offered by research on joint ventures in developing countries, where special attention is paid to the bargaining relationship between the multinational company (MNC) partner and the local government/partner. In this stream of inquiry, more often than not, the phenomenon of "fading out," whereby the MNC partner gradually reduces its ownership and/or management control, has been the central concern. From this viewpoint, structural reconfiguration results directly from an "obsolescing bargain" (Vachani 1995; Vernon 1977), which occurs when the foreign partner's relative bargaining power vis-à-vis the host government/partner erodes over time as it invests irreversible, transaction-specific resources in the local economy that become de facto hostage (Fagre and Wells 1982). As a result, the MNC's participation in a joint venture in terms of its ownership share and/or management control may be reduced, which eventually can lead to expropriation (Davidson 1982). Dymsza (1988) suggests that in joint ventures between developed and developing country partners, the importance of the former's contribution to the partnership tends to decline over time, at least from the local partner's perspective. When this occurs, structural changes are necessary in which major management responsibilities are turned over to the local partner. In turn, the foreign partner's management control over the venture will decrease over time as a result of obsolescing bargain, prompting structural instability.

It is important to note that although obsolescing bargain has been documented mainly in joint ventures in developing countries, the tendency for the local partner to hold the foreign partner's investment hostage is common in all international alliances. Obsolescing bargain is rooted in transaction costs theory, which argues that a partner's bargaining power decreases as the partner increases its commitment of transaction specific assets in a trading relationship (Williamson 1981). This explanation for restructuring in joint ventures views structural instability from the MNC partner's perspective, and argues that an obsolescing bargain should be anticipated at the outset of the collaboration.

Interpartner Competitive Learning

Finally, a fourth explanation for instability focuses on interpartner competition. Joint ventures are mixed-motive games (Hamel, Doz, and Prahalad 1989) in which the participants cooperate and compete simultaneously. Das and Teng (1999) argue that cooperation and competition become one of the key dilemmas existing throughout the lifetime of a joint venture. Kogut (1989) attributes joint venture failure to potential competition between the sponsors. While the expectation of reducing mutual competition may be a key motivator for forming partnerships, competitive factors also create a primary source of future instability. More specifically, instability and limited duration of joint ventures may be a direct result of interpartner competitive learning (Hamel 1991; Inkpen and Beamish 1997). From this perspective, structural changes in joint ventures are inevitable. Hamel (1991) argues that venture sponsors form alliances to extract and internalize the skills of their partners, and thus either improve their own competitive position or reduce their partners' capability for autonomous action within and without the partnership. Therefore, joint ventures provide an arena in which the partners are engaged in a "race to learn." This competitive motive, however, complicates the partnership. The potential for misunderstanding and mistrust increases when alliances involve learning-oriented versus output-oriented goals (Westney 1988). Learning changes partner interdependency, thereby creating pressure for recontracting or reorganizing. Interpartner asymmetries in learning can shift the relative bargaining power between the partners, and thus make the original bargain obsolete, because the faster learner is likely to raise its "price" for further cooperation (Hamel 1991). Consequently, reallocation of control becomes necessary, or interpartner jockeying for power will follow. In either case, stability will suffer (Inkpen and Beamish 1997). Yan and Gray's (1994) case studies suggest that learning can occur at several different levels: joint learning by the partners during the joint venture's localization, competitive learning between the partners to acquire each others' skills and competencies, and learning by the venture's own personnel to internalize its parents' intellectual contributions. Each of these learning activities is able to upset the original balance of bargaining power, and prompt structural change such that control will accrue to the faster, more effective learner.

Although the several stimuli discussed above conceptually and logically differ from each other, and thus exert separate effects on structural instability, mutual stimulation and interaction are possible among the forces, creating multiplicative effects as a result. For example, unforeseeable changes in the venture's environment (the first explanation) can either negatively or positively affect its performance, thus creating the performance justification for structural change (the second explanation). When the environmental effect is positive, the party in control may gain "undeserved" credit for the desirable performance, which helps enhance its control. When the environmental effect is negative, however, the party in control will become a wrong target for blame and its control position may be weakened or removed as a result. Similarly, competitive learning and obsolescing bargain can occur concurrently when the local partner internalizes the foreigner's expertise, whereas the latter increases its transaction-specific investment. In this case, the shift in bargaining power from the foreign partner to the local partner can be very significant.

The Structural Inertia Perspective

Now, let us shift to the other side of the paradox. Originated in the organization theory literature, the structural inertia perspective argues that there are forces in organizations that counter change and help retain certain organizational characteristics. Once these characteristics are acquired at the organization's founding, they are held unchanged over a long period of time. This phenomenon of organizational imprinting first received attention from Stinchcombe (1965), who argued that unique features of an organization "imprinted" at its birth have a lasting effect on its subsequent structure and even its chances of survival. Defining imprinting as the tendency of organizations to retain the features acquired at their origin, Scott (1992, 171) noted that "it is instructive to realize that the form organizations acquire at their founding is likely to affect the structure they retain over their life." Of particular interest are the stabilizing and sustaining forces that preserve organizational features from change, and the influence of these founding features on subsequent performance and ultimate survival.

Two environmental sources of structural inertia were initially identified: The initial combination of resources acquired by a firm from its task environment (Stinchcombe 1965), and forces from the firm's institutional environment at its birth (e.g., institutional rules, procedures and expectations to which the firm has to conform in order to gain legitimacy and support) (Covaleski and Dirsmith 1988; Meyer and Rowan 1977). More recent studies have suggested that organizational factors, such as the characteristics of the founding executives (Kimberly 1980; Mintzberg and Waters 1982) or the top management team (Eisenhardt and Schoonhoven 1990), as well as the firm's initial business strategy (Boeker 1989), can also create structural inertia.

The organizations in which imprinting has been studied have been limited to single, stand-alone, domestic firms. We believe, however, that international joint ventures are not immune to the effect of structural inertia. Although sponsored by more than one parent firm, joint ventures are economically and legally independent entities (Pfeffer and Nowak 1976). In many respects they are similar to individual organizations, particularly when its local environment is considered. As a separate entity, the venture has to deal with its own suppliers, customers, and competitors. Similarly, its legitimacy is governed by the political, social, and economic environments in the host country, which may be radically different from the institutional environments of its sponsors. Harrigan (1988b) observed that "a joint venture is normally considered more difficult than a contractual agreement to establish, terminate, and fundamentally change." Garrette and Dussuage (1995) found preliminary evidence of imprinting in strategic alliances formed in the aerospace and defense industries. The founding structure of alliances in these two industries varied from the beginning, and the difference was kept for over three decades.

Yet, international joint ventures are not completely independent organizations. Therefore, we expect that they necessarily have unique features of imprinting. By focusing on the international and interorganizational nature of these ventures, we identify four principal sources of structural inertia: the local political and legal environments at the venture's founding; partner initial resource contributions; the original match of interpartner bargaining power; and pre-venture relationships between the partners.

Local Political and Legal Environments

Institutional environment refers to the elaboration of social norms, laws, rules, and requirements to which individual organizations must conform in order to receive legitimacy and support (Meyer and Scott 1983). Organizations formed at the same time under the same institutional pressures exhibit isomorphic structural features (DiMaggio and Powell 1983; Tolbert and Zucker 1983). Thus, an organization's initial structure reflects institutional forces present at its founding. Even though the institutional environment may change over time, its imprint on the organization's structure is sustained. For example, Carroll and Delacroix (1982) provide evidence that the nature of the original economic circumstances and political needs that gave birth to newspapers remained as sustaining forces impacting their evolution and survival.

As is the case for single organizations, the institutional environment of an international joint venture may serve as a powerful source of imprinting. Although the process by which the structure is initially imprinted may vary among different joint ventures (e.g., by "invisible hands" versus by blunt intervention), the lasting effect of structural inertia is common to all. However, the environmental imprint may be particularly powerful for joint ventures in developing countries, in which political and ideological rules often play a more active role than economic principles in shaping policy. The strong influence of the local government may serve as a significant source of pressure for coercive isomorphism (DiMaggio and Powell 1983). Therefore, it is conceivable that the political environment at the time of the joint venture's founding directly affects how the venture is organized and structured. For example, Golich (1995) found differences between aerospace alliances in Europe and those in the United States, even though they were formed in the same time period. She attributed these differences to different political contexts of the respective countries.

We expect that joint ventures formed in the same country during different political climates will exhibit different structural features reflecting the conditions of the institutional environment at the time of their formation. Once formed, however, unique structural features become imprinted and resistant to change (Stinchcombe 1965). For example, the Chinese government stipulated in its 1979 international joint venture law that the venture's chairman of the board of directors must be Chinese regardless of the ownership split between the partners, but subsequently removed this restriction in the 1990 amendment to this law. While some new joint ventures have started to install a foreign partner–nominated chairman of the board, few of the existing ventures have changed their board structure. Another example is the "two-man office" concept observed in most, if not all, early-bird joint ventures in China, in which the expatriate general manager is assisted by a local deputy general manager; and the two, more often than not, physically share the same office space. This structure was proposed by the Chinese government presumably to support a cooperative spirit between the partners and the unity of management, as well as to facilitate mutual learning. While the structure is no longer enforced, no significant changes have been found in those ventures that started with this unique type of arrangement (Yan 1993, 1995). These suggest that structural features of a joint venture resulting from the political and institutional environment at its founding tend to remain unchanged over time, even when such influences are subsequently removed or disappear.

Partner Initial Resource Contributions

The economic, technical, and social resources acquired by an organization at founding reflect the characteristics of the environment at that specific time. At certain points in time, appropriate conditions converge to generate support for organizations that could not exist under different conditions (Stinchcombe 1965). Once acquired, as Scott (1992, 171) explains, "the mix of initial resources out of which an organizational structure is created has a lasting effect on the attributes of that structure."

Unlike single organizations whose initial resources are obtained directly from the environment, a joint venture's starting resources (including capital, technology, local and/or export marketing channels, and management expertise) are, for the most part, made available by its sponsors. Therefore, strictly speaking, this source of imprinting is interorganizational rather than environmental for joint ventures.

A more detailed analysis suggests that for international joint ventures, the initial resource mix has two critical features that may leave a lasting effect on the venture's control structure. First, the specific *types* of resource contributed by a partner may significantly affect the particular *domains* in the venture's operation in which this partner exercises control (Blodgett 1991; Hebert 1994). Second, the relative *amount* of critical resources contributed by the sponsors constitutes the key source of partner *relative bargaining power*, a primary determinant of management control structure (Child et al. 1997; Killing 1983; Yan and Gray 1994). Below we analyze the structural implication of resource type, while relative amount will be discussed subsequently in the context of the initial balance of partner bargaining power.

From a resource-dependence point of view, the partner who contributes the dominant share of resources to a functional area of the joint venture can earn the right to manage this area (Hebert 1994; Schaan 1983). However, from a resource protection viewpoint, joint venture sponsors are reluctant to transfer key technologies/expertise to the partnership, unless a status of sole or dominant control of the potential use, or misuse, of the resources is guaranteed (Blodgett 1991; Hamel, Doz, and Prahalad 1989). In any case, the specific combination of partner resources at the venture's founding may significantly affect the division of control between them. For example, when two partners contribute expertise in highly differentiated areas, a split control structure can be expected (Killing 1982).

We further argue that joint ventures will retain their initial configuration of resources for an extended period of time for several reasons. First, the availability of a specific resource to one (rather than the other) partner is relatively stable because of the imperfect imitability or imperfect mobility of the resource (Chi 1994). Therefore, once a sponsor initially contributes a specific type of resource, the same sponsor tends to continue this contribution over time. Second, contractual agreements may be reached between the sponsors that require them to continue their contribution of the resource committed at the venture's formation. For example, many joint ventures have a separate contractual agreement governing the transfers of technology from one or both parents. Third, it is likely that the joint venture's initial production/operation technology is designed in such a way that it depends exclusively upon the types of inputs available at founding. Therefore, the inflexibility of the venture's technological system may prevent it from shifting to resources other than the mix that was initially available. Finally, the anti-opportunism arrangements, such as guaranteed dominant control by the contributing partner over its resource contributions, as discussed above, help maintain the initial mix of resources. Collectively, these factors help to keep the initial areas of management control by each partner stable.

We speculate that the imprinting effect of the initial resource mix may be less lasting in joint ventures in developing countries than ventures in developed economies for two reasons. First, because of the relatively high level of environmental uncertainty in developing countries, the partners' initial resource commitments tend to be small, thus creating limited inertia. Second, the market growth potential is greater in developing countries than in developed countries. In both cases, radical reconfiguration of the initial resource base and significant additions of new resources become necessary. As a result, the structural inertia produced by the initial resource mix may be cut short.

The Initial Balance of Bargaining Power

Bargaining power refers to the negotiator's capability to change the bargaining relationship (Lax and Sebenius 1986), to win accommodations from the other (Dwyer and Walker 1981; Tung 1988), and to influence the outcomes of a negotiation (Schelling 1956). Partner resource contributions to joint ventures have been argued to be the most critical base of bargaining power (Harrigan 1986; Harrigan and Newman 1990). In addition, empirical evidence suggests that there is a positive relationship between bargaining power and parent control (Child et al. 1997; Fagre and Wells 1982; Lecraw 1984; Yan and Gray 1994).

By arguing for the imprinting effect of the initial balance of partner bargaining power, we are not suggesting that the bargaining power of each partner remains unchanged over time. As we indicated earlier in this chapter, many researchers have provided convincing arguments and empirical evidence that partner bargaining power does change as a result of environmental, interorganizational, or organizational dynamics (Hamilton and Singh 1991; Harrigan 1986; Inkpen and Beamish 1997; Yan and Gray 1994). What is stabilizing and resistant to change is the *balance* of relative bargaining power between the partners reached at the venture's inception. This initial equilibrium of bargaining power provides a reference point against which the relative power positions of the partners are monitored and, when imbalance occurs, adjustments made to achieve a new state of balance. Similar to a heating system in which the thermostat compares the actual and the preset temperature, and switches the furnace on and off so that self-regulation is achieved, the initial structure of bargaining power performs the role of the preset temperature, which is "prearranged information that guides subsequent behavior" (Beniger 1986, 36). Adjustment actions are expected to be taken by the sponsor whose relative bargaining power is worn out either because of an increase in its partner's power, or as a consequence of a loss of its own power. The interpartner competitive motive for bargaining power and control (Hamel et al. 1989; Lax and Sebenius 1986) provides the incentive for both partners to monitor the changes in their power positions, and for the power-losing partner to make replenishing actions.

With their comparative case data, Yan and Gray (1994) illustrated the process in which a dynamic equilibrium of bargaining power is maintained. In several cases, the joint venture depended upon the foreign parent for importing inputs. As they started to localize raw material sourcing, the foreign partner's bargaining power diminished while the local partner gained power. At the same time, however, new power accrued to the foreign partner, who either brought in new products or raised the price for future technology transfers when the technology agreement was open to renew. Although the power bases for each partner changed over time, the overall position of the partners in the bargaining relationship remained largely unchanged. The above discussion suggests that the initial control structure of a joint venture will be retained as a result of the partners' ongoing adjustments to replenish their bargaining power losses.

Interpartner Pre-venture Relationship

Another interorganizational source of imprinting may exist in the prior relationship between the partners which, according to its extensiveness, can range from cold calls to blind dates, arm's-length trade relationships, and contractual collaborations (Gray and Yan 1997). When creating a venture on cold calls, the sponsors have to spend a significant amount of time and resources on relationship building both during the negotiations and after the venture's founding. In contrast, when the partnership is built upon more extensive pre-venture relationships, these issues are addressed prior to its formation. More importantly, mutual commitment and trust are likely to develop. Prior relationships appear to be particularly significant in developing a trusting relationship between the partners (Gulati 1995; Parkhe 1993a, b; Ring and Van de Ven 1994).

The presence or absence of interpartner trust at the venture's founding will affect their subsequent relationship, the design of structure, and the perceived importance of the formal control structure. The preliminary sense of mutual commitment and trust derived from a previous relationship may set the venture on a fast lane toward the further development of trust. To this extent, trust is able to proliferate—trusting partners tend to behave in a trustworthy manner in dealing with each other, and expect to generate a trustworthy response in return. This spiral process enhances and further develops trust in the relationship. However, lack of trust between the partners at the venture's formation can be a major source of structural instability. In this case, the partners depend heavily on learning by doing. As they learn over time, however, surprises will emerge, which prompt conflict and instability. One party may feel that it was cheated or taken advantage of by the other, or that it made strategic or tactical errors during the founding negotiations. These feelings produce distrust, and because of the tit-for-tat nature of interpartner interaction (Kogut 1989), any attempts by a partner to "retaliate" against the other or to "correct" its own errors will set the partnership on a track to instability.

The pre-venture experience can also provide the partners insights in building consensus on what control structure should be adopted. Such a decision is likely to be made by considering the best interests of the entire partnership, rather than the unilateral interest of an individual partner in controlling the venture and safeguarding against the other's opportunism. In this case, the structure of control results from a rational analysis, rather than bipartisan bargaining. Therefore, a low degree of instability may be designed in the venture's initial structure, which, therefore, is expected to be sustained.

When a trusting relationship is established at the venture's founding, the partners tend to render the formal structure less important. As Gulati (1995) notes, interpartner trust reduces transaction costs among the partners and the concomitant need for formal governance structures to counteract opportunism. Therefore, it is predictable that parties in a trusting relationship will keep the control structure formed at founding, but act on interpartner consultation and good faith. In this case, important management decisions are made by consultation between the partners, rather than by imposing the division of power prescribed by the contracted formal control structure. As a result, the formal control structure becomes only nominal. When a structural change is proposed, the parties are likely to focus on its net impact on the venture, rather than guessing the proponent's partisan interests in the proposal. Bipartisan support for structural adjustments is possible. Therefore, system stability will remain unaffected. To summarize, the pre-venture relationship between the partners affects the joint venture's structure by leaving an imprint in its initial design, as well as by reducing the reliance on the formal control structure, thereby minimizing the need for structural reconfiguration.

The various stabilizing forces presented above may interact with each other jointly producing multiplicative interaction effects. For example, when the initial mix of resource contributions were decided based on a trusting/successful pre-venture relationship, the joint stabilizing effect would be particularly strong and lasting.

The Joint Effect of Stabilizing and Destabilizing Forces

We have proposed above that two sets of factors coexist in international joint ventures: One set drives towards structural reconfiguration, while the other stabilizes structures. A joint venture dynamically evolves under the influence of both sets of forces. However, one should not assume that the forces in each set would be equally powerful for any specific venture, nor equally important to all ventures. For example, in developed-developing country joint ventures, a strong interest in acquiring advanced technology by the local partner, coupled with the need for local knowledge by the foreign partner, may make interpartner learning an extremely critical driving force for structural reconfiguration.

It seems that structural inertia raises the threshold for change initiatives. Because of this threshold effect, the momentum for changing the structure in joint ventures has to be sufficiently strong to overcome the structural inertia. Therefore, driving forces derived from incremental sources may be less powerful in overcoming the resistance of structural inertia than forces derived from radical changes. Unusual events, such as sudden shifts in interpartner bargaining power or environmental jolts, may have a greater impact than a series of insignificant changes in focusing the partners' attention, triggering a motivation for structural reconfiguration and intensifying the perceived need for change. In addition, environmental forces may serve as a more effective stimulus for change than interpartner forces, because the political dynamics between partners tend to make a change proposed by one of the parties politically more suspicious than a change stimulus originating in the environment.

To summarize, we argue that, while both sets of forces influence the venture, actual changes in its structure depend upon the relative strength of the two sets of forces. In other words, structural reconfiguration will not occur unless the overall destabilizing forces are stronger than the overall stabilizing forces. Given the assumption that the effect of the forces is additive and interactive, the relative balance or imbalance between the driving and restraining forces for change determines the net momentum for restructuring. Constant changes may occur within the same set of forces over time; however, changes on different dimensions may act against each other, and thus mutually cancel out with no net effect on the overall structure. In other words, structural reconfiguration is possible only when the overall destabilizing forces exceed the overall stabilizing forces.

Conclusion: A Balanced Understanding of Joint Venture Development

The task of explaining how joint ventures structurally reconfigure, or how instability develops over time, requires a more balanced theoretical framework than has typically been formulated in the literature. Toward this end, an integrative model of structural instability in international joint ventures is offered in Figure 11.1, which accounts simultaneously for the stabilizing and destabilizing forces.

Structural Changes and Venture Success

Will structural changes contribute to success? Or will structural instability lead to failure? We agree with Gomes-Casseres (1987) and Blodgett (1992) that stability is not necessarily positive (like a situation in which a stable but stagnant structure is maintained by government restrictive policies). Similarly, it may be arbitrary to claim that a restructuring effort is good or bad because instability may have positive or negative effects on performance, or have nothing to do with it (Blodgett 1992, 481).

Frequent structural changes as a response to change stimuli increase transaction costs, prompt interpartner conflict, and reduce interpartner trust. With a strong mood for change, partners tend to escalate their sensitivity to their "share" of control over the venture and deploy changes based on unilateral interpretations of environmental and organizational events. In addition, changes can occur in series—as Blodgett (1992, 480) found out— "if a joint venture contract has been previously renegotiated, the chance is much greater that it will be adjusted again." Frequent changes in control structure usually are also associated with strategic, policy, and personnel changes. In addition to the direct cost of time, attention, and resources for implementation, discontinuity of management personnel and policies may send negative signals to the venture's stakeholders, and adversely affect its image and performance.

However, ignoring change stimuli and blindly maintaining the existing structure is no less damaging. False stability will promote perceptions of inequality, and thus create dissatisfied partners. As a result, the venture will become a political battlefield for the partners to jockey for power, and unsurprisingly, performance will suffer. Yan and Gray (1994) provided an example in which the U.S. partner repeatedly proposed to add

264

Figure 11.1 A Framework of Structural Reconfiguation in International Joint Ventures

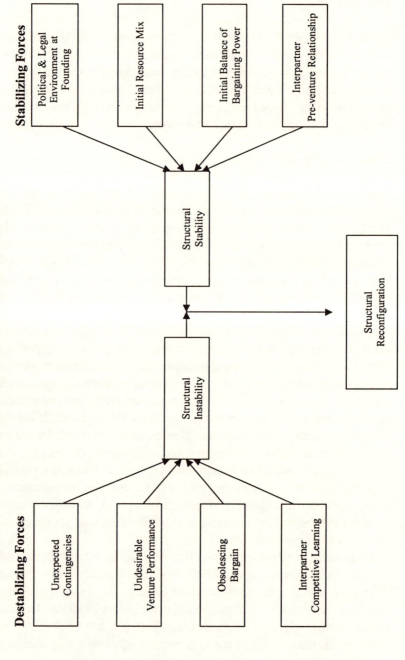

one more U.S. member to the venture's board of directors to justify the U.S. firm's increased bargaining power. However, the local partner refused the proposal every time it was presented. This consequently deteriorated the interpartner relationship, and hurt the venture's potential to grow. The unhappy U.S. firm threatened not to renew its technology transfer agreement with the venture, and started creating new ventures with different local firms.

A balanced view of joint venture development argues for a dynamic stability of the co-alignment between structure and environment, and the congruence between the partners' bargaining power and management control. A dynamic fit between internal structure and external environment will produce success (Lawrence and Lorsch 1967). Similarly, maintaining congruence between the structure of control and the partners' relative bargaining power creates a sense of equity and fairness, minimizes interpartner conflict, enhances trust, and consequently improves performance.

Implications and Future Research

This chapter was intended to make several contributions. First, the change-stability paradox (Poole Van de Ven 1989) in organization theory is adopted to enrich our theoretical explanations for joint venture development. It is our argument that conceptual construction of instability in international joint ventures needs to adopt multiple, alternative, and even competing theoretical lenses to capture the complexity and richness of joint venture evolution. The structural instability and the organizational imprinting perspectives discussed in this chapter are adapted from different organizational literatures. Until now, no attempts have been made to integrate these seemingly incompatible perspectives. Previous theoretical attempts that consider the stabilizing forces in international joint ventures have been rare. Even rarer are studies that examine both the driving and restraining forces in an integrative framework. Our use of the structural inertia perspective to examine joint ventures represents the first attempt to apply the theory beyond independent organizations in which it was originated. It is our belief that research on international joint ventures as a young field of study needs to enrich itself by drawing theoretical insights from other more established areas of organization science.

Second, by focusing on the specific forces affecting joint venture evolution, we call for increased attention to the process of organizational development in joint ventures. As shown in the review in the previous chapter, the current literature has paid considerable attention to either the very beginning of the venture (in the tradition of modal choices) or its ultimate end (as reflected in the current research on instability), while the mid-life of joint ventures has been left understudied at best. By focusing on only the opening and the closing games, previous research has missed the most exciting and arguably the most challenging part of the story. Studying the active forces and their interactions in joint ventures and the process by which ventures evolve over time promises to be one of the most important areas in which scholars can contribute to the state of the art in joint venture research.

In this chapter we also intended to contribute to a paradigm shift among researchers with respect to joint venture stability versus change. It is a dominant view in the literature that to maintain stability is a key task for joint venture sponsors. The term "instability" has been used with a negative connotation. Continuing the stance for a "neutral" conceptualization that we stated in the previous chapter, we strive for a balanced understanding of the stability-instability dichotomy by emphasizing the dual roles played by structural change; that is, a change in control structure can either increase or reduce overall system stability. We propose that joint venture researchers move away from the assumption that stability produces success, whereas instability produces failure. Stability may be stagnant and inflexible, while instability may signify change, development, and progress. Dynamic changes should be no surprise. Rather, it would be very surprising for a joint venture to remain unchanged over time.

The conceptual model we developed in this chapter might also offer useful implications for practitioners to whom the high instability of international alliances has long been a concern. What prior research is able to offer has been limited with respect to how to conduct ongoing diagnoses of instability for operational joint ventures (rather than already terminated ones) and, more importantly, how to undertake managerial actions in unstable ventures. In this regard, the stabilizing and destabilizing forces identified in this chapter provide useful insights in terms of cultivating a more thorough understanding of how interpartner dynamics unfold, and what needs to be done to enhance the partnership's sustainability and performance.

The model warrants further research. It is clear that future empirical examination of the variables and relationships must use longitudinal designs. Before large-scale, quantitative work is done for theory testing, rigorously designed qualitative studies may be necessary. For example, longitudinal comparative case studies that track a set of joint ventures in their natural field settings from beginning to end will prove particularly useful (Parkhe 1993b; Ring and Van de Ven 1994). The rich data collected this way will help refine conceptualization, verify and enrich the relationships proposed, operationalize the constructs by deriving appropriate measures, and generate thick descriptions and explanations for subsequent quantitative theory testing.

Future research should also compare and contrast the driving and restraining forces for structural change in different types of partnerships. For example, the relative criticality of the forces proposed in this paper should be examined in ventures in developed versus developing economies, in two-partner versus multipartner alliances, and in ventures in different industry sectors.

A Mini-Case Example

Changes in International Joint Ventures in China

It is arguable that China represents one of the most dynamic economies in the world today. Having closely traced the development of international joint ventures in China and having made frequent trips to the country in the past decade, we have been often surprised by the magnitude of changes. Based on our observations, below, we identify several new trends that may have significant implications for forming and managing international joint ventures in China in the upcoming century, therefore deserving the attention of joint venture researchers as well as practitioners.

Changes in Interpartner Relational Characteristics

Several salient changes have occurred over time with respect to the interpartner relational characteristics in joint ventures in China. For example, recent evidence suggests that the Chinese partners are becoming increasingly attracted by financial returns, and the desire for hard currency is losing motivation power. As a result of the recent proliferation of economic pragmatism in China, making a profit is quickly moving to the top of the list of the Chinese joint venture partner's strategic interests, replacing the objective of obtaining advanced Western technology. Technology may still remain a top objective in the Chinese central government's priority, but the more autonomous business enterprises and government officials at the local provincial or municipal levels tend to treat technology as more or less only a means to derive financial returns. This shift in the Chinese partner's strategic objectives may have a significant effect on both the existing joint ventures and partnerships yet to be formed. It can bring changes in the venture's strategic mission, as well as in the relationships between the partners. To a certain extent, this implies that the Chinese partner is moving closer to the foreign partner by sharing the same strategic expectations. The converging goals between the partners may significantly decrease interpartner conflict and opportunism, thereby enhancing venture performance. However, the increased compatibility of Chinese enterprises with international firms will potentially gain the Chinese more alternative partners to cooperate with, which may give rise to increased competition among international players in China.

China has kept a very high level of foreign exchange reserve over the recent years, only next to Japan. As a result, at the macro level, the Chinese government has significantly relaxed its state control over foreign exchange; at the corporate level, the Chinese joint venture partners have gradually downplayed the importance of earnings in hard currency as an important objective. We envision that these changes will have three important effects on joint ventures. First, the promise to export the joint venture's product will diminish in power as a bargaining chip for the international partner in negotiating with the local government for preferential treatment. Second, the foreign and Chinese partners will converge in their strategic interests in the joint venture, which may have a positive effect on performance. The decision on where to sell the venture's product, in the international or the local market, has been an area in which interpartner disagreements and controversies frequently occurred, but now it is no longer a serious concern. Finally, decreased Chinese interest in export may send a bad message to international partners who have a strong interest in deriving heavy returns by buying back the joint venture's product at internal transfer prices.

Changes in the Multinational Partner's China Strategies

A significant change has been observed recently in the multinational partners' overall China strategies in which they strive for a higher level of control over their joint ventures and for an increased degree of integration among their overall operation in China. There are two major factors contributing to this aggressive drive for control by the foreign joint venture sponsors. First, the lifting of the Chinese government's restriction on foreign ownership and governance structures has made these changes legally possible. Over a period of more than a decade, the highly positive effect of foreign invested businesses on China's economic development has convinced the Chinese government and eased its initial concerns about the possibility of loss of control or ideological contamination. Therefore, some important policy changes have been undertaken, one of which is the increased tolerance toward foreign-majority ownership in joint ventures. Although not strictly defined by law, the Chinese government's previous preference for equally shared ownership to foreign-majority ownership in equity joint ventures has created an overwhelming majority of 50–50–structured joint ventures. For the past several years, the number of foreign-majority joint ventures have rapidly increased. At the same time, the 1991 amendment to the joint venture law has allowed joint ventures to install a foreign chairman. These changes in government policy provide the legal and institutional backgrounds against which the multinationals' attempt to increase control is legitimately proposed. Second, many multinational firms have grown their joint ventures in China both in number and scale of operation to such a point that an overall strategy and a coordination structure are needed to integrate these different ventures/operations. For example, when BCG, a British conglomerate manufacturer of industrial gases, formed its first joint ventures in China, each venture was designated to serve a regional market. Because of the vast territory of the country, cross-joint venture competition had never been a concern at all until very recently. Now the company is operating more than a dozen joint ventures in China. At least occasionally, these sister joint ventures have engaged in competition against each other, which has caught the attention of the foreign parent and prompted actions undertaken to consolidate its overall control.

The multinational firms' attempt to increase control over their joint ventures has been made by pursuing a variety of strategies, two of which are observed most frequently: renegotiating for an increase in ownership, and creating majority or wholly owned holding companies. Increase or proposal for increase in the foreign partner's equity holding occurred in many of the early joint ventures in China. For example, Shanghai Foxboro changed its ownership structure from 49–51 (American-

Chinese) to 51–49. Although the change is hardly large in terms of absolute scale (2 percent), the shift of the symbolic majority positions carries much more significance. Xerox has been more aggressive, attempting to increase its control at both the individual joint venture level and the level of its overall operation in China. A wholly owned holding company was founded in Beijing in 1995 to control all its China operations, and the ownership structure at its first joint venture, Xerox Shanghai, was renegotiated from a symbolic majority (51 percent) to a significant majority (65 percent).

The foreign parent's consolidation of control over joint ventures may signify a landmark event in the history of direct foreign investment in China. It represents a significant step in which the Chinese business environment is upgraded toward maturity and internationalization. The Chinese market is no longer a clean slate of competition isolated from the rest of the world. As a result, fierce competition among international firms in China looms large. Meanwhile, the attempt for increased control over their joint ventures indicates that the early entrants into China have put an end to their initial strategy, that is, going to China to test the local market or simply to establish a presence in the country. Now they are getting serious. They start to take advantage of being the early entrants by building entry barriers against newcomers. However, the consolidation effort by the foreign joint venture partners is not conducted without resistance, as discussed below.

Changes in the Bargaining Power Structure

Significant changes have occurred in the relative bargaining power balance between the international partner and the local government/partner. In the early years of the Open Door policy, China was eager to attract foreign investors. Accordingly, favorable taxation policies and other preferential treatment were offered by the central and/or the local government to the joint venture early birds. Over time, as more and more international firms flew into China forming joint ventures or wholly owned foreign subsidiaries, many of these incentive offers have been reduced or eliminated. Especially in the more developed regions, such as the coastal areas, the local government has perceived a substantial increase in its bargaining power in negotiating with prospective foreign joint venture partners. A government official in a coastal city commented in a recent interview: "Originally it was us who pulled them [the foreign firms] here to make deals. So, they were very picky about us. . . . Now it's our turn, because it is them who want to team up with us. We have to compare at least three foreign candidates to decide with which one to form a joint venture."

Although it probably is the experience of most joint ventures in China that the local government's interference in the joint ventures' affairs, particularly in the operation and management areas, has been minor or minimal, this fact does not imply that the government would give up its influence on strategically critical issues. For example, the increased number of foreign wholly owned holding companies has captured significant attention by the government policy makers. Over the recent several years, government media (e.g., *China Daily*) have made it a topic for front-page commentaries that the emerging foreign holding companies are presenting a potential threat for Chinese domestic enterprises. At present, a holding company is allowed to form only when the foreign company is concurrently operating at least three separate joint ventures in China. The function of holding companies is also being subjected to significant constraints. It is our prediction that not only will the existing constraints for holding companies remain for a relatively long period of time, but that new and more detailed regulation measures are likely to be stipulated.

Local governments and the Chinese joint venture partners are highly reluctant to reduce their ownership holdings in joint ventures, particularly when joint ventures significantly outperform the wholly owned domestic divisions of the Chinese partner. Therefore, the Chinese stakes in, and returns from, the joint venture become extremely critical. For example, at Xerox Shanghai, the renegotiations around ownership restructuring were extremely painful and took a period of several years.

Changes in the Government's Roles

A significant change has occurred in recent years in China, that is, the role of the central and local governments in international joint ventures has been significantly reduced. In the earlier joint ventures, it was typical that one of the venture's directors and/or top level managers was a government official. Now not only is this type of arrangement rare for newly formed joint ventures, the local government has been calling back its nominees from those ventures that initially adopted this arrangement. Similarly, except for exceptional cases, such as venturing in the government-designated "pillar" industries, government officials no longer show up at the joint venture negotiation tables.

Finally, the improved legal environment represents another major change. As more formal rules in the form of laws and policies concerning international joint ventures are adopted, baseless government interventions in the venture's business negotiations and operations have been minimized. For example, in the early days of the "open door" policy, the Chinese companies found it ridiculous to see a lawyer in the foreign partner's negotiation team: "We haven't gotten married yet, but you are preparing for a divorce!" Now we witness more Western law firms setting up their offices in China in the form of joint ventures. Therefore, American companies should not be surprised when they find an America-trained lawyer sitting on the Chinese side of the table!

We had followed closely the recently settled dispute between McDonald's and the municipal government of Beijing regarding the relocation of the former's largest restaurant in the Chinese capital. The controversy started when the local government contracted with a giant Hong Kong real estate developer to build a business center (to be named the Oriental Plaza) in the larger area in which the restaurant was built under a twenty-year lease of the piece of land. The settlement, which involves a payment by the city's government to McDonald's of approximately $12 million (RMB 100 million yuan), ended a years-long, highly publicized negotiation. The relocation of the restaurant per se (the new site is only several blocks away) and the amount of compensation involved are far less significant than the political implications of the case, in our view. As the first high-profile case in which a Chinese government ended up compensating a foreign company, it carries an encouraging message for foreign investors and businesses.

—— 12 ——

Exit Strategies and Procedures

Termination of international joint ventures does not necessarily signal failure. As a transitional form of organization, joint ventures evolve over time, and from time to time participants exit from partnerships. However, not all joint venture participating firms have mechanisms in place to guide the exit process. The previous two chapters have discussed the joint venture evolution and instability from a conceptual perspective. In this chapter, using specific examples, we discuss the reasons why joint ventures are dissolved and stress the importance of exit strategies. Apart from the possibility that the partners have all achieved their objectives, other reasons for termination range from unnoticed yet irreconcilable interpartner differences to changes in partner strategies, inability to meet partner expectations, and unrealized partner commitment. Then we reiterate exit approaches and procedures involved in equity transfer, liquidation, or reconfiguration of joint ventures.

Lack of Exit Mechanisms

As we discussed in the last two chapters, conventional wisdom often treats the dissolution of joint ventures as a failure. Ring and Van de Ven (1994) argue that investments in interfirm cooperation include not only economic and technological resources of participating firms, but also social commitments and entanglements of individual agents. Therefore, social-psychological motivations can be powerful for preserving relationships even if the partnership is not economically successful. Consequently, "it is not only in the economic but also in the psychological best interests of the organizational parties to find ways to preserve their socially embedded relationship" (p. 107). Clearly, to these authors, termination of partnerships is undesirable, at least from the perspective of interorganizational social relationship. From a field study of several cross-border joint ventures, Lane and Beamish (1990) concluded that a successful joint venture indicates a stable business relationship that meets the needs of both partners over the long term. Geringer and Hebert (1991) in a study of alternative performance measures in joint ventures found that international joint ventures that were perceived by the partners as successful were more likely to live longer than ventures that were evaluated as being less than successful. Therefore, a positive relation was proposed for the linkage between success and the longevity of the venture.

However, international joint ventures are neither designed, nor should be expected, to have an extremely long duration (Harrigan 1986). As we discussed in the previous chapter, joint venture instability is not always tantamount to collaborative failure as is widely assumed. Exit via termination, dissolution, or divestment is a natural outcome for most joint ventures. While some joint ventures do end bitterly, breakups do not automatically imply a flop. For instance, when Hercules sold its equity stake in Himont, its 50–50 joint venture with Montedison that manufactured and marketed polypropylene worldwide, joint venture skeptics quipped that "another corporate partnership has failed." Yet Alexander Giacco, former CEO of Hercules, argued differently: "An underlying motivation for all joint venture partners is to create wealth. Success should not and does not depend on whether the entity continues indefinitely as a joint venture. Longevity is not a measure of success."

Ironically, however, scholars and practitioners alike have paid little attention to the end games of joint ventures and have overlooked the venture's termination mechanisms and processes. In fact, we have witnessed numerous cases in which termination is a natural and probably an appropriate event, but there are no mechanisms in place to guide the process. Parent companies often fail to plan for termination when the venture is being set up. Increasingly, insightful executives realize that reaching clear agreement at the outset on the way in which the end game will be handled is an important organizational mechanism to ensure joint venture success.

Exit Reasons

Similar to the case of marriage, in which couples expect a life-long partnership but many enter the business of divorce shortly thereafter, joint venture partners usually establish long-term objectives but have to face a premature termination of the venture. Clearly, it is important to be alert to conditions that potentially lead to the demise of the venture, which may be hidden at the start but become more evident over time. Below we discuss several such conditions.

Unnoticed Yet Irreconcilable Interpartner Differences

It is quite often that two firms create a partnership before they fully understand each other, particularly the significant differences between them. Then it is too late when they become informed. This would fit the scenario of "a Martini merger and the morning after." There are several areas in which the partners can differ significantly. First, incompatible strategic goals and directions set for a joint venture can intensify as the venture evolves. When such incompatibility cannot be overcome, partners are often left with no choice but divorce. For example, practitioners and academics alike have attributed many of the problems in U.S.-Japanese joint ventures in the auto parts industry to incompatibility of partner goals. U.S. suppliers often have a narrow focus on gaining access to the Japanese auto transplants in the United States. Their Japanese counterparts, however, have broader goals of securing a foothold in the U.S. market. Such incompatibility can occur at the operational level as well. Take the example of a cross-equity partnership between AT&T and Italtel, in which the latter liquidated its stake in AT&T's Dutch-based operation in 1993. The two partners differed significantly on how the European telecommunications market would develop and how the venture should capitalize on market opportunities. Specifically, they disagreed on what strategy and technology should be employed: AT&T was pushing its digital 5ESS switch system whereas Italtel had its own Linea UT digital telephone exchanges. Soon after the termination of the partnership, Italtel chose Siemens to form a joint venture because the latter also produces Linea UT exchanges.

Second, joint venture partners often find significant differences in terms of how to run the joint venture. For example, one partner may prefer to replicate its operational procedures within the joint venture whereas the other stresses the venture's need for autonomy to adapt to new markets, technologies, or products. Conflict is likely to ensue, which can lead to the dissolution of the joint venture. Also, the partners may be unable to reach an agreement on management appointments. For example, in a majority-minority joint venture, the dominant partner may impose its own choices. On the other hand, if both partners seek to avoid conflict over personnel appointments, they may end up giving the venture's management more free rein than either partner wished. In this instance, the parents become dependent on a small number of managers who, over time, become irreplaceable. When problems arise, disagreement over management selection becomes more severe. In the Corning-Vitro joint venture, for instance, neither party anticipated the extraordinarily low speed of decision making, which in fact resulted from inconsistent management practices. There was confusion over how each partner's internal decision-making process works, who has what decision power, and how far down in the joint venture's structural hierarchies decision-making authority can be delegated. Corning usually decentralizes decision power to lower managerial levels; but Vitro's managers at the same levels would still have to take the issue to more senior executives. Therefore, there was plenty of confusion over whether and by whom decisions have to be made.

Third, the challenge of overcoming differences in managerial culture and styles between cross-border partners is often formidable. When partners face adverse market conditions and hazardous institutional environment, there can be insufficient time to devote to the task of bridging such differences. For instance, strains in Western-Japanese joint ventures from corporate, industrial, and national cultural differences abound. Disputes arise over clashes in work ethics, corporate culture, human resource practices, decision-making styles, incentive structure, and rewarding systems. Interpartner conflicts in these areas can swell into insurmountable problems and cause the failure of the venture. Again, in the case of the Corning-Vitro joint venture, both partners did agree that the venture needed to boost the competitiveness of its operations. However, cultural differences made it difficult to agree on what the key issues were and how to solve them. The two partners had different ideas on how to define and provide "service" to customers. Corning was concerned about service to retailers, such as Wal-Mart and Kmart. Once a manufacturer agrees to deliver merchandise on a given date, the company must honor its commitment to maintain its reputation and business. Yet, Vitro had different ideas. Having operated for years in a closed Mexican economy with little competition, service, as defined as reliability and promptness, was not a major issue.

Finally, the partners may each subscribe to different conflict resolution mechanisms. For example, the partner firms may operate in radically different legal environments. In the Western societies, with the

United States being the extreme, individuals and firms rely heavily, if not exclusively, on the legal code to protect and promote their interests. Other societies, for historical or cultural reasons, may shy away from open confrontation in general, and from court arbitration of dispute in particular. In many foreign joint ventures in China, for instance, the Chinese side prefers not to pre-specify explicit conflict resolution terms, especially judiciary or arbitration resolutions, in a joint venture contract. When a lawyer on the U.S. negotiation team is introduced to the Chinese negotiators, the hosts are typically found stunned—"We are not yet married, you are already prepared for divorce!" However, leaving legal terms ambiguous may create problems down the road. For example, in 1994, Lehman Brothers sued its joint venture partners, Sinochem and Sinopec, two giant state-owned Chinese firms, for failing to honor their obligations in swap transactions. This accusation, however, was rejected by the Chinese partners who argued that there were no explicit stipulations in the contract with respect to these transactions. As a result of open confrontation, the partnerships were broken out.

Changes in Partner Strategies

It should not be a surprise that, as joint ventures evolve, significant changes may occur in the parent firms as well as in the venture's operational environment. These changes prompt new dynamics around the partnership and often contribute to a venture's termination. Westinghouse Mitsubishi Power Products Inc., a 50–50 joint venture between Westinghouse and Mitsubishi and Toshiba, is such an example. This joint venture was initially designed to pursue a collective strategy in the volatile market for high-voltage circuit breakers. A few years after the venture's inception, however, Westinghouse switched from this mature market to new high-growth markets, which led to its withdrawal from a business that did not fit its new strategy. Similarly, Ciba-Corning Diagnostics, a 50–50 joint venture between Corning and Ciba-Geigy of Switzerland, derailed because of the growing differences in the two partners' ambitions and commitment. When the joint venture was launched to offer medical services, Ciba merged part of its therapeutics business with Corning's diagnostics operations. Much to the surprise of both partners, however, as the venture progressed, Ciba found itself in a position to escalate its contributions in proprietary therapeutics know-how to make the venture a success. Realizing the potential implications of an escalation of commitment, the Swiss pharmaceuticals giant decided to exit from the partnership and to go it alone. As a result, the partners negotiated for the sale of Corning's share to Ciba.

A joint venture can become a "victim" of a parent firm's pursuit of other, more important interests. For instance, Rohm and Haas (R&H) subsidiary Elga Ronal (Milan) decided to exit from its joint venture with Tokyo Okha Kogyo (Kawasaki, Japan) to accommodate the regulatory concerns of the European Union. R&H's pending acquisition of Morton International made the European Union concerned about the antitrust implications of R&H's businesses in Europe, because there are possible overlaps in R&H's and Morton's dry-film photo-resist businesses. Hoping to ease the government concerns, R&H shut its joint venture in the electronic chemicals business.

Inability to Meet Partner Expectations

Nonperformance can doom a joint venture to failure. Targets may be missed as a result of inadequate resources, time, or effort, or perhaps because of unrealistically ambitious goals. Rather than signal the end of the game, nonperformance should be seen as an opportunity to reset goals or evaluate inadequacies more closely. The targets set for the venture may be shifting due to rapid market developments, changing strategies, or uncontrollable events. In practice, there are a number of reasons the partners' interests diverge. Unexpected change in market demand was a major force behind the decision by Du Pont and Philips to terminate their 50–50 joint venture in optical media. When the partners formed Philips Du Pont Optical in 1986, predicted sales in the global audio, video, and data markets were higher than $4 billion by 1990. However, as their hopes for the high sales faded, the partners were so disappointed that they started immediately concentrating on how to disband the joint venture. Similarly, Shell recently planned to pull out of its three joint ventures in Europe (Rovin with Akzo Nobel at Rotterdam and Berre, Wavin with Waterleiding Mij Overijssel of the Netherlands, and Dorlyl with Elf Atochem in France and Italy). The underlying reason was that Shell had the objective of becoming a leader in the specific business sector, but has fallen short of achieving this objective. As a result, it is convinced that a divestment in this sector could strengthen its leading positions in other business sectors.

Unrealized Partner Commitment

When one or more partners fails to make a financial commitment as specified in the founding agreement, the venture can collapse. From a parent firm's perspective, it often has to ensure its overall corporate interests at the expense of the financial demands of a particular international joint venture. For instance, many Japanese and Korean joint ventures in Asian countries and Europe had to be dissolved during 1997–1999 due to the financial problems that the parent firms suffered as a result of the Asian financial crisis. Another example is Chrysler. Under an acute need to raise cash inflow, Chrysler sold its 50 percent stake in its joint venture, Diamond Star Motors, to its partner, Mitsubishi Motors, for approximately $100 million. Interestingly, in many respects, the joint venture was a thorough success—Chrysler gained valuable exposure to Japanese management techniques while Mitsubishi secured an important foothold in the U.S. market.

Another case of unrealized partner commitment concerns the partners' resource contributions to the joint venture. Most joint ventures are formed out of the assumption that the partner firms will provide organizational strengths that are needed by other partners. However, false expectations about partner capabilities can cause joint venture termination. Since the partners fully expect that the resources they contribute to the venture would be effective, when one or both partners' presumed competencies or strengths fail to generate expected results, joint ventures have to confront the risk of dissolution. The wider the perceived gaps between what partners pledged and what they actually deliver, the greater the difficulties for the joint venture. For example, in the former AT&T-Philips NV venture that produced telecommunications equipment in Europe, AT&T believed that Philips's reputation as a European champion would stimulate AT&T's foothold in other European countries. This belief was found to be quite naive. In an unsuccessful bid for a slice in the French telecommunications market, AT&T discovered that the national limits in the European markets were extremely strict and that Philips NV's clout did not go far beyond the Dutch national territories.

Mission Fulfilled

The best scenario of joint venture dissolution is that the venture has achieved its strategic goals set by the parties. In particular, when the parties join forces for acquiring knowledge from each other, there is no reason to expect the partnership will last long. For instance, Hercules and Montedison, two former competitors in polypropylene products, pooled together $900 million in assets to create Himont in November 1983. Before the joint venture, Montedison developed a novel technology, which was expected to radically change the production cost structure of polypropylene as well as to pave the way for new product extensions. However, the company had lacked the market presence outside of Western Europe. Hercules, meanwhile, had a sophisticated worldwide marketing network, yet had been short of sophisticated technology and resources to develop superior products in-house. The joint venture helped sharpen the competitive edge for both partners. Through research and technological breakthroughs, Himont added new properties and applications for polypropylene and grew worldwide to include more than 3,000 employees, 38 manufacturing plants, and distribution capabilities in 100 countries. As a leader in the chemical industry with a return on equity of 38 percent, Himont earned at least $150 million per annum from new products. Meanwhile, Hercules successfully acquired the sophisticated technologies from the partnership. After successfully fulfilling its mission for both partners, the joint venture was happily dissolved.

Exit Approaches and Procedures

Dissolution is planned in some joint ventures, but not in many others. A planned termination by both parties may represent a more successful and happier end of a joint venture than unplanned ones. New United Motor Manufacturing Inc. (NUMMI), a manufacturing joint venture between GM and Toyota, provides an interesting example of a planned divorce scenario. In 1984, the U.S. Federal Trade Commission authorized the formation of NUMMI with a provision that the joint venture would have a limited span of twelve years. Since both partners knew from the very outset that the partnership had a limited life span, they were well prepared for the contracted divorce. Such planned terminations, however, are the exception rather than the rule. Divorces in joint ventures usually are unanticipated and premature. Most companies enter a joint venture without really knowing how long it will last. The dissolutions of the collaborative partnerships between GM and Daewoo, Meiji and Borden, and AT&T and Olivetti are examples of unplanned divorces.

The second issue concerns whether or not the termination is friendly. The divorce between Vitro and Corning, as mentioned earlier in the chapter, is an example of an alliance that ended on friendly terms. Both companies amicably agreed to terminate their equity ventures, and Corning paid Vitro its original investment in the joint venture. In addition, both companies agreed to continue their distributorship. Friendly separations typically are handled through negotiated settlements. For instance, Teijin of Japan announced in March 1999 the dissolution of its joint venture with Molecular Simulations (MSI) of the United States, the world's largest player in computerized chemistry. The joint venture was effectively dissolved when Teijin transferred its stock shares in the venture to MSI. The negotiated settlements stipulated that Teijin sold all of its rights in the venture, for approximately $10 million, to Pharmacopeia, the company that acquired MSI in January 1998. Teijin willingly accepted the deal because its original objectives of starting up a computerized chemistry business had been met, and adequate expertise had been built up as a result of the cooperation.

In contrast, unfriendly divorces are often contested in courts or end up in arbitration. One such case is the ongoing dispute between Coors Brewing Company and its Canadian partner and licensee, Molson Breweries. Coors sued and served Molson with an arbitration notice after the latter agreed to form a partnership with Miller Brewing Company. According to Coors, Miller's purchase of a 20 percent stake in Molson contributed to a consolidation of the North American beer industry and endangered Coors's competitive position. Coors also maintained that the Miller-Molson alliance provided Miller, a key competitor of Coors in the United States, with highly confidential marketing strategies and brand performance information that Coors had given Molson under their licensing agreement.

The third issue concerns whether or not all parties agree to a termination. Hercules (U.S.) and New Japan Chemical, for instance, agreed in 1999 to disband their joint venture, Rika Hercules. When the partners decided that managing the joint venture's businesses separately would allow the individual partners to better preserve and expand their advantageous market positions, a peaceful agreement was reached between them. Following the dissolution, Hercules Japan has assumed independent control of the oil-derived hydrocarbon resin and terpene resin businesses while New Japan Chemical has been in control in the business of rosin derivatives. Having a partner refusing to terminate a joint venture relationship presents a more challenging scenario. To illustrate, a major U.S. computer company attempted to terminate its alliance with a Japanese partner. Although the venture was doing well financially, the U.S. partner decided to exit from the alliance because of a major shift in its strategic focus. Although the joint venture's contract allowed the U.S. firm to exit, the Japanese partner refused the termination proposal and insisted on maintaining the alliance. To the Japanese partner, acceptance of the proposal would mean a loss of face.

In general, there are three forms of termination of joint ventures: termination by acquisition (equity transfer), termination by dissolution, and termination by reconfiguration. In the first case, the joint venture is terminated with one of the partners acquiring the stake of the other partner. Termination by acquisition could also take the form of one partner selling its equity stake in the joint venture to a third company (e.g., British Aerospace selling its equity stake in Rover to BMW), or both partners selling their shares to a third party. In general, however, most multinational firms prefer reallocation of joint venture ownership between the existing parent firms. These changes in ownership and resource commitments are a function of both firms' evolving relationships to the venture. Termination by acquisition is most common in international joint ventures. The case of Rika Hercules in which New Japan Chemical bought out its partner, Hercules, is such an example. Termination may also occur through reconfiguring the joint venture's agreement. In lieu of termination, partners to an international alliance may agree to redefine or restructure their original agreement. For example, Matsushita Electric Industries Co. of Japan (MEI) and Solbourne Computer Inc. of Colorado entered into an ambitious partnership in 1987 to compete with Sun Microsystem's SPARC computers. When the venture failed, MEI and Solbourne agreed in 1992 to redraft their initial agreement into a more limited partnership arrangement.

Regardless of the specific conditions that have provoked termination or the particular type of termination, the process should be managed in accordance with procedures stipulated in the initial joint venture contract. These procedures generally include conditions of termination, timing, disposition of assets, disposition of liabilities, and dispute resolution mechanisms. In many countries, both developed and developing, the regulations governing termination and dissolution of joint ventures are contained in the joint venture law and its implementing regulations. According to the Chinese Equity Joint Venture Law, for instance, a joint venture may be dissolved when it incurs "heavy losses" or when one party fails to execute its obligations. If a loss is incurred due to a breach of contract, the violating party has to bear financial liability for the loss. Other conditions in most countries' corporate or joint venture laws concerning joint venture dissolution include expiration of duration, inability to continue operations due to losses caused by *force majeure*, inability to obtain the desired objectives of the operation while simultaneously seeing no future for development, and occurrence of other reasons for dissolution as prescribed by the contract or articles of association.

The board of directors of a joint venture must agree unanimously to dissolve the venture. In some developing countries, joint venture management must also file an application for dissolution with the relevant governmental authority (normally the same authority that initially approved the joint venture formation). In a liquidation process, an auditor is required according to the joint venture contract or relevant rules set by the parties. The joint venture board or its designated committee must notify known creditors so that they may declare their claims. In case a multinational firm involved in the dissolution of an existing joint venture wants to form a new arrangement, it has to fully comply with all the legal requirements. Otherwise, its new venture may become legally exposed to claims by the dissolving joint venture's creditors.

Envisioning the less than desirable scenarios, joint venture partners better agree at the venture's formation on the circumstances that would allow each partner to exit or call for dissolution. As we listed in chapter 3 on founding negotiations, numerous events can trigger such a call, such as material breach of agreement, breach of law, repeated deadlocks on the board of directors, changes in the laws and regulations, or failure to meet targets. In addition, the partners must agree on voting rights and procedures for dissolving an alliance. For example, termination may require either a majority or unanimous approval by the board of directors.

In addition, the timing of a possible termination can establish upfront the amount of commitment and flexibility of each party with respect to the joint venture. If two companies agree not to retract their participation in the joint activity, they have sent a strong signal to each other about their level of dedication to the project. A benchmark event may be set, such as termination of the venture being allowed only when it has reached a stage of self-sufficiency.

Moreover, the partners should specify the methods to be used in valuing assets. Partners should negotiate how the joint venture will liquidate its assets and how the partners will share in the assets. Asset valuation or pricing is a major source of disagreement during a divorce. The contract should stipulate whether one partner will be given the opportunity to bid on the equity share of the other. The basis for asset valuation should also be clarified. It may be based on the actual amounts invested by the partners, the assessment of an independent appraiser, or an offer placed by an external buyer.

Further, a clause needs to stipulate liabilities disposition. How partners deal with the liabilities of the joint venture and how the venture deals with contingent liabilities should be clarified. For example, terminating a venture in host countries such as Italy, Spain, or Belgium can be very expensive because of significant severance benefits that the governments of these countries require employers to pay terminated employees. To illustrate, terminating a forty-five-year-old manager with twenty years of service and a salary of $50,000 per year can cost as much as $130,000 in Italy, $125,000 in Spain, and $94,000 in Belgium, compared to an average of $19,000 in the United States. Partners to a joint venture must be prepared to address these and other types of liabilities related to termination.

Collecting Your Belongings

Protection of proprietary information and property is also an important factor in the termination decision. This is particularly important in joint ventures that involve an exchange of intellectual property (e.g., patents, know-how, trademarks, copyrights, trade names). Questions such as the following must be addressed: What intellectual property rights will belong to each of the partners? What will remain in the joint venture as an independent organizational entity? How will the various types of license be handled? In addition, rights over sales territories and obligations to customers should also be considered. Upon termination of a joint venture, it is important to specify each party's responsibility for continuing support for the dissolving joint venture's customers. Such long-term considerations should be addressed way before the partnership is on the brink of dissolution.

In addition to the business considerations, the partners to an international joint venture must be prepared to address issues with the local government. International joint venture partners must be aware of relevant governmental policies regarding termination, which determine whether or not a multinational firm can achieve a quick exit at a minimal costs. For instance, according to the "Liquidation Measures for Foreign Invested Enterprises," the Chinese government classifies joint venture liquidation into "ordinary" and "special" categories. In an ordinary liquidation, the joint venture's board of directors appoints the members of a liquidation task force, which reports back to the board on the outcomes of the liquidation. In a special liquidation, however, a relevant government authority performs the function of the task force, and the chairman of the task force exercises power on behalf of the legal representative of the joint venture. An ordinary liquidation is conducted in cases where the joint venture assets can satisfy its liabilities and the board of directors is able to agree on the organization of a liquidation task force. The procedures for a special liquidation apply when a joint venture is unable to organize a liquidation task force, or when "serious problems" arise that prevent the venture from carrying out an ordinary liquidation. In Vietnam, the notice of termination must be sent to the Ministry of Planning and Investment (MPI) by one or both owners, depending on the reasons for liquidation. The owners must have MPI's authorization before they proceed with the liquidation. MPI may issue a decision approving the liquidation and withdrawing the investment license. It may, at its discretion, appoint a professional body to reevaluate the results of liquidation prior to issuing such a decision. Similar to policies in China, joint venture liquidation in Vietnam must be carried out by a liquidation committee appointed by the venture's board of directors.

Foreign investors should be aware that the dissolution process is difficult and time-consuming. In most countries, joint venture or corporate laws allow for unilateral termination if the partners cannot reach consent. Nonetheless, when facing refusal by a local government authority, the partner has little choice but to come up with a new strategy. For instance, a smooth dissolution of a joint venture generally takes at least six months in China. It is always true that governmental authorities tend to be charming and friendly when foreign investors come to shop for a place to invest. However, they become reluctant to advocate for foreign investors' interests when dispute arise and dissolution is filed.

Finally, it is important to note that joint venture partners should appropriately assess the gains and losses associated with the termination of a joint venture. Since multiple relationships might be developed between the same partners, the negative effect of the termination of one of these relationships should be minimized. For example, Westinghouse and Mitsubishi have been linked through a variety of cooperative ties for more than seventy years. Yet difficult market conditions and new competitive pressures forced the breakup of one of their 50–50 joint ventures. As Jon Elmendorf, a former president of Westinghouse Energy Systems in Japan and current director for Westinghouse's environmental compliance operations, explains, "The collapse of the circuit-breaker venture was a true test of the relationship. There was a great deal of unhappiness and frustration. But the long-standing trust and commitment between the partners enabled us to deal with the immediate problems and focus on the future. In fact, the breakup of the circuit-breaker venture potentially could have destroyed the entire alliance. Yet this mutual trust and respect prevented any ill will or resentment from boiling over and ruining our other collaborative activities in nuclear energy and gas and steam turbines."

Mini-Case Examples

Case 1: Pepsi's Joint Venture in India

Up until the late 1970s, Coca-Cola led the Indian soft drink industry. It conducted business by importing concentrate from the United States. to its bottling plant in India, where carbonated water was added. Socialists in government at the time asked Coca-Cola to leave India because it refused to divulge its soft drink formula and it was repatriating its profits back to the United States. The Indian government believed that local businesses could make money for their people by producing a similar product. The government's aim was to transfer technology and retain the added value within the country.

With Coca-Cola out, Pepsi soon began plans for entering the Indian market. Pepsi worked several years with an Indian business group seeking government approval over the objections of both domestic soft drink companies and anti-multinational legislators. Pepsi made an offer that the Indian government found hard to refuse. It promised to focus considerable effort on rural areas to help their economic development; to transfer food processing, packaging, and water-treatment technology to India, to develop and export Indian made, Agro-based products; and, through the joint venture, to create ample employment opportunities for the unemployed youth of Punjab, many of whom were involved in criminal activities. Pepsi's specific commitment included: (1) employing 50,000 people nationally, with 25,000 personnel drawn from Punjab; (2) investing 74 percent of the total investment in food and agro-processing, with manufacturing of soft drinks limited to 25 percent; (3) bringing advanced technology in food processing; (4) marketing Indian products abroad, including export of 50 percent of the total value of production; (5) establishing an Agro-research center in consultation with two other Indian firms; (6) not using any foreign brand names in domestic sales; and (7) maintaining an export-import ratio of 5:1 over ten years.

Clearly, Pepsi's strategy was to bundle a set of benefits that would win the support of various interest groups in India. All in all, Pepsi put forth a strong argument for why it deserved to enter the Indian market. Since this agreement would secure peace and economic development, it was well received in the political circles of the Indian government.

The joint venture cleared the Indian government in September 1988 in an agreement between Pepsi, the government-owned Punjab Agro Industrial Corporation (PAIC), an agency specializing in food engineering services (specifically the manufacturing of dried egg products), and Voltas India Ltd., a publicly traded organization specializing in air conditioning, machine tools, chemicals, home appliances, and water treatment. In the initial agreement on sharing arrangement, PAIC held 36.11 percent, Voltas 24 percent, and Pepsi 38.89 percent.

The joint venture, called Pepsi Foods Ltd., produced fruits and vegetables as well as sold cola under the name Lehar Pepsi. The joint venture seemed to support the national priorities of India through export, agriculture, employment, and technology, all of which were important to the developing economy. However, beginning in 1991, the Indian government began to dismantle barriers to foreign investment, making terms much more favorable to foreign multinationals.

Pepsi's local partners contributed market knowledge, distribution channels, market power, quality capital (in the form of refrigeration equipment), and, most importantly, a strong relationship with the government. Their value to Pepsi was that the government would not have allowed Pepsi to enter without them.

However, the joint venture became the center of much attention and controversy soon after its formation because of Pepsi's failure to keep its promises. First, a dramatic reorientation of the Indian economic policy in the early 1990s made entry into India's marketplace much more attractive to foreign firms. Tariff rates were reduced from 100 percent to

25 percent. Wholly owned foreign subsidiaries were now allowed. India also became a signatory to the GATT treaty. Pepsi took these changes as an opportunity to get rid of its involvement in agriculture, in which the soft drink company lacked expertise. It made offers to both Voltas and PAIC to buy their equity back. Voltas sold all its shares to Pepsi, while PAIC agreed to hold less than 1 percent of the total equity in the virtually collapsed partnership. As a result, Pepsi legitimately changed the name of its cola back to its original name, and attempted to sell off its food processing plant.

Second, Pepsi's decision to concentrate its efforts on the soft drink industry was compounded by the fact that the indigenous soft drink industry began to take off after Coca-Cola exited. A host of native colas and other sodas proliferated in a cutthroat domestic market sheltered from external competition while Pepsi was still negotiating its entry. Pepsi found later that it was difficult to break into the new market. Leading the pack was Parle, with a dominant 55 percent market share. Pepsi soon found that it was playing catch-up; it was more difficult to carve out a niche than expected.

Third, Pepsi's major promise that the joint venture would create 50,000 jobs nationally stood nowhere close to reality. In 1996, the total employment figure of direct employment by Pepsi was 2,400, only 5 percent of its initial promise. Pepsi's claim that it had generated employment for over 26,000 people in India through indirect employment can be challenged because, in most cases, the joint venture simply enabled the existing vendors to add Pepsi products to their other goods. Adding Pepsi items and putting up signs in shops, however, cannot be interpreted as creating jobs.

The fact that the joint venture did not meet its promises has strengthened certain bitterness felt by the Indian public. The legacy of Britain's East India Co. has bred a suspicion of foreigners that applies to companies, ideas, and even tourists. In fact politicians in opposition parties rally support against "foreign devils" by smashing symbols of Western imperialism such as bottles of Pepsi and Coca-Cola. Such incidents provide propaganda for the Indian industry, which is fearful of foreign competition. Surprisingly, Japanese and German companies encounter few such problems.

Pepsi is learning that as new markets open, worldwide opportunities exist. Developing markets like India offer potential for businesses to capitalize on new markets, new sources of labor, and key raw materials for production. However, it is important to stick with contracted commitments, especially when political leaders are expressing xenophobic sentiments and nationalistic rhetoric that encourage citizens to distance themselves from American products. Reform in government does not necessarily lead to a change in the public's attitude towards foreigners and foreign companies. It is expected that Pepsi would have been much more successful if it had stuck to its commitments and helped build the Indian economy the way it had originally agreed. It would have then built the trust of the government and ultimately the public. After all, the public is the ultimate consumer of its soft drinks.

In retrospect, this could be tracked back to partner selection. Pepsi should have selected partners with similar business practices or more complementary skills. In this way they would not have had to spread their business to areas that were unfamiliar and would not have had to withdraw from its original agreements. Partners in joint ventures need to be like a couple getting married; if their personalities do not complement each other, their relationship will end in a bitter divorce.

Case 2: Warner-Lambert and Glaxo: A Happy Divorce

Warner-Lambert is based in Morris Plains, NJ. It signed a 50–50 joint venture agreement in 1993 with two London-based companies, Glaxo Holdings PLC and Wellcome PLC, to market and sell nonprescription drugs in the United States. The two PLC companies merged two years later to form Glaxo Wellcome. In 1996, Warner paid $1.05 billion to Glaxo to acquire total ownership of numerous medications covered by the joint ventures, including Sudafed, Actifed, and Neosporin. Glaxo's net investment in the joint venture was GB£7 million by the end of 1997. The joint venture expanded to include several over-the-counter prescriptions such as Zovirax Cold Sore Cream for the use in the treatment of herpes and a hay fever remedy. In 1998, Warner-Lambert and Glaxo Wellcome PLC agreed to end their five-year old joint venture, which was set up to sell over-the-counter versions of the ulcer medication Zantac.

Glaxo Wellcome is currently the world's largest maker of prescription pharmaceuticals, with an estimated 5 percent of the global market and $13 billion in revenues. It is the leader in the respiratory, antiviral, and anti-ulcerant categories. On the other hand, Warner-Lambert is a global provider of health care and consumer products. It is one of the world's leading makers of prescription drugs, over-the-counter medications, gums, and mints. It primarily engages in pharmaceuticals (44 percent of 1997 sales), consumer products (23 percent of sales), and confectionery products (23 percent of sales). It distributes products such as Lipitor, Rezulin, Listerine, Sudafed, Benadryl, Rolaids, Hall's, Trident, Certs, and Dentyne. On a global scale, Warner is seen as a small and relatively unprofitable pharmaceutical company, however.

The joint venture was started for several reasons. Warner-Lambert was looking for a way to expand into nonprescription drugs, while Glaxo was looking for a way to distribute Zantac 75 in the United States. Since Glaxo is a global producer of pharmaceuticals, it was an easy choice of partners for Warner-Lambert. Glaxo in return received a very knowledgeable partner that had significant distribution channels and was well positioned in the U.S. market. It also was looking to move a majority of drugs such as Zantac that were close to patent expiration. In addition, numerous joint ventures with various pharmaceutical companies throughout the world were showing how lucrative the U.S. market was becoming.

Dissolution of the joint venture was mutually agreed upon. Warner contended that it was exiting from the venture because it had reached its original goal of strengthening its position in the nonprescription drug market. It had become one of the market leaders in the over-the-counter market thanks to the breadth of Glaxo's product line. Glaxo, on the other hand, wanted to terminate the partnership because it wanted more flexibility to adopt different marketing strategies in different countries.

Another contributing factor is that the Zantac patent ran out in July 1997. Zantac was the world's top-selling pharmaceutical, but with the expiration of the patent, sales began slumping. Increased generic competition squeezed trade margins. Glaxo was losing one of its most popular and most profitable products. The situation was no better in the United States. Sales for Zantac were down 76 percent for the first half of 1998.

Glaxo had relied mainly upon Zantac for its sales growth and a majority of its earnings. It was now shifting to five new products. Overall, Glaxo was disappointed with the earnings from the joint venture. It believed that it could make more money without the restrictions of the alliance.

Under the dissolution agreement, Warner-Lambert retained domestic and Canadian rights to sell Zantac 75, the over-the-counter version of Glaxo's Zantac. Sales from the over-the-counter version accounted for roughly $211 million in 1997. In exchange for the right to market Zantac,

Warner paid Glaxo an undisclosed amount of cash. Glaxo could continue to sell nonprescription forms of Zantac, Zovirax, and the hay fever medication.

In conclusion, the joint venture was formed between two companies with different goals. These goals, however, were not in the best interests of the joint venture. Glaxo entered for defensive purposes while Warner had offensive purposes. Glaxo wanted to protect its world position, while Warner wanted to look into different pharmaceuticals. In addition, the joint venture had a limited time frame since the patents for Zantac and Zovirax were going to expire soon.

The companies have each established many joint ventures with other companies throughout the world. Interpartner trust was not present in this venture. The companies were bound by a couple of products. Both companies could rely on other ventures to keep them afloat when the patent ran out on Zantac.

References

Adler, Nancy J.; Brahm, Richard; and Graham, John L. 1992. "Strategy Implementation: A Comparison of Face-to-Face Negotiations in the People's Republic of China and the United States." *Strategic Management Journal* 13: 449–466.

Alchian, Armen, and Demsetz, Harold. 1972. "Production, Information Costs, and Economic Organization." *American Economic Review* 62 (5): 777–795.

Aldrich, Howard E. 1977. "Visionaries and Villains: The Politics of Designing Interorganizational Relations." *Organizations and Administration* 8 (2 and 3): 23–40.

Anderson, Erin. 1990. "Two Firms, One Frontier: On Assessing Joint Venture Performance." *Sloan Management Review* (winter): 19–30.

Anderson, Erin, and Gatignon, Hubert. 1986. "Modes of Foreign Entry: A Transaction Cost Analysis and Propositions." *Journal of International Business Studies* 18 (3): 1–26.

Arrow, Kenneth J. 1974. *The Limits of Organization.* New York: W.W. Norton.

Astley, W. Graham, and Fombrun, Charles F. 1983. "Collective Strategy: Social Ecology of Organizational Environments." *Academy of Management Review* 8 (4): 576–587.

Bacharach, Samuel B., and Lawler, Edward J. 1984. *Bargaining: Power, Tactics, and Outcomes.* San Francisco: Jossey-Bass.

Badaracco, Joseph L., Jr. 1991. *The Knowledge Link: How Firms Compete Through Strategic Alliances.* Boston: Harvard Business School Press.

Banner, David K., and Gagne, T. Elaine. 1995. *Designing Effective Organizations: Traditional & Transactional Views.* Thousand Oaks, CA: Sage.

Barkema, Harry, and Vermeulen, Freek. 1997. "What Differences in the Cultural Backgrounds of Partners Are Detrimental for International Joint Ventures?" *Journal of International Business Studies* 28 (4): 845–864.

Barney, Jay B., and Hansen, Mark H. 1994. "Trustworthiness as a Source of Competitive Advantage." *Strategic Management Journal* 15: 175–190.

Bartlett, Christopher A., and Ghoshal, Sumantra. 1986. "Tap Your Subsidiaries for Global Reach. *Harvard Business Review* 6: 87–94.

Beamish, Paul W. 1984. *Joint Venture Performance in Developing Countries.* Unpublished Ph.D. diss., University of Western Ontario, London, Ontario, Canada.

———. 1985. "The Characteristics of Joint Ventures in Developed and Developing Countries." *Columbia Journal of World Business* (fall): 13–19.

———. 1987. "Joint Ventures in LDCs: Partner Selection and Performance." *Management International Review* 27: 23–37.

———. 1988. *Multinational Joint Ventures in Developing Countries.* New York: Routledge.

————. 1993. "Characteristics of Joint Ventures in the People's Republic of China." *Journal of International Marketing* 1 (1): 29–48.

Beamish, Paul W., and Banks, John C. 1987. "Equity Joint Ventures and the Theory of the Multinational Enterprises." *Journal of International Business Studies* (summer): 1–16.

Beamish, Paul W., and Delios, Andrew. 1997. "Incidence and Propensity of Alliance Formation." In *Cooperative Strategies: Asian Pacific Perspective*, ed. Paul W. Beamish and J. Peter Killing. San Francisco: New Lexington Press, pp. 91–114.

Beamish, Paul W., and Inkpen, Andrew C. 1995. "Keeping International Joint Ventures Stable and Profitable." *Long Range Planning* 28 (3): 26–36.

Beamish, Paul W., and Lane, Harry W. 1983. *Need, Commitment and the Performance of Joint Ventures in Developing Countries*. Working paper no. 330, School of Business Administration, University of Western Ontario.

Bedeian, Arthur G. 1984. *Organizations: Theory and Analysis*. Chicago: Dryden Press.

Beniger, James R. 1986. *The Control Revolution: Technological and Economic Origins of the Information Society*. Cambridge: Harvard University Press.

Berg, Stanford V., and Friedman, Philip. 1978. "Joint Ventures in American Industry." *Mergers and Acquisitions* 13 (2): 28–41.

Blau, Peter M. 1964. *Exchange and Power in Social Life*. New York: John Wiley and Sons.

Bleeke, Joel, and Ernst, David. 1991. "The Way to Win in Cross-Border Alliances." *Harvard Business Review* 69 (6): 127–135.

Blodgett, Linda L. 1991. "Partner Contributions as Predictors of Equity Share in International Joint Ventures." *Journal of International Business Studies* 22 (1): 63–78.

————. 1992. "Factors in the Instability of International Joint Ventures: An Event History Analysis." *Strategic Management Journal* 13 (6): 475–481.

Boddewyn, Jean J., and Brewer, Thomas L. 1994. "International-Business Political Behavior: New Theoretical Directions." *Academy of Management Review* 19 (1): 119–143.

Boeker, Warren. 1989. "Strategic Change: The Effects of Founding and History." *Academy of Management Journal* 32 (3): 489–515.

Bresser, Rudi K., and Harl, Johannes E. 1986. "Collective Strategy: Vice or Virtue?" *Academy of Management Review* 11 (2): 408–427.

Brett, J. M., and Okumura, T. 1998. "Inter- and Intracultural Negotiation: U.S. and Japanese Negotiators." *Academy of Management Journal* 41: 495–510.

Brewer, Thomas, L. 1992. "An Issue-Area Approach to the Analysis of MNC-Government Relations." *Journal of International Business Studies* 23 (2): 295–309.

Brouthers, Keith D., and Bamossy, Gary J. 1997. "The Role of Key Stakeholders in International Joint Venture Negotiations: Case Studies from Eastern Europe." *Journal of International Business Studies* 28 (2): 285–308.

Buckley, Peter J., and Casson, Mark. 1988. "A Theory of Cooperation in International Business." In *Cooperative Strategies in International Business*, ed. Farok J. Contractor and Peter Lorange. Lexington, MA: Lexington Books, pp. 31–53.

Burt, Ronald S. 1982. *Toward a Structural Theory of Action*. New York: Academic Press.

Campbell, John P. 1977. "On the Nature of Organizational Effectiveness." In *New

Perspectives on Organizational Effectiveness, eds. Paul S. Goodman and Johannes M. Pennings. San Francisco: Jossey-Bass, pp. 13–55.

Carroll, Glen R., and Delacroix, Jacques. 1982. "Organizational Mortality in the Newspaper Industries of Argentina and Ireland: An Ecological Approach." *Administrative Science Quarterly* 27: 169–198.

Chandler, Alfred D., Jr. 1962. *Strategy and Structure: Chapters in the History of American Industrial Enterprise*. Cambridge: MIT Press.

Chatterjee, Sayan; Lubatkin, Michael H.; Schweiger, David M.; and Weber, Yaakov. 1992. "Cultural Differences and Shareholder Value in Related Mergers: Linking Equity and Human Capital." *Strategic Management Journal* 13 (5): 319–334.

Chi, Tailan. 1994. "Trading in Strategic Resources: Necessary Conditions, Transaction Cost Problems, and Choice of Exchange Structure." *Strategic Management Journal* 15 (4): 271–290.

Chi, Tailan, and McGuire, Donald J. 1996. "Collaborative Ventures and Value of Learning: Integrating the Transaction Cost and Strategic Option Perspectives on the Choice of Market Entry Modes." *Journal of International Business Studies* 27 (2): 285–308.

Child, John. 1972. "Organizational Structure, Environment and Performance: The Role of Strategic Choice." *Sociology* 6 (January): 1–21.

Child, John, and Markoczy, Livia. 1991. "Host Country Managerial Behavior in Chinese and Hungarian Joint Ventures: Assessment of Competing Explanations." Working paper, University of Aston, England.

Child, John; Yan, Yanni; and Lu, Yuan. 1997. "Ownership and Control in Sino-Foreign Joint Ventures." In *Cooperative Strategies: Asian Perspectives*, ed. Paul W. Beamish and J. Peter Killing. San Francisco: New Lexington Press, pp. 181–225.

China Daily. 1996. "Woguo Jiakuai Yu Shijie Jingji Jiegui (Our Country Has Accelerated Its Interconnection with the World Economy)" (December 31): 2.

Chowdhury, M.A. Jafor. 1988. *International Joint Ventures: Some Interfirm-Organization Specific Determinants of Success and Failures—A Factor Analytic Exploration*. Unpublished Ph.D. diss., Temple University.

Contractor, Farok J. 1990. "Ownership Patterns of U.S. Joint Ventures Abroad and the Liberalization of Foreign Government Regulations in the 1980s: Evidence from the Benchmark Surveys." *Journal of International Business Studies* 21 (1): 55–73.

Contractor, Farok J., and Lorange, Peter. 1988. "The Strategy and Economics Basis for Cooperative Ventures." In *Cooperative Strategies in International Business*, ed. Farok J. Contractor and Peter Lorange. Lexington, MA: Lexington Books, pp. 3–28.

Cook, Karen S. 1977. "Exchange and Power in Networks of Interorganizational Relations." *Sociological Quarterly* 18: 62–82.

Covaleski, Mark A., and Dirsmith, Mark W. 1988. "An Institutional Perspective on the Rise, Social Transformation, and Fall of a University Budget Category." *Administrative Science Quarterly* 33: 562–587.

Cressey, Donald R. 1953. *Other People's Money*. Glencoe, IL: Free Press.

Cummings, Larry L. 1977. "The Emergence of the Instrumental Organization." In *New Perspectives on Organizational Effectiveness*, ed. Paul S. Goodman and Johannes M. Pennings. San Francisco: Jossey-Bass, p. 57.

Cyert, Richard M., and March, James G. 1963. *A Behavioral Theory of the Firm*. Englewood Cliffs, NJ: Prentice-Hall.

Dang, Tran. 1977. *Ownership, Control, and Performance of the Multinational Corporations: A Study of U.S. Wholly-Owned Subsidiaries and Joint Ventures in Philippines and Taiwan*. Unpublished Ph.D. diss., University of California, Los Angeles.

Darrough, Masakon N., and Stoughton, Neal M. 1989. "A Bargaining Approach to Profit Sharing in Joint Ventures." *Journal of Business* 62 (2): 237–270.

Das, T.K., and Bing-Sheng Teng. 1999. "Between Trust and Control: Developing Confidence in Partner Cooperation in Alliances." *Academy of Management Review* 23 (3): 491.

Datta, Deepak K.; Grant, John H.; and Rajagopalan, Nandini. 1991. "Management Incompatibility and Postacquisition Autonomy: Effects on Acquisition Performance." In *Advances in Strategic Management*, vol. 7, ed. Paul Shrivastava. Greenwich, CT: JAI Press, pp. 157–182.

Davidson, William H. 1982. *Global Strategic Management*. New York: John Wiley and Sons.

———. 1987. "Creating and Managing Joint Ventures in China." *California Management Review* 24 (4): 77–94.

DiMaggio, Paul J., and Powell, Walter W. 1983. "The Iron Cage Revisited: Institutional Isomorphism and Collective Rationality in Organizational Fields." *American Sociological Review* 48: 147–160.

Doz, Yves L. 1996. "The Evolution of Cooperation in Strategic Alliances: Initial Conditions or Learning Processes?" *Strategic Management Journal* 17 (summer): 55–85.

Doz, Yves L., and Hamel, Gary. 1998. *Alliance Advantage*. Boston: Harvard Business School Press.

Dunning, John H. 1995. "Reappraising the Electic Paradigm in an Age of Alliance Capitalism." *Journal of International Business Studies* 26 (3): 461–491.

Dwyer, F. Robert, and Walker, O.C. 1981. "Bargaining in an Asymmetrical Power Structure." *Journal of Marketing* (winter): 104–115.

Dymsza, William A. 1988. "Successes and Failures of Joint Ventures in Developing Countries: Lessons from Experiences." In *Cooperative Strategies in International Business*, ed. Farok J. Contractor and Peter Lorange. Lexington, MA: Lexington Books, pp. 403–424.

Eisenhardt, Kathleen M. 1985. "Control: Organizational and Economic Approaches." *Management Science* 31 (2): 134–149.

———. 1989. "Building Theories from Case Study Research." *Academy of Management Review* 14 (4): 532–550.

Eisenhardt, Kathleen M., and Schoonhoven, Claudia B. 1990. "Organizational Growth: Linking Founding Team Strategy, Environment, and Growth Among U.S. Semiconductor Ventures, 1978–1988." *Administrative Science Quarterly* 35 (3): 504–29.

Ellis, Shmuel, and Shenkar, Oded. 1996. "Death of the 'Organization Man': Temporal Relations in Strategic Alliances." *International Executives* 38 (1): 537–553.

Emerson, Richard. 1962. "Power-Dependence Relations." *American Sociological Review* 27: 31–41.

Erramilli, M. Krishna. 1996. "Nationality and Subsidiary Ownership Patterns in Multinational Corporations." *Journal of International Business Studies* 27 (2): 225–248.

Fagre, Nathan, and Wells, Louis T., Jr. 1982. "Bargaining Power of Multinationals and Host Governments." *Journal of International Business Studies* 3 (fall): 9–23.

Fama, Eugene F. 1980. "Agency Problems and the Theory of the Firm." *Journal of Political Economy* 88: 288–305.

Fayerweather, John. 1982. *International Business Strategy and Administration*. Cambridge, MA: Ballinger.

Fayerweather, John, and Kapoor, Ashok. 1976. *Strategy and Negotiation for the International Corporation*. Cambridge, MA: Ballinger.

Fayol, Henri. 1949. *General and Industrial Management*. Trans. C. Scorrs. London: Pitman.

Fisher, George. 1980. *International Negotiations: A Cross-Cultural Perspective*. Chicago: Intercultural Press.

Fisher, Roger, and Ury, William. 1981. *Getting to YES: Negotiating Agreements Without Giving In*. New York: Penguin Books.

Flamholtz, Eric G.; Das, T.K.; and Tsui, Anne S. 1985. "Toward an Integrative Framework of Organizational Control." *Accounting, Organizations and Society* 10 (1): 35–50.

Fox, R.P. 1984. "Agency Theory: A New Perspective." *Management Accounting* 62 (2): 36–38.

Frances, June N. P. 1991. "When in Rome? The Effects of Cultural Adaptation on Intercultural Business Negotiations." *Journal of International Business Studies* 22: 403–428.

Franko, Lawrence G. 1971. *Joint Venture Survival in Multinational Corporations*. New York: Praeger.

Galaskiewicz, Joseph. 1985. "Interorganizational Relations." *Annual Review of Sociology* 11: 281–304.

Galbraith, Jay R., and Nathanson, Daniel A. 1979. "The Role of Organizational Structure and Process in Strategy Implementation." In *Strategic Management: A New View of Business Policy and Planning*, ed. Dan Schendel and Charles W. Hofer. Boston: Little Brown, pp. 249–283.

Garrette, Bernard, and Dussuage, Pierre. 1995. "Patterns of Strategic Alliances Between Rival Firms." In *Interorganizational Joint Ventures: Economic and Organizational Perspectives*, ed. Kalyan Chatterjee and Barbara Gray. Norwell, MA: Kluwer Academic Publishers.

Georgopoulos, Basil S., and Tannenbaum, Arnold S. 1957. "A Study of Organizational Effectiveness." *American Sociological Review* 22: 535–536.

Geringer, J. Michael. 1988. *Joint Venture Partner Selection*. New York: Quorum Books.

———. 1991. "Strategic Determinants of Partner Selection Criteria in International Joint Ventures." *Journal of International Business Studies* (first quarter): 41–62.

Geringer, J. Michael, and Hebert, Louis. 1989. "Control and Performance of International Joint Ventures." *Journal of International Business Studies* 20 (2): 235–254.

———. 1991. "Measuring Performance of International Joint Ventures." *Journal of International Business Studies* 22 (2): 249–263.

Geringer, J. Michael; Beamish, Paul, W.; and da Costa, Richard C. 1989. "Diversification Strategy and Internationalization: Implications for MNE Performance." *Strategic Management Journal* 10 (2): 109–119.

Glaser, Barney G., and Strauss, Anselm L. 1967. *The Discovery of Grounded Theory*. Chicago: Aldine.

Golich, Vicki L. 1995. "Transnational Patterns in Commercial Class Aircraft Manufacturing: Why and How." In *Interorganizational Joint Ventures: Economic and Organizational Perspectives*, ed. Kalyan Chatterjee and Barbara Gray. Norwell, MA: Kluwer Academic Publishers.

Gomes-Casseres, Benjamin. 1987. "Joint Venture Instability: Is It a Problem?" *Columbia Journal of World Business* (summer): 97–102.

———. 1990. "Firm Ownership Preferences and Host Government Restrictions: An Integrated Approach." *Journal of International Business Studies* 21 (1): 1–22.

Gouldner, Alvin W. 1959. "Organizational Analysis." In *Sociology Today: Problems and Prospects*, eds. Robert K. Merton, Leonard Broom, and Leonard S. Cottrell, Jr. New York: Basic Books, p. 420.

Graham, John L. 1987. "A Theory of Interorganizational Negotiations." *Research in Marketing* 9: 163–183.

Granovetter, Mark. 1985. "Economic Action and Social Structure: The Problem of Embeddedness." *American Journal of Sociology* 91: 481–510.

Gray, Barbara, and Yan, Aimin. 1997. "Formation and Evolution of International Joint Ventures: Examples from U.S.-Chinese Partnerships." In *Cooperative Strategies: Asian Perspectives*, ed. Paul W. Beamish and J. Peter Killing. San Francisco: New Lexington Press, pp. 57–88.

Guetzkow, Harold. 1966. "Relations Among Organizations." In *Studies on Behavior in Organizations: A Research Symposium*, ed. Raymond V. Bowers. Athens: University of Georgia Press.

Gulati, Ranjay. 1995. "Does Familiarity Breed Trust? The Implications of Repeated Ties for Contractual Choice in Alliances." *Academy of Management Journal* 38 (1): 85–112.

Hall, R. Duane. 1984. *The International Joint Venture.* New York: Praeger.

Hamel, Gary. 1991. "Competition for Competence and Inter-Partner Learning Within International Strategic Alliances." *Strategic Management Journal* 12 (special issue): 83–104.

Hamel, Gary; Doz, Yves L.; and Prahalad, C.K. 1989. "Collaborate with Your Competitors—and Win." *Harvard Business Review* 67: 133–139.

Hamilton, William F., and Singh, Harbir. 1991. "Strategic Alliances in Technological Innovation: Cooperation in Biotechnology." *Journal of High Technology Management Research* 2: 211–221.

Harrigan, Kathryn R. 1984. "Joint Ventures and Global Strategies." *Columbia Journal of World Business* (summer): 7–13.

———. 1985. *Strategies for Joint Ventures.* Lexington: MA: D.C. Heath.

———. 1986. *Managing for Joint Venture Success.* Lexington, MA: Lexington Books.

———. 1988a. "Strategic Alliances and Partner Asymmetries." In *Cooperative Strategies in International Business*, eds. Farok J. Contractor and Peter Lorange. Lexington, MA: Lexington Books, pp. 205–226.

———. 1988b. "Joint Ventures and Competitive Strategy." *Strategic Management Journal* 9: 141–158.

Harrigan, Kathryn R., and Newman, William H. 1990. "Bases of Interorganization Cooperation: Propensity, Power, Persistence." *Journal of Management Studies* 27 (4): 417–434.

Harrison, Jeffrey S.; Hitt, Michael A.; Hoskisson, Robert E.; and Ireland, R. Duane.

1991. "Synergies and Post-Acquisition Performance: Differences Versus Similarities in Resource Allocations." *Journal of Managment* 17 (1): 173–190.

Hebert, Louis. 1994. *Division of Control, Relationship Dynamics and Joint Venture Performance*. Unpublished Ph.D. dissertation, University of Western Ontario, London, Ontario, Canada.

Hebert, Louis, and Beamish, Paul W. 1994. *The Control-Performance Relationship in International vs. Domestic Joint Ventures*. Paper presented at the annual meeting of the Academy of Management, Dallas.

Hennart, Jean-Francois. 1988. "A Transaction Costs Theory of Equity Joint Ventures." *Strategic Management Journal* 9 (4): 361–374.

Hennart, Jean-Francois, and Zeng, Ming. 1997. *Is Cross-Cultural Conflict Driving International Joint Venture Instability? A Comparative Study of Japanese-Japanese and Japanese-American IJVs in the United States*. Paper presented at 1997 Academy of Management Meeting, Boston.

Hennart, Jean-Francois; Kim, Dong-Jae; and Zeng, Ming. 1998. "The Impact of Joint Venture Status on the Longevity of Japanese Stakes in U.S. Manufacturing Affiliates." *Organization Science* 9 (3): 1–14.

Hennart, Jean-Francois; Roehl, Thomas; and Zietlow, Dixie S. 1999. " 'Trojan Horse' or 'Work Horse'? The Evolution of U.S.-Japanese Joint Ventures in the United States." *Strategic Management Journal* 20 (1): 15–29.

Herbert, Theodore T. 1984. "Strategy and Multinational Organization Structure: An Interorganizational Relationships Perspective." *Academy of Management Review* 9 (2): 259–270.

Hill, Charles W. L. 1990. "Cooperation, Opportunism, and the Invisible Hand: Implications for Transaction Cost Theory." *Academy of Management Review* 15 (3): 500–514.

Hill, Charles W. L.; Hwang, Peter; and Kim, W. Chan. 1990. "An Eclectic Theory of International Entry Mode." *Strategic Management Journal* 11: 117–128.

Hill, Robert C., and Hellriegel, Don. 1994. "Critical Contingencies in Joint Venture Management: Some Lessons from Managers." *Organization Science* 5: 594–607.

Hofstede, Geert. 1984. "Cultural Dimensions in Management and Planning." *Asia Pacific Journal of Management* (January): 81–99.

Hrebiniak, Lawrence G.; Joyce, William F.; and Snow, Charles C. 1989. "Strategy, Structure, and Performance: Past and Future Research." In *Strategy, Organization Design, and Human Resource Management*, ed. Charles C. Snow. Greenwich, CT: JAI Press.

Inkpen, Andrew C. 1995. *The Management of International Joint Ventures: An Organizational Learning Perspective*. London: Routledge.

———. 1998. "Learning, Knowledge Acquisition, and Strategic Alliances." *European Management Journal* 16 (2): 223–229.

Inkpen, Andrew C., and Beamish, Paul W. 1997. "Knowledge, Bargaining Power, and the Instability of International Joint Ventures." *Academy of Management Review* 22 (1): 177–202.

Inkpen, Andrew C., and Currall, Steven C. 1998. "The Nature, Antecedents, and Consequences of Joint Venture Trust." *Journal of International Management* 4 (1): 1–20.

Janger, Allen R. 1980. *Organization of International Joint Venture*. New York: Conference Board.

Jemison, David B., and Sitkin, Sim B. 1986. "Corporate Acquisitions: A Process Perspective." *Academy of Management Review* 11 (1): 145–163.

Jensen, Michael C., and Meckling, William H. 1976. "Theory of the Firm: Managerial Behavior, Agency Costs, and Ownership Structure." *Journal of Financial Economics* 3: 305–360.

Jones, Gareth R., and Hill, Charles W.L. 1988. "Transaction Cost Analysis of Strategy Structure Choice." *Strategic Management Journal* 9 (2): 159–172.

Jones, Kevin, and Shill, Walter. 1993. "The Dilemma of Foreign Affiliated Companies: Surviving Middle Age in Japan." In *Collaborating to Compete: Using Strategic Alliances and Acquisitions in the Global Marketplace*, ed. Joel Bleeke and David Ernst. New York: John Wiley and Sons.

Kelley, Harold H. 1966. "A Classroom Study of the Dilemmas in Interpersonal Negotiation." In *Strategic Interaction and Conflict: Original Papers and Discussion*, ed. K. Archibald. Berkeley: Institute of International Studies, 49–73.

Kilduff, Martin. 1992. "Performance and Interaction Routines in Multinational Organizations." *Journal of International Business Studies* 23: 133–145.

Killing, J. Peter. 1982. "How to Make a Global Joint Venture Work." *Harvard Business Review* 3: 120–127.

———. 1983. *Strategies for Joint Venture Success*. New York: Praeger.

———. 1988. "Understanding Alliances: The Role of Task and Organizational Complexity." In *Cooperative Strategies in International Business*, ed. Farok J. Contractor and Peter Lorange. Lexington, MA: Lexington Books, pp. 55–67.

Kimberly, John R. 1980. "Initiation, Innovation, and Institutionalization in the Creation Process." In *The Organizational Life Cycle: Issues in the Creation, Transformation, and Decline of Organizations*, ed. John R. Kimberly and Robert H. Miles. San Francisco: Jossey Bass, pp. 134–160.

Kobrin, Stephen J. 1988. "Trends in Ownership of U.S. Manufacturing Subsidiaries in Developing Countries: An Interindustry Analysis." In *Cooperative Strategies in International Business*, ed. Farok J. Contractor and Peter Lorange. Lexington, MA: Lexington Books, pp. 129–142.

Kochan, Thomas A., and Katz, H. C. 1988. *Collective Bargaining and Industrial Relations*, 2d ed., Homewood, IL: Irwin.

Kogut, Bruce. 1988. "Joint Ventures: Theoretical and Empirical Perspectives." *Strategic Management Journal* 9 (4): 319–332.

———. 1989. "The Stability of Joint Ventures: Reciprocity and Competitive Rivalry." *Journal of Industrial Economics* 38 (2): 183–198.

———. 1991. "Joint Ventures and the Option to Expand and Acquire." *Management Science* 37 (1): 19–32.

Kogut, Bruce, and Zander, Udo. 1992. "Knowledge of the Firm, Combinative Capabilities, and the Replication of Technology." *Organization Science* 3 (2): 383–397.

Kusewitt, John B., Jr. 1985. "An Exploratory Study of Strategic Acquisition Factors Relating to Performance." *Strategic Management Journal* 6 (2): 151–169.

Lane, Harry W., and Beamish, Paul W. 1990. "Cross-Cultural Cooperative Behavior in Joint Ventures in LDCs." *Management International Review* (special issue): 87–102.

Lawrence, Paul R., and Lorsch, Jay W. 1967. *Organization and Environment: Managing Differentiation and Integration*. Boston: Harvard Business School.

Lax, David A., and Sebenius, James K. 1986. *The Manager as Negotiator*. New York: Free Press.

Lecraw, Donald J. 1984. "Bargaining Power, Ownership, and Profitability of Transactional Corporations in Developing Countries." *Journal of International Business Studies* 15 (1): 27–43.

Lee, Chol, and Beamish, Paul W. 1995. "The Characteristics and Performance of Korean Joint Ventures in LDCs." *Journal of International Business Studies* 26 (3): 637–654.

Lei, David; Slocum, John W., Jr; and Pitts, Robert A. 1997. "Building Cooperative Advantage: Managing Strategic Alliances to Promote Organizational Learning." *Journal of World Business* 32 (3): 203–223.

Levinthal, Daniel A., and Fichman, Mark. 1988. "Dynamics of Interorganizational Attachments: Auditor-Client Relationships." *Administrative Science Quarterly* 33: 345–369.

Li, Jiatao. 1995. "Foreign Entry and Survival: Effects of Strategic Choices on Performance in International Markets." *Strategic Management Journal* 16: 333–351.

Li, Jiatao, and Guisinger, Stephen E. 1991. "Comparative Business Failures of Foreign-Controlled Firms in the United States." *Journal of International Business Studies* 22 (2): 209–224.

Li, Jiatao, and Shenkar, Oded. 1996. "The Perspectives of Local Partners: Strategic Objectives and Structure Preferences of International Cooperative Ventures in China." In *Cooperative Strategies: Asian Pacific Perspectives*, ed. Paul W. Beamish and J. Peter Killing. San Francisco: New Lexington Press, pp. 300–322.

Lincoln, Yvonna S., and Guba, Egon G. 1985. *Naturalistic Inquiry*. Beverly Hills: Sage.

Liu, Chu. 1980. "China's Joint Venture Policies." In *Business with China: An International Reassessment*, ed. Nian Tsu Wang. New York: Pergamon Press, pp. 73–77.

Lubatkin, Michael. 1987. "Merger Strategies and Stockholder Value." *Strategic Management Journal* 8 (1): 39–53.

Luo, Yadong. 1997. "Partner Selection and Venturing Success: The Case of Joint Ventures with Firms in the People's Republic of China." *Organization Science* 8 (6): 648–662.

———. 1998. "Joint Venture Success in China: How Should We Select a Good Partner?" *Journal of World Business* 33 (2): 145–166.

Lyles, Marjorie A. 1994. "The Impact of Organizational Learning on Joint Venture Formations." *International Business Review* 3 (4): 459–467.

Madhok, Anoop. 1995. "Revising Multinational Firms' Tolerance for Joint Ventures: A Trust-based Approach." *Journal of International Business Studies* 26 (1): 117–137.

Makino, Shige. 1995. *Joint Venture Ownership Structure and Performance: Japanese Joint Ventures in Asia*. Unpublished Ph.D. diss., the University of Western Ontario, London, Ontario, Canada.

Makino, Shige, and Delios, Andrew. 1996. "Local Knowledge Transfer and Performance: Implications for Alliance Formation in Asia." *Journal of International Business Studies* 27 (5): 905–927.

Mann, Jim. 1989. *Beijing Jeep*. New York: Simon and Schuster.

March, James G. 1991. "Exploration and Exploitation in Organizational Learning." *Organization Science* 2: 71–87.

Meyer, John W., and Rowan, Brian. 1977. "Institutionalized Organizations: Formal Structure as Myth and Ceremony." *American Journal of Sociology* 83: 340–363.

Meyer, John W., and Scott, Richard. 1983. *Organizational Environments: Ritual and Rationality*. Beverly Hills: Sage.

Miles, Robert H. 1980. *Macro Organizational Behavior*. Glenview, IL: Scott, Foresman.

Miles, Raymond E., and Snow, Charles C. 1978. *Organizational Strategy, Structure, and Process*. New York: McGraw-Hill.

Milgrom, Paul, and Roberts, John. 1992. *Economics, Organization and Management*. Englewood Cliffs, NJ: Prentice-Hall.

Mintzberg, Henry. 1983. *Power In and Around Organizations*. Englewood Cliffs, NJ: Prentice-Hall.

Mintzberg, Henry, and Waters, James A. 1982. "Tracking Strategy in an Entrepreneurial Firm." *Academy of Management Journal* 25: 465–499.

Mjoen, Hans, and Tallman, Stephen. 1997. "Control and Performance in International Joint Ventures." *Organization Science* 8 (3): 257–274.

Moe, Terry M. 1984. "The New Economics of Organization." *American Journal of Political Science* 28: 737–777.

Moran, Robert T., and Stripp, W.G. 1991. *Successful International Business Negotiations*. Houston: Gulf Publishing Company.

Moxon, Richard W., and Geringer, J. Michael. 1985. "Multinational Consortia in High Technology Industries: Commercial Aircraft Manufacturing." *Columbia Journal of World Business* (summer): 55–62.

Nelson, Richard R., and Winter, Sidney G. 1982. *An Evolutionary Theory of Economic Change*. Cambridge: Harvard University Press.

Newman, William H. 1992. "Focused Joint Ventures in Transforming Economies." *Academy of Management Executive* 6 (1): 67–75.

Nordberg, Markus; Campbell, Alexandra; and Verbeke, Alain. 1996. "Can Market-Based Contracts Substitute for Alliances in High Technology Market?" *Journal of International Business Studies* 27 (5): 963–979.

O'Connor, Kathleen M. 1997. "Motives and Cognitions in Negotiation: A Theoretical Integration and an Empirical Test." *International Journal of Conflict Management* 8: 114–131.

Osborn, Richard N., and Hagedoorn, John. 1997. "The Institutionalization and Evolutionary Dynamics of Interorganizational Alliances and Networks." *Academy of Management Journal* 40 (2): 261–278.

Osland, Gregory E., and Cavusgil, S. Tamer. 1996. "Performance Issues in U.S.-China Joint Venture." *California Management Review* 38 (2): 106–130.

Ouchi, William G. 1980. "Markets, Bureaucracies, and Clans." *Administrative Science Quarterly* 25: 129–141.

Ouchi, William G., and Bolton, Michele K. 1988. "The Logic of Joint Research and Development." *California Management Review* (spring): 9–33.

Park, Seung Ho. 1996. "Managing an Interorganizational Network: A Framework of the Institutional Mechanism for Network Control." *Organization Studies* 17 (5): 795–824.

Park, Seung Ho, and Russo, Michael V. 1996. "When Competition Eclipses Cooperation: An Event History Analysis of Joint Venture Failure." *Management Science* 42 (6): 875–890.

Park, Seong Ho, and Ungson, Gerardo R. 1997. "The Effect of National Culture, Organizational Complementarity, and Economic Motivation on Joint Venture Dissolution." *Academy of Management Journal* 40 (2): 279–308.

Parkhe, Arvind. 1991. "Interfirm Diversity, Organizational Learning, and Longevity in Global Strategic Alliances." *Journal of International Business Studies* 22 (4): 579–601.

———. 1993a. "Strategic Alliance Structuring: A Game Theoretic and Transaction Cost Examination of Interfirm Cooperation." *Academy of Management Journal* 36: 794–829.

———. 1993b. "'Messy' Research, Methodological Predispositions, and Theory Development in International Joint Ventures." *Academy of Management Review* 18 (2): 227–268.

Pearson, Margaret M. 1991. *Joint Ventures in the People's Republic of China: The Control of Foreign Direct Investment Under Socialism*. Princeton, NJ: Princeton University Press.

Peng, Mike W., and Heath, Peggy S. 1996. "The Growth of the Firm in Planned Economies in Transition: Institutions, Organizations, and Strategic Choice." *Academy of Management Review* 21 (2): 492–528.

Peng, Mike; Yuan, Lu; and Shenkar, Oded. 1998. *Treasures in the China House: A Review of Management and Organizational Research on Greater China, 1978–1997*. Paper presented at the Academy of International Business Conference, October 8, Vienna, Austria.

Pennings, Johannes M., and Goodman, Paul S. 1977. "Toward a Workable Framework." In *New Perspectives on Organizational Effectiveness*, ed. Paul S. Goodman and Johannes M. Pennings. San Francisco: Jossey-Bass.

Pennings, Johannes M.; Barkema, Harry; and Douma, Sytse. 1994. "Organization Learning and Diversification." *Academy of Management Journal* 37 (3): 608–640.

Perrow, Charles. 1987. *Complex Organizations: A Critical Essay.* 3d ed., New York: McGraw-Hill.

Pfeffer, Jeffrey. 1977. "Power and Resource Allocation in Organizations." In *New Directions in Organizational Behavior*, ed. Barry M. Staw and Gerald R. Salancik. Chicago: St. Clair.

Pfeffer, Jeffrey, and Nowak, Phillip. 1976. "Joint Ventures and Interorganizational Interdependence." *Administrative Science Quarterly* 21: 398–418.

Pfeffer, Jeffrey, and Salancik, Gerald R. 1978. *The External Control of Organizations: A Resource Dependence Perspective*. New York: Harper and Row.

Pisano, Gary. 1989. "Using Equity Participation of Support Exchange: Evidence from the Biotechnology Industry." *Journal of Law, Economics and Organization* 5: 109–126.

Poole, Marshall S., and Van de Ven, Andrew H. 1989. "Using Paradox to Build Management and Organization Theories." *Academy of Management Review* 14 (4): 562–578.

Porter, Michael E. 1990. *The Competitive Advantage of Nations*. New York: Free Press.

Powell, William W. 1990. "Neither Market nor Hierarchy: Network Forms of Organization." In *Research in Organizational Behavior*, ed. Larry L. Cummings and Barry M. Staw. Vol. 12. Greenwich, CT: JAI Press, pp. 295–336.

Prahalad, C. K., and Doz, Yves L. 1981. "An Approach to Strategic Control in MNC's." *Sloan Management Review* (summer): 5–13.

Pruitt, Dean G., and Lewis, S. 1975. "Development of Integrative Solutions in Bilateral Negotiation." *Journal of Personality and Social Psychology* 31: 621–633.

Rafii, Farshad. 1978. *Joint Ventures and Transfer of Technology to Iran: The Impact of Foreign Control*. Unpublished Ph.D. diss., Harvard University.

Ramaswamy, Kannan. 1997. "The Performance Impact of Strategic Similarity in Horizontal Mergers: Evidence from the U.S. Banking Industry." *Academy of Management Journal* 40 (3): 697–715.

Reddin, William J. 1970. *Managerial Effectiveness*. New York: McGraw-Hill.

Reynolds, John I. 1979. *Indian-American Joint Ventures: Business Policy Relationships*. Washington, DC: University Press of America.

Ring, Peter Smith, and Van de Ven, Andrew H. 1994. "Developmental Processes of Cooperative Interorganizational Relationships." *Academy of Management Review* 19 (1): 90–118.

Root, Franklin R. 1988. "Some Taxonomies of International Cooperative Arrangements." In *Cooperative Strategies in International Business*, ed. Farok J. Contractor and Peter Lorange. Lexington, MA: Lexington Books, pp. 69–80.

Rubin, Jeffrey Z., and Brown, Bert R. 1975. *The Social Psychology of Bargaining and Negotiation*. New York: Academic Press.

Salacuse, Jeswald W. 1991. *Making Global Deals: Negotiating in the International Marketplace*. Boston: Houghton Mifflin.

Schaan, Jean-Louis. 1983. *Parent Control and Joint Venture Success: The Case of Mexico*. Unpublished Ph.D. diss., University of Western Ontario, London, Ontario, Canada.

———. 1988. "How to Control a Joint Venture Even as a Minority Partner." *Journal of General Management* 14 (1): 4–16.

Schelling, Thomas. 1956. "An Essay on Bargaining." *American Economic Review* 46: 281–306.

Scherer, F.M., and Ross, David. 1990. *Industrial Market Structure and Economic Performance*. 3d ed. Boston: Houghton Mifflin.

Scott, W. Richard. 1992. *Organizations: Rational, Natural, and Open Systems*, 3d ed. Englewood Cliffs, NJ: Prentice-Hall.

Shane, Scott A. 1993. "The Effect of Cultural Distances in Perceptions of Transactions Costs on National Differences in the Preference for International Joint Ventures." *Asia Pacific Journal of Management* 10 (1): 57–69.

Shenkar, Oded, and Ronen, Simcha. 1987. "The Cultural Context of Negotiations: The Implications of Chinese Interpersonal Norms." *Journal of Applied Behavioral Science* 6: 263–275.

Shenkar, Oded, and Zeria, Yoram. 1992. "Role Conflict and Role Ambiguity of Chief Executive Officers in International Joint Ventures." *Journal of International Business Studies* 23 (1): 55–75.

Singh, Harbir, and Montgomery, Cynthia A. 1987. "Corporate Acquisition Strategies and Economic Performance." *Strategic Management Journal* 8 (4): 377–386.

Stinchcombe, Arthur L. 1965. "Social Structure and Organizations." In *Handbook of Organizations*, ed. J. G. March. Chicago: Rand NcNally, pp. 142–193.

Stopford, John M., and Wells, Louis T. 1972. *Managing the Multinational Enterprise*. New York: Basic Books.

Strauss, Anselm L. 1978. *Negotiations: Varieties, Contexts, Process, and Social Order*. San Francisco: Jossey Bass.

———. 1987. *Qualitative Analysis for Social Scientists*. New York: Cambridge University Press.

Tallman, Stephen B., and Shenkar, Oded. 1994. "A Managerial Decision Model of International Cooperative Venture Formation." *Journal of International Business Studies* (first quarter): 91–113.

Tannenbaum, Arnold S. 1968. *Control in Organizations*. New York: McGraw-Hill.

Teagarden, Mary B., and Von Glinow, Mary Ann. 1990. "Sino-Foreign Strategic Alliance Types and Related Operating Characteristics." *International Studies of Management and Organization* 20 (1–2): 99–108.

Thomas, Kenneth. 1976. "Conflict and Conflict Management." In *Handbook of Industrial and Organizational Psychology*, ed. Marvin D. Dunnette. Chicago: Rand McNally, pp. 889–915.

Thompson, James D. 1967. *Organizations in Action*. New York: McGraw-Hill.

Tolbert, Pamela S., and Zucker, Lynne G. 1983. "Institutional Sources of Change in the Formal Structure of Organizations: The Diffusion of Civil Service Reform, 1880–1935." *Administrative Science Quarterly* 28: 22–39.

Tomlinson, James W.C. 1970. *The Joint Venture Process in International Business: India and Pakistan*. Cambridge: MIT Press.

Tomlinson, James W.C., and Thompson, M. 1977. *A Study of Canadian Joint Ventures in Mexico*. Office of Science and Technology, Department of Industry, Trade and Commerce, Ottawa, Canada.

Tomlinson, James W.C., and Willie, C.S.W. 1978. *Cross Impact Simulation of the Joint Venture Process in Mexico*. Office of Science and Technology, Department of Industry, Trade and Commerce, Ottawa, Canada.

Triandis, Harry C. 1986. "Collectivism vs. Individualism: A Reconceptualization of a Basic Concept in Cross-Cultural Psychology." In *Personality, Cognition and Values*, ed. C. Bagby and G. Vernma. London: Macmillan.

Tung, Rosalie L. 1982. "U.S.-China Trade Negotiations: Practices, Procedures, and Outcomes." *Journal of International Business Studies* (fall): 25–38.

———. 1984. *Business Negotiations with the Japanese*. Lexington, MA: Lexington Books.

———. 1988. "Toward a Conceptual Paradigm of International Business Negotiations." *Advances in International Comparative Management* 3: 203–219.

Turner, Louis. 1987. *Industrial Collaboration with Japan*. London: Routledge.

United Nations, 1989. *Joint Ventures as a Form of International Economic Cooperation*. New York: Taylor and Francis.

U.S.-China Business Council 1990. *Special Report on U.S. Investment in China*. Washington, DC: China Business Forum.

Vachani, Sushil. 1995. "Enhancing the Obsolescing Bargain Theory: A Longitudinal Study of Foreign Ownership of U.S. and European Multinationals." *Journal of International Business Studies* 26 (1): 159–180.

Venkatraman, N. 1989. "The Concept of Fit in Strategy Research: Toward Verbal and Statistical Correspondence." *Academy of Management Review* 14 (3): 423–444.

Vernon, Raymond. 1977. *Storm over Multinationals*. Cambridge: Harvard University Press.

———. 1983. "Organizational and Institutional Responses to International Risk." In *Managing International Risk*, ed. R. Harring. New York: Cambridge University Press.

Vickers, John. 1985. "Pre-emptive Parenting, Joint Ventures, and the Persistence of Oligopoly." *International Journal of Industrial Organization* 3 (3): 261–273.

Weiner, Norbert. 1954. *The Human Use of Human Beings: Cybernetics and Society.* Garden City, NY: Doubleday.

Weiss, Stephen E. 1987. "Creating the GM-Toyota Joint Venture: A Case in Complex Negotiation." *Columbia Journal of World Business* (summer): 23–37.

———. 1990. "The Long Path to the IBM-Mexico Agreement: An Analysis of the Microcomputer Investment Negotiations, 1983–86." *Journal of International Business Studies* 21 (4): 565–596.

———. 1993. "Analysis of Complex Negotiations in International Business: The RBC Perspective." *Organization Science* 4: 269–600.

Westney, D. Eleanor. 1988. "Domestic and Foreign Learning Curves in Managing International Cooperative Strategies." In *Cooperative Strategies in International Business*, ed. Farok J. Contractor and Peter Lorange. Lexington, MA: Lexington Books, pp. 339–346.

Williamson, Oliver E. 1975. *The Economic Institutions of Capitalism: Firms, Markets, Relational Contracting.* New York: Free Press.

———. 1979. "Transaction-Cost Economics: The Governance of Contractual Relations." *Journal of Law and Economics* 22: 233–261.

———. 1981. "The Economics of Organization: The Transaction Cost Approach." *American Journal of Sociology* 87: 548–577.

———. 1985. *The Economic Institutions of Capitalism.* New York: Free Press.

———. 1991. "Comparative Economic Organization: The Analysis of Discrete Structural Alternatives." *Administrative Science Quarterly* 36: 269–296.

Williamson, Oliver E., and Ouchi, William G. 1981. "The Markets and Hierarchies Program of Research: Origins, Implications, Prospects." In *Perspectives on Organization Design and Behavior*, ed. Andrew Van de Ven and William F. Joyce. New York: John Wiley and Sons.

Yan, Aimin. 1993. *Bargaining Power, Management Control, and Performance in International Joint Ventures: Development and Test of a Negotiations Model.* Unpublished Ph.D. diss., Pennsylvania State University, University Park, PA.

———. 1995. "The Formation Dynamics of U.S.-China Manufacturing Joint Ventures." *China Business Review* (December): 31–49.

———. 1998. "Structural Instability and Reconfiguration of International Joint Ventures." *Journal of International Business Studies* 29 (4): 773–796.

Yan, Aimin, and Gray, Barbara. 1994. "Bargaining Power, Management Control, and Performance in United States–China Joint Ventures: A Comparative Case Study." *Academy of Management Journal* 37: 1478–1517.

———. 1995. "Reconceptualizing the Determinants and Measurement of Joint Venture Performance." *Advances in Global High-Technology Management* 5: 87–113.

Yan, Aimin, and Zeng, Ming. 1999. "International Joint Venture Instability: A Critique of Previous Research, a Reconceptualization, and Directions for Future Research." *Journal of International Business Studies* 30 (2): 397–414.

Yin, Robert K. 1989. *Case Study Research: Design and Method.* Rev. ed. Newbury Park, CA: Sage.

Yuchtman, Ephraim, and Seashore, Stanley E. 1967. "A System Resource Approach to Organizational Effectiveness." *American Sociological Review* 32: 891–903.

Zeira, Yoram, and Shenkar, Oded. 1990. "Interactive and Specific Parent Characteristics: Implications for Management and Human Resources in International Joint Ventures." *Management International Review* 30 (special issue): 7–22.

Index

About the Authors

Aimin Yan (Ph.D. in business administration from Penn State) is associate professor in Boston University's School of Management. His research has focused on interorganizational relations, international joint ventures, and firms in transforming economies. His study of U.S.-China joint ventures won him the Barry M. Richman Award for Best Dissertation from the Academy of Management in 1994. He has published in leading management journals and taught global management courses in undergraduate, MBA, doctoral, and executive programs. He is a consultant to business firms and governmental agencies on international organizational development and strategic alliances. Professor Yan is the founding director of BU's International Management Program—China.

Yadong Luo (Ph.D. in business administration from Temple University) is associate professor in the School of Business, University of Miami. His research interests include international strategy and businesses in emerging markets. He has published nine books and dozens of articles in major referred journals. He was a former provincial official in China in charge of international business.